# DARING
## MISSIONS
## *of* WORLD
# WAR II

# DARING
# MISSIONS
## *of* WORLD
# WAR II

**William B. Breuer**

CHARTWELL
BOOKS

Brimming with creative inspiration, how-to projects, and useful information to enrich your everyday life, Quarto Knows is a favorite destination for those pursuing their interests and passions. Visit our site and dig deeper with our books into your area of interest: Quarto Creates, Quarto Cooks, Quarto Homes, Quarto Lives, Quarto Drives, Quarto Explores, Quarto Gifts, or Quarto Kids.

Inspiring | Educating | Creating | Entertaining

This edition published in 2017 by Chartwell Books
an imprint of The Quarto Group
142 West 36th Street, 4th Floor
New York, New York 10018
T (212) 779-4972   F (212) 779-6058
www.QuartoKnows.com

This edition published by arrangement with and permission of:
John Wiley & Sons, Inc.
111 River Street
Hoboken, New Jersey

This publication is designed to provide accurate and authoritative information in regard to the subject matter provided. It is sold with understanding that the publisher is not engaged in rendering professional services. If professional advice or other expert assistance is required, the services of a competent professional person should be sought.

ISBN-13: 978-0-7858-3550-9

10 9 8 7 6 5 4 3 2

Printed in the United States of America

Certified Sourcing

www.sfiprogram.org

SFI-01681

Label applies to text stock

*Dedicated to*
GENERAL WILLIAM C. WESTMORELAND *(Ret.)*,
*who fought with distinction in*
*World War II*
*and led freedom forces in the*
*Vietnam War*
*with great honor and*
*exceptional proficiency*

# Contents

# Daring Missions
## of World War II

# Introduction

WORLD WAR II, the mightiest endeavor that history has known, was fought in many arenas other than by direct confrontation between opposing forces. One of the most significant of these extra dimensions was a secret war-within-a-war that raged behind enemy lines, a term that refers to actions taken a short distance to the rear of an adversary's battlefield positions or as far removed as a foe's capital or major headquarters.

Relentlessly, both sides sought to penetrate each other's domain to dig out intelligence, plant rumors, gain a tactical advantage, spread propaganda, create confusion, or inflict mayhem. Many ingenious techniques were employed to infiltrate an antagonist's territory, including a platoon of German troops dressed as women refugees and pushing baby carriages filled with weapons to spearhead the invasion of Belgium. Germans also wore Dutch uniforms to invade Holland.

The Nazi attack against Poland was preceded by German soldiers dressed as civilians and by others wearing Polish uniforms. In North Africa, British soldiers masqueraded as Germans to strike at enemy airfields, and both sides dressed as Arabs on occasion. One British officer in Italy disguised himself as an Italian colonel to get inside a major German headquarters and steal vital information.

In the Pacific, an American sergeant of Japanese descent put on a Japanese officer's uniform, sneaked behind opposing lines, and brought back thirteen enemy soldiers who had obeyed his order to lay down their weapons. Near the end of the conflict in Europe, Germans wearing American garb and riding in American jeeps, trucks, and tanks created enormous panic in the Allied camp during the Battle of the Bulge.

Other than infiltration by foot, during the war both sides used a wide variety of conveyances to get behind enemy lines: folding canoes, two-man submarines, human torpedoes, fishing trawlers, trucks, frogmen, jeeps, horses, mules, parachutes, gliders, and even a train.

Not all ventures behind enemy lines were planned. Often individuals and groups were cut off to the rear of an opposing force and had to utilize clever methods for escaping, including eight GIs who got back through German lines dressed as French policemen.

Escapes from prisoner-of-war camps and holdovers far to the rear of the front were not uncommon, but in most instances, the escapers were recaptured. There were amazing exceptions, however, including a French general in his sixties who fled in civilian garb and three GIs who spent eight days trapped in an attic of a small house without food or water with German soldiers occupying the first floor.

Spies were integral components of the war-within-a-war. Many of these bold people were caught and executed. Women played a key role in espionage activities, including several who organized and directed underground escape lines that saved hundreds of downed Allied airmen in Nazi-occupied Europe.

Many books have been published relating to high-level strategic designs and episodes of heroism on the battlefield, in the air, and at sea during World War II. This volume helps fill a reportorial void: a comprehensive focus on capers behind enemy lines, many of which were so bizarre or illogical that their telling would have been rejected by Hollywood as implausible—yet they happened.

# Part One

## Darkness Falls over Europe

# Post Office Shoot-Out
# Launches a War

DURING THE FIRST HALF OF 1939, an atmosphere of foreboding hovered over Europe. There was the sense of an approaching storm. A revered British figure, Winston S. Churchill, who had held a number of cabinet posts but was now out of politics, warned that "ferocious passions" were "rife in Europe." He was referring to Adolf Hitler and his Nazi cohorts in Berlin.

The preparations for war were everywhere in England, and in London, the high-pitched moans of air-raid sirens were heard for the first time as defense officials tested the nation's early warning system against attack by the powerful Luftwaffe.

At the same time, another force was at work, this one invisible to the eye. For many months, Admiral Wilhelm Canaris, chief of the Abwehr, Germany's intelligence agency, had been feeding a stream of accurate reports on the military and political situation in the Third Reich to MI-6, Great Britain's secret service for foreign operations. Canaris was a leader of the Schwarze Kapelle (Black Orchestra), the conspiracy of prominent Germans pledged to curb or halt Hitler's dream of conquest.

Soon after the führer sent his booted legions to gobble up defenseless Czechoslovakia in March 1939, Canaris implemented a new strategy in an effort to prod Great Britain into taking action against the Reich. Now he ceased sending factual reports and planted false information on MI-6.

On April 3, Canaris, a small, nervous man, stated that Hitler might send his Luftwaffe to attack the Royal Navy, Great Britain's first line of defense. A second haunting report "disclosed" that German U-boats were prowling in the English Channel and even penetrating far up the Thames Estuary, the water passage to London.

This time, the crafty German master spy got action, minimal as it may have been. Lord Stanhope, the first lord of the Admiralty, swallowed the bait. That same day, he gave orders for the fleet to "man the antiaircraft guns" and "be ready for anything that might happen."

Yet another false report planted by Canaris stated that Hitler planned to launch a war against Great Britain by a sneak bombing raid on London. This time, the wily admiral overplayed his hand. When none of his concocted scenarios developed, he lost credibility with MI-6 and other British leaders. Many in London believed, wrongly, that the admiral was hatching these fanciful tales as part of a devious Hitler deception scheme to mask the führer's true intentions.

Meanwhile in early 1939, Hitler was preparing to launch Fall Weiss (Case White), the code name for a massive invasion of neighboring Poland. Army ranks were swelled by new men called up for "summer training." The great German armament works were humming, turning out guns, tanks, airplanes, and ships.

The führer's highly capable general staff had put together an invasion plan which could be spearheaded by the infiltration of a large number of Germans behind Polish lines to create confusion, sabotage key facilities, and protect bridges needed for the advancing panzers.

Earlier, notice had gone out from the *Heer* (army) that volunteers were being accepted for a special commando-type unit. It was headed by Oberst (Colonel) Theodor von Hippel, head of Section II, the intelligence branch responsible for clandestine operations.

Within a few weeks, Hippel organized a force of picked men, who were chosen not only for their combat skills, but also for their resourcefulness and fluency in at least one foreign language. This project was designated top secret.

To mask the true function of this crack outfit, it was designated Lehr und Bau Kompagnie (Special Duty Training and Construction Company). Its headquarters was in the old Prussian city of Brandenburg, giving the organization the name it would carry during the war—the Brandenburgers. Specific missions for the outfit would be decided by the high command, Oberkommando der Wehrmacht.

On a large country estate outside Brandenburg, the future commandos were taught the techniques of stealth and individual sufficiency, how to move silently through woods, live off the land, and navigate by the stars. They learned to handle parachutes, kayaks, and skis, and how to create explosives from potash, flour, and sugar.

The first real test of the Brandenburgers came in mid-1939 when small parties of these men, disguised as coal miners and laborers, began stealing into Poland and infiltrating the mines, factories, and electric power stations. Hitler, in essence, had a large covert sabotage force deep behind Polish lines along the frontier.

X-Day for Case White was set for September 1, 1939, but the conflict that would become known as World War II erupted a half hour ahead of the scheduled kickoff. Curiously, participants on both sides in this opening round would be wearing civilian clothes, not military uniforms.

On the evening of August 31, a group of Brandenburgers in civilian disguise prepared to go into action in the Baltic port of Danzig, which the victors of the First World War had awarded to Poland to prevent that country from being landlocked.

At 4:17 A.M. on X-Day, the Brandenburgers surrounded the Danzig post office and demanded its surrender. The Polish postal workers were armed, and a shoot-out erupted that would rage all day.

While the gunfire was in progress at the post office, the German battleship *Schleswig-Hohlstein,* supposedly in the harbor on a goodwill visit, began blasting targets in Danzig at point-blank range. It may have been the only instance in history where a warship, in essence, got behind enemy lines on a combat mission. By nightfall, Danzig—and its post office—were in German hands.

At the same time, Brandenburgers who had been working as civilians inside Poland collected the explosives smuggled in from Germany in recent weeks and blew up the key facilities where they had been employed.

Elsewhere, other Brandenburgers slipped across the frontier from Germany, got behind Polish defensive positions, and seized the crucial Vistula River bridges. At five o'clock in the morning, five German armies plunged across the border with the panzer spearheads charging over the Vistula spans secured by the Brandenburgers.

It was a brutal, overwhelming assault. The Polish army and air force were antiquated and greatly outnumbered; those of Germany were the most modern that history had known. Adolf Hitler had introduced the term blitzkrieg (lightning war) to the languages of many nations.

The Poles fought with desperate courage, but their valor was largely futile. On one occasion, a contingent of horse cavalry armed with lances attacked a group of German panzers.

Aided by his infiltrators masquerading as Polish civilians, Adolf Hitler's legions conquered a nation of thirty-three million people in only twenty-seven days. In the Third Reich, the führer reached a new pinnacle of popular admiration.[1]

# Wiping Out Hitler's Spy Network

AFTER ADOLF HITLER had curtly rejected a British ultimatum to withdraw his mechanized juggernaut from Poland, England and France declared war on Nazi Germany on September 3, 1939. At the time, the Abwehr, the crack German intelligence agency, had an espionage network in the British Isles of 256 men and women.

Since 1937, the Abwehr had been laying the groundwork for war against Great Britain by infiltrating or recruiting the vast array of secret agents in England, many of whom had been ordered to remain deep undercover until they were needed.

*"Turned" Nazi spies in England resulted in follow-up agents being apprehended almost as they arrived. (National Archives)*

Largely responsible for creating the widespread espionage apparatus had been German Navy Captain Joachim Burghardt, chief of the Abwehr branch in Hamburg, which was in charge of extracting intelligence from Great Britain. Burly and unkempt, Burghardt was not the stereotype of a spymaster. But he had a keen mind, was innovative, and had a knack for attracting able and zealous young officers to his staff. Despite his great success in creating a spy network in Britain, Burghardt was bounced from his post in 1938, having been caught in the middle of an Abwehr internal power struggle.

Burghardt was replaced by Navy Captain Herbert Wichmann, also a dedicated and brainy operative. Like Burghardt before him, Wichmann possessed a key trait for success as a spymaster: an intense passion for anonymity.

The Abwehr espionage apparatus in Britain was organized into two networks. One was called the R-chain, consisting of mobile agents who had posed as sightseers and commercial salesmen, moving in and out of the country and collecting intelligence while seemingly involved in legitimate business.

The other Abwehr network was the S-chain of "silent" or "sleeper" agents—Germans, citizens of neutral nations, and British traitors, all of whom had blended into everyday life. There were at least ten women in the S-chain, including a pair in their fifties who were maids in the homes of two British admirals. While serving tea to the navy leaders and their guests, the female servants overheard countless scraps of secret information.

By the time Hitler decided to invade Poland, these few hundred Abwehr operatives had located most of the airfields, port facilities, military bases, munitions and aircraft factories in southern and eastern England. When war broke out, the Abwehr and Wehrmacht (armed forces) intelligence had pieced together a remarkably accurate portrait of British military capabilities.

On September 3, only hours after Great Britain went to war, agents of Scotland Yard (the London Metropolitan Police) and MI-5 (Britain's counterespionage service) began fanning out across the British Isles. It would be one of history's largest roundup of spies.

During the first ten days of the operation, British sleuths apprehended nearly every one of the 356 persons on their Class A espionage list. Hundreds of others classified as "unreliables" were deported or detained.

Most Abwehr spies (or suspected spies) were hauled from their homes or places of work unaware that British security agents had been keeping an eye on them for years. A few Nazi operatives, seeing the handwriting on the wall and hoping to save their necks (literally), turned themselves in to authorities.

In just a fortnight, the espionage apparatus in Great Britain that the Abwehr had painstakingly built for nearly three years, had been wiped out.[2]

# The Gestapo Cracks
# an Espionage Ring

As war clouds were gathering over Europe in mid-1939, Folkert Van Koutrik, a young Dutchman who had been spying against Germany for two years from The Hague, had a new girlfriend and a problem. She had a taste for extravagant living, including jewelry, so Van Koutrik had a serious need for much more money than he was being paid by MI-6, the British secret service for foreign operations.

Consequently, the Dutchman approached Captain Traugott Protze, chief of a special branch of the German Abwehr known as IIIF, and cut a deal. He would spy for the Germans against the British—for double the pay he was getting from MI-6.

Even Van Koutrik's much larger income could not keep up with his lady friend's material desires. So he said nothing to MI-6 about his arrangement with IIIF and spied for and collected money from both sides. Then his "loyalties" tilted toward the Germans (with their much higher pay), and he began tipping off Protze to each British spy being slipped into the Third Reich from The Hague.

Inside Germany, the Gestapo kept tabs on these British agents and their contacts. Within hours after Great Britain declared war on Germany on September 3, 1939, Gestapo agents swooped down on the spies.

However, not all of the British agents had been caught in the dragnet. But a renegade Englishman, John "Jack" Cooper, who had been a trusted aide to a top officer in the MI-6 post in The Hague and had been fired for stealing funds, disclosed the remainder of the agents to Protze. Before being kicked out by MI-6, Cooper had made copies of secret files and used that knowledge to sell out his country to Nazi Germany—for a modest amount of gold.

Within thirty days, the widespread British espionage network in Germany, built up for five years, was demolished.[3]

# Masquerading Germans
# Pace the Invasion

AFTER POLAND WAS CRUSHED by the mighty German Wehrmacht in less than a month in September 1939, Adolf Hitler turned his attention to the west and built up his forces along the border of the Third Reich facing British and French armies. There the two sides coexisted peacefully for several months. Hardly a shot was fired. World newspapers labeled it the Phony War or the Sitzkrieg (a play on the new word blitzkrieg which the Germans had introduced in Poland).

The Dutch, unlike their neighbors the Belgians, had survived World War I with their neutrality intact. They saw no reason why they could not do the same in the present situation. But the Dutch were determined to fight if the Germans did invade, although the army had no tanks, artillery was drawn by horses, and infantrymen were issued only three grenades each.

Queen Wilhelmina and other Dutch leaders were jolted in early November 1939 when Major Gijsbert Jacob Sas, an assistant military attaché at the Dutch embassy in Berlin, sent back word that the Germans were going to invade the Netherlands on the twelfth.

Strangely, General Izaak H. Reijnders, the Dutch army chief of staff, discounted the Sas bombshell. He thought that the Germans were cleverly using Sas as part of their *Nervenkrieg* (war of nerves).

Prime Minister Dirk Jan de Geer was equally skeptical. When November 12 passed quietly, he took to the radio to recall World War I, when similar fears of invasion had proved equally unfounded.

What Major Sas could not disclose to Dutch leaders was that his information had been received from Colonel Hans Oster, a top aide to Admiral Wilhelm Canaris, the director of the Abwehr, the Reich's intelligence agency.

A *propaganda sign in view of the opposing French forces during the "Sitzkrieg" reads:* "The German people won't attack the French people, if the French don't attack the Germans." (Hearst Metronome News)

Both Canaris and Oster belonged to the Schwarze Kapelle (Black Orchestra), the conspiracy among high German military and government leaders to get rid of Adolf Hitler one way or another. In his crucial post, Canaris was privy to full details of the führer's military plans.

In the weeks ahead, Sas passed along some fifteen dates for Hitler to launch Fall Gelb (Case Yellow), a mammoth offensive against the French and British armies and an invasion of three neutral nations, the Netherlands, Belgium, and Luxembourg. But as one "Zero Day" after another came and went, Sas's credibility continued to sink from his continually crying wolf.

Sas became a prophet without honor in his own country. Dutch leaders concluded that he was a victim of a nefarious Abwehr plot to provoke the Dutch into taking some sort of action that would give Hitler a reason to invade.

Actually, Sas's warnings had been authentic. Each time the führer had postponed Case Yellow on account of the weather, which was extremely capricious that winter and early spring. But Sas could not pass along this information for fear that it would result in exposure of the Schwarze Kapelle and the execution of the conspirators.

Even though Sas's warnings had been rejected, Dutch intelligence uncovered an alarming scheme being carried out by the Abwehr. The Germans had been smuggling across the border and into the Third Reich a large number of Dutch uniforms belonging to the army, the police, and the rail system.

This curious German project had an ulterior goal: German soldiers would wear the uniforms to sneak behind Dutch lines along the border and create massive confusion in the rear areas at the time Case Yellow was launched.

Now Dutch leaders began to take an invasion threat seriously. This intensity heightened on May 4, 1940, when Major Sas reported from Berlin that the Germans would invade the Netherlands within two weeks.

After dining at his residence in The Hague on November 8, Foreign Minister Eelco van Kleffens was summoned to the telephone. Sas was on the line. His message was frightening and brief: "Tomorrow at dawn—hold tight!"

At 3:00 A.M. on May 9, a small convoy of vehicles with Adolf Hitler aboard rolled to a halt in front of a large concrete bunker located on a heavily forested mountain south of the ancient German border city of Aachen. Code-named Felsennest (Aerie on the Cliffs), this bleak structure would be Hitler's command post for directing Case Yellow.

An hour before the Nazi warlord arrived at the bunker, German soldiers wearing the Dutch army uniforms that had been collected for months, began infiltrating behind Dutch lines along the border. In one instance, three Germans dressed in the garb of Dutch military policemen escorted six disarmed German soldiers from the border region toward Gennep.

Dutch army checkpoints made no effort to challenge the group; presumably it was thought that the six prisoners had inadvertently strayed over the frontier and after a mild warning, they would be returned to the Reich. Actually, the nine Germans were engaged in a *ruse de guerre* (war trick) to pave the way for the invaders.

Led by Lieutenant Wilhelm Walther, the band of Germans kept going until they reached the railroad bridge across the Meuse River. As a defensive measure against a German invasion, the Dutch had wired the key span with demolition charges.

A squad of genuine Dutch soldiers stood by to ignite the explosives at the approach of a German troop train. However, the arrival of Walther and his men aroused no suspicions at the bridge. So the three Germans dressed as policemen walked up to the guardhouse on the eastern bank and disposed of the sentries. Then the six German "prisoners" swarmed over the bridge and rapidly cut the wires leading to the explosives.

Just before dawn, a few hundred thousand German soldiers and scores of panzers charged across the Dutch border, gaining total surprise. Soon the first armored train, loaded with infantrymen chugged unimpeded into Holland and roared over the Meuse Bridge.

At the same time the "Dutch policemen" and their "German prisoners" were seizing a key bridge by deception, nearly one hundred Brandenburgers were invading neighboring Belgium ahead of the German Army. Dressed in civilian clothes, the Brandenburgers had infiltrated Belgium defenses along the border and joined the ragged columns of refugees fleeing from the approaching violence.

Many of the masquerading Germans pushed baby carriages that had weapons concealed under the mattresses. According to preconceived plans, they maneuvered through the crowds to secure their objectives: the main bridges over the Meuse River and the Scheldt River tunnel near the port of Antwerp.

Another contingent of Germans, clad in berets and topcoats, infiltrated Belgian lines, seized a commercial bus, and raced toward Nieuport. The mission was to prevent an episode like the one that had occurred in World War I. When the kaiser's army had invaded Belgium in that conflict, the defenders of Nieuport opened the floodgates on the Yser River, inundating the low-lying regions and blocking a rapid German advance. This time, the Brandenburgers won out, capturing the floodgates before the Belgians could open them.[4]

# A Streetcar Spearheads an Attack

SOON AFTER DAWN on the first day of the German invasion of the Netherlands, citizens of Rotterdam were astonished to see twelve ancient Heinkel floatplanes flying low along the New Maas River in the middle of the city and landing near the Willems Bridge far in back of the battle lines. One hundred and twenty infantrymen and engineers quickly scrambled out, inflated rubber rafts, and paddled ashore. It was May 10, 1940.

Pedestrians on the way to work and unaware that their country was under a massive German assault thought the seaplanes were British, and they even helped some of the invaders scramble up the steep riverbank.

Soon a larger Dutch force arrived and engaged in a shoot-out with the Germans, who took refuge in nearby houses and behind bridge piers. To the commander of the seaplane contingent it looked like his unit would be wiped out unless help were to arrive soon.

Meanwhile, a company of *Fallschirmjaeger* (paratroopers) led by First Lieutenant Horst Kerfin landed in and around a soccer stadium a short distance south of the river. After shucking their parachutes, the troopers formed up and rushed to help the beleaguered seaplane group at the Willems Bridge.

Dutch fire was so heavy that Kerfin and his men were pinned down before they could get even halfway to the span. But he and his men climbed into and on top of a streetcar that had been abandoned when the parachute drops began. With bells clanging furiously and the Germans firing their weapons, the streetcar sped to the south end of the Willems Bridge. Soon the trapped seaplane contingent was rescued.

The episode may well have been the only time in the war that a streetcar spearheaded an infantry attack.[5]

# Hitler Order:
# Kidnap Queen Wilhelmina

A FLIGHT OF Luftwaffe transport planes carrying Lieutenant General Hans Graf von Sponeck and elements of his German 22nd Air Landing Division was winging over eastern Holland and approaching The Hague, the seat of the Netherlands government and the official residence of Queen Wilhelmina. The historic city lies on the southwestern coast, about three miles inland from the North Sea. It was the first day of the German invasion.

Adolf Hitler had assigned a special mission to General von Sponeck. After he and his paratroopers had landed, they were to charge into The Hague and kidnap Wilhelmina. The führer issued strict orders that "no harm be done to the queen." At this stage of the war, Nazi Germany was playing a "correct" role. Hitler did not need a dead sixty-year-old queen on his hands.

Sponeck was conspicuous among the paratroopers who landed with him. In anticipation of being "received" by Wilhelmina, the general was wearing a dress uniform, complete with a large array of decorations. His men were clad in combat garb.

Even before the Wehrmacht charged into the Netherlands, the British secret service had learned of Hitler's scheme to "take Queen Wilhelmina into protective custody." The source of this electrifying intelligence was code-named Franta, and he was a senior official in the Abwehr, Germany's intelligence agency.

For four years, Franta had been passing along Hitler's top-secret plans to Major Josef Bartik, chief of the counterintelligence section of the Czech secret service. Bartik, in turn, had been shuttling this high-grade information to Major Harold L. Gibson, chief of the British secret service in Prague.

After the German military juggernaut occupied Czechoslovakia in March 1939, Franta apparently established another secret contact to get his information to the British. It was the mysterious Franta (his true identity would never be known) who had warned of Hitler's scheme to kidnap Wilhelmina.

Consequently, even while General von Sponeck was having his boots shined for an anticipated audience with the queen, British secret service agents arranged to escort Wilhelmina to a waiting British destroyer that took her across the English Channel to Great Britain.

In London, the queen set up a Dutch government-in-exile and continued the struggle against Nazi Germany.[6]

*Nazi kidnap target: Queen Wilhelmina. (Netherlands Information Service)*

# A Legal Diamond Thief

LIEUTENANT COLONEL Montague R. Chidson was one of the most experienced and productive officers in the Continental service of MI-6, Great Britain's overseas intelligence operation. On May 10, 1940, the forty-eight-year-old officer was seated at his desk in The Hague, Holland, when he received word that Adolf Hitler's powerful military machine had invaded the country.

The news came as no surprise to Chidson: his high-level moles in the German secret service had alerted him that the offensive was imminent.

Chidson, who had been with MI-6 since World War I, rapidly changed into civilian clothes and launched a personal operation for which he had been prepared. He hurried to Amsterdam, the capital and largest city (850,000 population). Founded in about 1275, Amsterdam had been a world center of the diamond industry for centuries.

At the Amsterdam Mart, where most of the Dutch diamond cache was safeguarded, Chidson found the main door locked and the place deserted. Using a key he had had the foresight to "borrow" a few weeks earlier, the secret agent entered the building. From information he had obtained a month before for just such a crisis, he spent twenty-four hours fiddling with the combination in the huge master vault.

Down the hall, he heard shouts and the scuffling of many boots on the floor. He surmised that these were German soldiers whose mission was to seize the same priceless diamonds that he was coveting—wealth to help fuel the Nazi war juggernaut. The footsteps drew closer. If caught in civilian clothes, Chidson would probably be shot on the spot as a spy. Just then, the vault opened and he fled with the entire stock of Dutch industrial diamonds.

Although the Wehrmacht had swarmed all over the Netherlands, Chidson managed to sneak the diamonds, which were of colossal value to an industrial power at war, to London. There this valuable cache was turned over to Queen Wilhelmina, who, along with top members of her government, had just escaped from her country on a British destroyer.

For Chidson's incredible exploit, he was awarded the Distinguished Service Order—in secret. Public recognition would have unmasked one of Great Britain's most skilled and innovative undercover operatives.[7]

# Rommel Personally Captures a Unit

MAJOR GENERAL Erwin Rommel was in the lead tank of his German 7th Panzer Division as it plunged over the Belgian border into France on May 16, 1940, a week after Adolf Hitler had unleashed his war juggernaut along the Western Front. Already other Wehrmacht commanders were complaining that the forty-eight-year-old Rommel was needlessly risking his life by being at the point of his advancing spearhead. Some said jealousy triggered the criticisms.

Rommel was no novice to the battlefield. As a young infantry platoon leader in World War I, he had been wounded twice and received the Iron Cross 1st Class and other high decorations for valor. The young officer had been described by a superior as "the perfect fighting animal—cold, cunning, ruthless, untiring, quick-witted, incredibly brave."

Although Adolf Hitler had met Rommel briefly four years earlier, it was not until September 1939 that the führer grew to admire the newly promoted major general, who commanded the troops guarding Hitler's mobile headquarters during the invasion of Poland. Rommel immediately hated the "atmosphere of intrigue," but his close association with Hitler resulted in his being given command of the 7th Panzer Division.

Now, at the head of his panzers, Rommel rolled westward at speeds up to forty miles per hour. It was a new type of warfare. His tanks, instead of halting when confronted by determined opposition, fought on the move, swiveling their turrets to fire in different directions.

Night fell. Rommel's men were near exhaustion. Keep going, the leader ordered. By the light of the moon, he could discern the shadowy figures of French soldiers, panic-stricken by the roar of the panzers, which were supposed to be forty miles to the east.

It was not until 6:15 A.M. that Rommel finally called a halt. His panzers had fought and driven nearly fifty miles during the past twenty-four hours. Although he had not realized it because of a breakdown in radio communications, he and his spearheading tanks had far outrun the main body of his division. He was twenty miles behind French lines.

Without pausing to rest, the indefatigable Rommel got into an armored car and raced off to the rear to bring up his straggling panzers. No longer shielded by darkness, he had to run a gauntlet of skirmishes with French units.

At one crossroad, Rommel spotted a group of French soldiers in a field. Halting the vehicle, he stood up, waved his arms, and shouted in passable French for the enemy troops to lay down their arms. Dispirited, the soldiers readily agreed and climbed into a large number of French trucks.

Led by the German general, the convoy headed to a nearby town where the French contingent officially surrendered. No doubt it was the largest group of enemy soldiers captured personally by a general on either side during the war—and the feat was accomplished behind enemy lines.[8]

# A General's "Impossible" Escape

THE FRENCH OFFICER was inspecting a frontline machine-gun position nine days after Adolf Hitler had triggered the Wehrmacht's invasion of Belgium, the Netherlands, and France. Suddenly, German infantry poured out of a nearby woods and surrounded the emplacement. A captain called out for the Frenchmen to surrender. To his astonishment, among those who emerged with hands in the air was a ramrod-straight man with the five stars of a general on his kepi—Henri Honoré Giraud. It was May 19, 1940.

For the second time in twenty-five years, Giraud was a prisoner of the Germans. As an infantry captain in World War I, he had been seriously wounded and captured. Two months later, despite his injury, he escaped from a POW enclosure. In various disguises—magician in a traveling circus, stable boy, butcher, and coal salesman, he made his way through the Netherlands to England. A few months later, the young captain rejoined his outfit in France.

After his second capture a war later, General Giraud was treated with great deference by the Germans in keeping with the Frenchman's lofty rank. Perhaps because of his reputation as an escape artist, he was ensconced in an "escape-proof" prison, the towering Koeningstein Castle, near Dresden, in eastern Germany not far from the Czechoslovak border.

Fleeing from the frowning castle, perched on a sheer cliff 130 feet high, would seem to be an impossibility. Every exit was double-guarded, and regular checks were made of the general's room. If he did manage to get out of the castle, he knew, hundreds of Gestapo agents and policemen throughout Germany would be searching for him. His photo would be widely distributed to aid in identifying the Frenchman. Moreover, he was sixty-one years of age, and the limp he had sustained from his wound in World War I had steadily become more pronounced and painful.

But Giraud refused a German request to give his word "as an officer" that he would not try to escape. To the contrary, he began to scheme almost

*General Henri Honoré Giraud (left), although in his sixties, escaped from a German "escape-proof" castle deep in the Third Reich. He shakes hands with General Charles de Gaulle after reaching Allied forces. (U.S. Army)*

immediately to make a getaway. Preparations would be long and tedious. Giraud practiced his German daily until he could speak without an accent. Maps of the surrounding area were smuggled into the fortress, and his keen mind memorized every contour, town, and river. With twine from Red Cross packages, he patiently wove a rope that would support his six-foot-three, two hundred-pound frame.

The Germans allowed Giraud to write letters, but they did not know that a French officer in the castle who had become an invalid and had been sent back to France, had contacted the general's wife with a secret code. Using this code in scores of seemingly innocent letters, Giraud sent details of his escape plan and asked his wife to contact the British secret service and ask for assistance. At great personal risk, she kept in touch with a Briton who was working undercover in France.

With the arrival of 1942, Giraud began covertly assembling his escape garments. His military raincoat could pass as a civilian garment, and a pair of civilian trousers was smuggled into the castle for him. Food packages reaching him, thanks to the British secret service, contained a Tyrolean hat, one typical of those worn by German civilians.

Early on the morning of April 7, Giraud was ready to launch his escape plan. Fellow POWs helped him strap on a package containing bread, cheese, and his civilian garb. Then he strolled out onto a high balcony, just as he had done countless times. When no guards could be seen, the general tied his homemade rope to the balustrade, and two fellow inmates lowered him one hundred feet to the ground, a hair-raising achievement. He could easily have lost his grip and plunged to his death.

After the conspirators hauled the telltale rope back up, Giraud limped to a cluster of trees, shaved off his trademark mustache that he had cultivated for decades, and donned his civilian clothes. Two hours later, he reached a bridge, five miles away, where, according to plan, a young man carrying a suitcase approached. Both men gave a prearranged signal of recognition.

Giraud and his companion then walked a short distance to a railroad station, boarded a train, and went to the men's lavatory. There Giraud opened the suitcase and found his own civilian clothes that had been provided by his wife. There were also fake, but genuine-looking, identity papers, bearing the name of an industrialist and a photograph that looked like Giraud without his traditional mustache. Also provided was real German money.

Now the French general had become a distinguished-looking businessman. But he knew that the alarm had been spread, and that German police and frontier guards were alert. So the escaper traveled on trains that crisscrossed Germany almost continuously for ten days until the uproar over the escape of the Third Reich's most prominent French prisoner faded.

On one occasion, Gestapo agents began working through the train on which Giraud was a passenger. Watching them casually, he determined that they were looking for identity cards of men who were about six feet, three inches tall. He quickly sat down next to a German army lieutenant and engaged him in amiable conversation. When the Gestapo man asked for Giraud's papers, the highly-decorated young officer told them the stranger was a friend of his and that he would vouch that he was a loyal German. The policeman moved on.

A day later, Giraud was about to board a train in Stuttgart when he noticed that Gestapo agents were searching each passenger. He waited until the train was starting to pull out, then dashed toward it, straining not to give himself away by limping, an affliction for which the Germans had been watching. As he neared one of the moving cars, he called out something about how he had a business appointment in another town and it was crucial that he catch the train. One of the Gestapo men actually helped the elderly, huffing and puffing "businessman" aboard.

A week after his railroad safari had begun, Giraud crossed the border into northern France, which was occupied by the Wehrmacht under the terms of an armistice that had been arranged in May 1940. He hoped to slip over the demarcation line into unoccupied southern France, where his home was located. But when he learned that German guards were closely examining the identities of all men over five feet eleven inches, he caught another train and headed across southeastern Germany to the Swiss frontier.

Giraud got off the train and, avoiding border guards, struck out across a seldom used mountain trail. It would have been a tortuous climb even for a younger man, but he continued to negotiate the craggy peaks. Suddenly, he bumped into three soldiers who had rifles aimed at him. They spoke, not in German, but in a Swiss dialect. He was safe.

Taken to the city of Basel, Giraud made his true identity known. Berlin was furious and demanded his return. Swiss authorities refused to surrender him.

Obtaining a driver and an old car, the general made a dash for the border of unoccupied France, which was governed by a puppet regime under senile, eighty-six-year-old Marshal Henri Philippe Pétain, who had been a hero of World War I in France. Early in May, almost two years since his capture, General Giraud rejoined his wife in their home in Lyon. Although he kept a low profile, the Gestapo staked out his house and made several attempts to murder him.

In a desperate effort to "save face," the Germans dispatched Pierre Laval, a French traitor who had been designated as de facto head of the puppet Vichy government, to pass along a bizarre proposal to Giraud. He proposed that the general placate the Nazis by returning to captivity in Germany. The suggestion was promptly rejected.[9]

# "The Cat" Was a Triple Agent

MAJOR ROMAN GARBY-CZERNIAWSKI was a dashing figure who had been an Olympic skier for Poland. As a Polish Air Force officer with cryptanalytical training, he escaped to Paris in October 1939 when the German Wehrmacht seized militarily weak Poland. When France fell seven months later, he went undercover and was asked by the Special Operations Executive (SOE), Britain's cloak-and-dagger agency, to organize a Paris-based espionage ring, code-named Interallié (Allied Circle), which grew to 120 agents.

Mathilde Carré, an alluring French woman in her mid-thirties who held a law degree, was recruited by Garby-Czerniawski as a radio operator. Carré had no way of knowing it at the time, but she would be the only female triple agent of the war and would work behind the lines of both sides.

In the weeks ahead, Carré gathered important intelligence through social contacts with top German officers who were bent on demonstrating their importance to this beautiful and vivacious young woman. She would later state that she received a sexual thrill from danger.

Interallié's first radio message to London was broadcast from near the Trocadero on January 1, 1941. Almost daily from that point, Carré radioed her own intelligence tidbits and those gathered by Garby-Czerniawski (code-

*Mathilde "the Cat" Carré, possibly
the war's only female triple agent.
(National Archives)*

named Valentin). She introduced her messages with "the Cat reports," so she was given the code name La Chatte (the Cat).

Meanwhile, the German intelligence agency, Abwehr, sent to Paris one of its operatives described as "a human ferret" to dig out the broadcast source and wipe out Interallié. He was Hugo Bleicher, a middle-aged man, who adopted the alias "Colonel Henri" (although he was only a sergeant).

Interallié had been so successful that Garby-Czerniawski received Poland's highest award for valor when he was brought to London in November 1941 for an intelligence planning session. While he was gone, disaster struck in France. Abwehr agents arrested Raoul Kiffer, the Interallié chief in Cherbourg, who betrayed more than twenty of his agents.

Unaware of the Cherbourg episode, Garby-Czerniawski returned to Paris on the night of November 17. He was sleeping soundly when Hugo Bleicher and a squad of his men burst into his apartment and seized the network leader. Apparently, Kiffer had also disclosed Valentin's hideout. (Some have said the Cat had betrayed the handsome Garby-Czerniawski in a fit of jealousy over another woman.)

Later that day, Bleicher arrested the Cat in the Interallié headquarters in the Rue Léandre. She evaded torture and execution by agreeing to become a double agent for Bleicher.

The Cat launched her perfidious role by failing to inform London promptly of Valentin's arrest. After London learned of the disaster, the Cat proposed continuing to broadcast for Interallié under the code name Victorie. Unaware that she had been turned, London quickly approved.

Predesignated security phrases were embedded in the Cat's messages to show that the operator was not under enemy control as Bleicher stood next to her.

About six weeks after the Cat's first radio broadcast to London, a member of Interallié who was still on the loose, Pierre de Vomecourt (code-named Lucas), suspected that she was working for the Germans and sending messages to London dictated by the Abwehr. Angrily confronting the woman, Lucas accused her of being in bed with the Germans. She vigorously denied the charge, but then she broke down in tears and confessed. Lucas thought about killing her on the spot. Then he had a better idea: turn her into a triple agent.

Had the Cat not been involved in the espionage business, she would have been a remarkable actress. She persuaded the Abwehr to allow Lucas to take her to London, where, she promised, she would get details about a meeting of British agents in Paris that Lucas was planning on his return to France.

Lucas and his female companion were picked up by a British torpedo boat on a remote beach in Britanny on the night of February 26, 1942. In London, British intelligence officers treated her like a queen. She was put up in a luxury apartment where she spent three happy months unaware that her rooms had been bugged with hidden microphones.

One day came the rude awakening. The British had obtained all the information they wanted, and the Cat was hustled from her ornate apartment and thrown, clawing and scratching, into a dingy prison for the remainder of the war.[10]

# Prowling behind German-Held Coast

ENGLAND WAS AN ISLAND under siege. Her expeditionary force that had been sent to the Continent in late 1939 to whip Adolf Hitler had just been withdrawn in total disarray from the English Channel port of Dunkirk. Nearly all weapons, tanks, and vehicles had to be left behind. Contingency plans had been developed to evacuate the royal family and government to Canada. It was June 1940.

On the far shore of the Channel was poised the German Wehrmacht, the most powerful armed force known to that time. It was preparing to bolt across the relatively narrow body of water and conquer England, a task Hitler and his generals estimated would take about six weeks.

In this haunting climate of impending doom for an entire nation, sixty-six-year-old, rotund Winston S. Churchill, the first lord of the Admiralty, was summoned by King George VI and appointed prime minister to replace the fumbling, elderly Neville Chamberlain.

Churchill immediately plunged into his task: saving Great Britain. He surrounded himself with a youthful, blue-blooded staff and began establishing an apparatus known as special means. This included the creation of "troops of the hunter class," who became known as Commandos—tough, resourceful men with killer instincts. Their function was to keep the Feldgrau (field gray, the average German soldier) across the Channel jittery and awake nights by launching hit-and-run raids and sneaking behind enemy lines to collect intelligence.

The task of organizing the Commandos was given to forty-one-year-old Lieutenant Colonel Dudley Clarke. There was no time to lose. Churchill was demanding that the cross-Channel raids be launched within three weeks. Clarke hastily recruited the toughest men he could find, and by June 15, a training base was established on England's southern coast. There were only forty-one submachine guns in the British Isles, and the fledgling Commandos were loaned twenty of them—but only after Clarke took a blood oath that he would return the weapons following the first raid.

Assault boats were nonexistent. So Royal Navy Captain Garnons-Williams quickly scraped up a motley collection of small vessels that had been used for sailing in quiet inland waters. Their seagoing qualities and the reliability of their engines were open to question.

The first raid was laid on for the night of June 23/24—barely three weeks since Dunkirk. A party of 120 Commandos under Major Ronald J. F. Todd, carried in four small boats, would strike at beaches to both sides of Boulogne opposite Dover. Colonel Clarke would accompany the raiders, but he had received strict orders not to go ashore. A movie company furnished the Commandos with black makeup, and at dusk, the raiders set sail.

Just before reaching the dark coast of France, the four boats split, according to plan, each heading for its own beach. There were patches of fog, and the pale rays of the moon were filtering through a haze. The dim silhouettes of Luftwaffe airplanes could be seen overhead. One boat stumbled into the center of a German seaplane anchorage, was detected, and had to pull out before reaching shore.

Commandos in two other craft stole inland for hours. Men in the boat carrying Colonel Clarke and Major Todd were spotted by a German bicycle patrol. A shoot-out erupted, and a bullet pierced Clarke's car, causing a stream of blood to cascade down his neck and saturate his clothing. The Commando leader was angry and roundly cursed the Germans: they had ruined his uniform.

The Commando force returned to England in broad daylight, each boat to a different port. At one harbor, permission was denied for a boat to enter; no one knew the identity of the sinister-looking, black-faced men in a craft with no identifying markings. The boat had to lay off the boom at the entrance; all the time it was covered by shore gun batteries. The Commandos were soaked to the skin, exhausted, and famished. They unfurled their most colorful profanity for the idiots in the port who would not let them dock.

As the morning rolled by, the waiting men got drunk, having consumed jars of rum that someone had stowed on board. Finally, the Commandos were allowed to enter the port, and as they staggered onto the docks, they were arrested as deserters by red-capped British military police.[11]

# Cat-and-Mouse Game

JUST AFTER MIDNIGHT, four men in two rubber rafts scrambled over the railing of a German trawler seven miles off the coast of southeastern England and paddled to shore. These men were Nazi spies, the vanguard of a team of some twenty-five agents who were to be sneaked into Great Britain by the Abwehr branch in Hamburg. It was September 3, 1940, precisely one year after the British had declared war on Germany.

The leader of the spy quartet was José Rudolf Waldberg, who was fluent in German and French, but could not speak English. Earlier in the year, he had been an Abwehr spy behind Allied lines in France.

Each of the four agents had been assigned a specific mission. Waldberg, regarded by Hamburg as the brightest of a not-too-astute group, was to ferret out the identity of British divisions deployed along the southern coast of England, the type of fortifications there, and the number, caliber, and range of coastal and antiaircraft artillery.

Carl Meier, a German who had been involved with the underground in the Netherlands, was to collect information on the status of the Royal Air Force. Sjord Pons, a former ambulance driver for the Dutch Army, and Charles van den Kieboom, a mild-mannered Dutchman who had been a bookkeeper in Amsterdam, had been told to snoop around southern England and report anything that might be of interest to German intelligence.

Their training as spies had been minimal—two weeks. At an Abwehr-operated hotel in Hamburg called the Klopstock, the four men had been given a crash course in basic cryptography (their assigned codes were childlike in simplicity) and on "recognition," how to identify British airplanes, equipment, guns, and unit insignia.

All four men had one handicap in common: they could speak minimal or no English and could understand it only when it was spoken slowly.

Now the spies were ashore in England shortly before dawn. Each man carried an Afu radio set for communicating with Hamburg. Waldberg also lugged with him an incredible amount of luggage as though he were on an extended vacation.

With the zeal of an amateur spy, Waldberg promptly set up his Afu on the shore and flashed an upbeat message back to Hamburg. It was a foolish act;

the transmission could have been intercepted by British monitors, which focused on the English Channel coast.

As a warm autumn sun ascended into a bright blue sky, Waldberg became thirsty. He told Carl Meier to go into the nearby town of Lydd and bring him back some cider.

Unaware that British pubs had their open hours regulated by government decree, Meier strolled confidently into a bar and ordered two bottles of cider in his flawed English words. The proprietress became suspicious and she explained what every Briton should know: nothing could be bought until mid-morning.

"Why don't you wait around, sir?" the woman suggested pleasantly. "You might want to look over the old church just down the street."

An hour later, Meier returned to the pub and into the arms of two constables who had been summoned by the proprietress. His career as a spy had lasted five hours.

Meier admitted that he had landed in a dinghy, but, using his cover story supplied at the Klopstock in Hamburg, he said he had come to England to join the new Dutch Army to fight the Nazis. He hated Hitler, he exclaimed vehemently.

Meier said nothing about Waldberg, who presumably was on the outskirts of Lydd awaiting a refreshing drink of cider. But the next morning, a police search party spotted him shuffling along a road under the burden of a radio and a few pieces of luggage holding his clothing.

Sjord Pons and Charles van den Kieboom, who had split from the other two spies, were jolted by an even more abrupt finish to their brief espionage careers. They inadvertently walked into a bivouac of the Somerset Light Infantry, and, when it was discovered that neither man could speak English or even knew precisely where he was, the pair was taken into custody.

Waldberg, Meier, and Van den Kieboom, were hanged a short time later, all brave men but not overly burdened with brains. Curiously, Pons convinced a jury that he was really a Dutch patriot who had joined the spy band for the cross-Channel trek merely to escape Nazi oppression in the Netherlands. Pons was exonerated, no doubt as the result of some machination in which he would become a double agent for the British.

In the weeks ahead, several other spy teams hastily trained in Hamburg proved equally inept. One pair, flown to a remote locale along the Scottish coast in a seaplane, got soaked to the skin wading ashore. When they purchased railroad tickets at a nearby depot, the clerk saw that their garments were thoroughly wet, although it had not been raining. Suspicious, he telephoned a constable, who rushed to the depot. After finding telltale errors in the pair's forged British identity cards, the officer took the two men to the jail.

A quick search nailed the pair. On one man was a half-eaten German sausage, a German-made Mauser pistol, and a German-built Afu radio set.

In Hamburg, Captain Wichmann was appalled by the disappearance of the spies he was sending into England. Rightfully, he suspected that they had been captured and probably hanged because no radio dispatch ever came from any of them. Then, almost as if by magic, the Abwehr's luck changed. Not only were succeeding spies sent to England avoiding capture, but they were sending Hamburg a wealth of seemingly useful intelligence.

Wichmann, a brainy and experienced cloak-and-dagger operative, no doubt should have suspected that some unknown development was taking place in Great Britain. But he and his aides were perhaps too occupied in congratulating themselves for what Nazi bigwigs in Berlin thought was impossible: penetrating the tight security in England and collecting information of great value to the German armed forces.

The key figure in this seeming counterespionage triumph—and Abwehr disaster—was forty-year-old Arthur George Owens, who was operating a legitimate business in London, the Owens Battery Equipment Company. A high-living free spirit accustomed to expensive clothing, fine wines, and curvacious girlfriends, he was married and had a family in England.

Owens, bright, energetic, and devious, had been known to MI-6, the British secret service responsible for overseas operations, since 1936, when Adolf Hitler began to openly rearm Germany. At that time, Owens had offered to spy against Germany, where he often traveled on business. MI-6 ignored his proposal.

So Owens's "loyalty" did a flip-flop. On his next trip to Berlin, he contacted the Abwehr and was paid a monthly fee to spy against England. His motive was uncomplicated—financial greed to support his high style of living.

"Snow," as he was code-named by the Abwehr, grew alarmed after England declared war on Germany on September 3, 1939, when he learned that British authorities were rounding up scores of Nazi spies in England. So he hatched a scheme to avoid an appointment with the hangman. He telephoned an inspector at Scotland Yard and asked the sleuth to meet him at Waterloo Station. The detective kept the rendezvous and promptly arrested Owens, who was ensconced in prison.

Owens was engaged in a subtle game of high-stakes poker, with his life on the table. He had expected to be imprisoned, so he played another trump card, figuring that if he disclosed the location of the rooming house where he had stashed his Afu radio, his captors would be appreciative and release him.

The scheme backfired. MI-6 recovered the Afu, but it displayed no sign of benevolence. Owens was a prime candidate for the gallows. But there was a way to save his neck, MI-6 informed him. He could become a double agent and radio misleading or false information to his Abwehr controllers in Hamburg. The prisoner promptly accepted.

Owens's Afu was brought to his cell and with British agents providing him with a script and hovering over him, he radioed Hamburg. The phony information was accepted as authentic by the Abwehr because it was based on facts that the British knew were already known to the Germans.

In Hamburg, Captain Wichmann was delighted with Snow's report, and the others that followed. He did not suspect that his ace spy had been "turned." MI-6 operatives were delighted, too—they had apparently hoodwinked the Abwehr in this first wartime duel of wits. Owens was the most elated of all. In one fell swoop, he had saved his own neck and ingratiated himself with both his German and British masters.

Owens was quietly released from prison a few days after being taken into custody and told to resume his role as a seemingly hard-working London businessman. In the time ahead, he continued to send Hamburg fake intelligence reports, all carefully crafted by British operatives.

It was through instructions radioed to Snow by the unsuspecting Abwehr in Hamburg that the British secret service learned in advance the identities of the German spies to be infiltrated into England, their arrival dates, and points they would enter on the coast.

A welcoming committee of British security men was always on hand to greet the German spies as soon as they stepped onto the beaches.[12]

# A Personal Telegram for the Führer

JUST PAST MIDNIGHT, a flotilla of five Royal Navy destroyers and two steamers that had been used to cross the English Channel in peacetime, the *Princess Beatrix* and the *Queen Emma*, stole out of Scapa Flow at the northern tip of Scotland. On board the steamers were five hundred British Commandos, a contingent of Royal Engineers, and fifty-two Norwegian volunteers. It was March 1, 1941.

The force was bound for the Lofotens, a group of German-held Norwegian coastal islands. There the Commandos were to blow up factories that processed herring and cod oil into glycerine that Germany used to manufacture munitions, and into vitamin A and B pills for the Nazi armed forces.

Just before dawn on March 4, the raiding force was offshore from two targeted islands. The Commandos lowered landing craft and headed for land. Bundled up against the arctic blasts, the men were grim. Although no German activity could be seen, the raiders were convinced that an ambush had been laid for them.

Indeed there was an ambush ashore: crowds of excited Norwegian civilian men and women who reached down and hoisted the Commandos onto the docks.

While the Royal Engineers methodically went about their business of blowing up eighteen fish oil factories along with storage tanks holding nearly a million gallons of fuel oil, the Commandos rounded up German stragglers, mostly merchant sailors.

Meanwhile, the Britons took over the German-operated telegraph station and telephone exchange. Before returning to the flotilla offshore, Commando Lieutenant R. L. Wills sent a telegram addressed to A. Hitler, Berlin: "You said in your last speech German troops would meet the English wherever they landed. Where are your soldiers?"[13]

# Who Was the Mysterious Max?

AT DAWN ON JUNE 22, 1941, Adolf Hitler's powerful Wehrmacht plunged across Russia's border along a front extending from Finland southward for hundreds of miles to the Black Sea. Soviet dictator Josef Stalin, who had signed a friendship pact with Hitler a year earlier, was taken totally by surprise. In the first phase alone of the offensive (code-named Barbarossa), the Red Army lost three million men, 22,000 guns, and a few thousand tanks.

Under a plan code-named Walli I, German intelligence had assigned each army a unit of front agents, or line crossers. These covert operatives would slip through Russian lines to a depth of twelve to fifteen miles, returning a couple of days later to report on Soviet defenses and troop concentrations.

Walli I agents were assisted by specialists called *Schleusenderer* (sluicers), who picked out parts of the front to insert the spies, usually areas that were not heavily manned.

In the weeks ahead, the Wehrmacht dug deeper into the vastness of the Soviet Union and were approaching Barbarossa's primary objectives: Moscow, Leningrad, and Stalingrad. It was in the capital of Moscow that the Germans had a highly effective mole known only as Max.

Max radioed his messages almost daily. Judging by the caliber of high-grade information he was sending, Max had intimate contact with the high and the mighty in the Soviet government and armed forces. The mysterious mole reported the Soviet high command's crucial decision to allow the German armies to advance deep into the sprawling country, trading terrain for time to mount a huge counteroffensive.

In late 1942, Max reported with incredible accuracy on plans drawn up by a war council in the Kremlin at which Stalin and his foremost generals planned a winter offensive that would doom 250,000 German soldiers at Stalingrad. The warning had been ignored by Hitler, who had decided the Soviet Army was breathing its last gasp.

Later, Hitler demanded to know from Admiral Wilhelm Canaris, a veteran spymaster and head of the Reich's Abwehr, the identity of Max. Canaris, who had been involved in behind-the-scenes contacts with agents of the Western Allies since the war began in September 1939, claimed ignorance of the mole's identity—which may or may not have been the case.

Canaris told the führer that all he knew was that Max's messages were sent by radio and eventually were passed along to Abwehr headquarters in Berlin by a shadowy Viennese figure who claimed his name was Fritz Kauders.

Because of certain expressions used by Max in his radio messages, some at Abwehr headquarters thought he was a physician who attended top-level Kremlin meetings. Others felt that the mole might even be Stalin himself who, for whatever devious reasons, was playing on both sides of the fence.

Yet other Abwehr leaders thought the mystery man might be someone in a position to tap the Kremlin telephone lines. Or perhaps he had covert connections to Japanese intelligence which had planted spies in Moscow many years earlier.

Whoever Max may have been, his identity would remain secret and probably will never be known. One factor was certain, however: Max was one of the war's greatest superspies.[14]

# Underwater War at Gibraltar

IN EARLY JULY 1941, Giuseppe Pierleoni arrived at the French consulate in Barcelona, Spain, to take up his new duties as a diplomat. Actually, that assignment was a cover. He was a commander in the Italian Navy, and he had been sent to Spain to organize and direct sabotage activities against the British bastion of Gibraltar.

Popularly known as the Rock, the British crown colony is perched on a peninsula just off the southern coast of Spain in the narrow entrance to the Mediterranean Sea. A limestone mass rising 1,408 feet above the water, the fortress is connected to the Spanish mainland by a low, sandy isthmus a mile and a half long.

Gibraltar was also a naval base, protected against submarine attacks by heavy steel nets. At any given time, there might be scores of Royal Navy vessels, from battleships to small boats, nestled in the relative safety of the harbor.

Commander Pierleoni, dressed in civilian clothes, spent most of the winter of 1941–1942 building up his sabotage organization in Spain. Then he was ready to launch his first land-based secret mission against British ships at Gibraltar. It would be an attack by twelve members of a combat swimming group known as the Gamma.

According to plan, the swimmers sneaked into a villa in Spanish territory just north of the Rock. They donned thick woolen undergarments, neck-to-toe rubber suits, camouflage-net helmets, and breathing equipment. Just before midnight on July 13, the Italian raiders left the villa and headed for the beach.

*An underwater war raged in this harbor of the British bastion of Gibraltar. (Author's collection)*

Strapped to the back and chest of each man were five-pound explosive devices known as "bed-ring bombs." Although small, the bombs could blow holes in steel plates.

Led by Vago Giari, tough and broad-shouldered with the proven dexterity of a seal, the swimmers knew they were on a perilous mission. The Rock was bristling with weapons, and large numbers of sentries were always on high alert—watching for saboteurs.

Nearing the Rock undetected, Giari and the others could see the dark silhouette of perhaps thirty Allied ships in the harbor. Each man was told his own target. Then the swimmers edged noiselessly into the water.

Back on the beach an hour later, Giari and five other frogmen heard four booms in the harbor. They knew the explosions would not sink the ships, but would put them out of action for a few months.

The operation was only moderately successful. Bombs were placed on ships only to have the explosives swept away by the current. Six swimmers did not return.

Giari was disappointed over the results of the raid and vowed to return. Two months later, he and another frogman sneaked into Gibraltar Harbor and badly damaged two British ships.

Now Commander Pierleoni turned his focus toward human torpedoes, using one of the war's strangest bases for his operations. It was the Italian tanker *Olterra*, which had been scuttled in shallow water by her captain just inside the Spanish harbor at Algeciras, within sight of Gibraltar. He had taken that action to keep the ship out of British hands after Italy declared war against England in 1940.

Italian Navy Lieutenant Licio Visintini brought to the submerged ship a human-torpedo crew that had crossed Spain in civilian clothes and with fake passports. Although Spain was officially neutral, it cooperated wherever possible with Nazi Germany. So a few Spanish soldiers who had been assigned to keep an eye on the *Olterra* were far more interested in scrounging cigarettes and consuming brandy.

Visintini's plan was to convert the half-sunken vessel into a base to launch underwater attacks against ships in Gibraltar Harbor. Keeping his mission as secret as possible, he told the Spanish soldiers that he was a civilian engineer who had been sent to try to salvage parts of the *Olterra*. The guards shrugged.

Working mainly at night to conceal their activity against any hostile eyes, the Italians used pumps to empty tons of water from the bow compartment until it rose out of the water. Then they cut out a door in the side of the compartment. Torpedoes would be kept in the bow, and when a night attack on Gibraltar Harbor was ready, they could be passed out of the ship through the door and lowered with pulleys to the water.

When renovation of the "base" was completed, Lieutenant Visintini explained to the Spanish soldiers that he was bringing boiler tubes from Italy by land. They again showed total disinterest. Actually, each crate contained a twenty-two-foot torpedo.

On December 7, 1942, all was ready for the first human-torpedo attack from the *Olterra* base against the closely guarded harbor. To discourage frogmen or human torpedoes, the Royal Navy dropped explosive charges into the harbor at irregular intervals. A steel net which could be lowered when an Allied ship approached, ringed the harbor.

Hidden by the veil of night, two torpedoes were lowered from the bow of the *Olterra* into the water. The Italians called a torpedo a *maiale* (pig).

Powered by an almost silent engine, a pig could travel at about three miles per hour and had a range of ten miles. It could travel on the surface or dive to a maximum of ninety feet. There was a warhead in the front section that could be detached by releasing an airscrew. Then the explosive could be attached to the hull of a ship.

Now Lieutenant Visintini got onto a seat at the front of one torpedo, and his partner took the rear seat. The back of one seat held steel cutters (to carve a hole in the harbor's net) and magnetic clamps to fix a warhead to a ship's hull. The man astride the pig in the forward position had controls for speed, steering, and diving, along with a luminous depth gauge for use below the surface.

Visintini and his companion cast off and reached the outer harbor in about an hour. They prepared to use the cutter on the steel net, but at that moment, the barrier was lowered to allow a destroyer to enter, so the silent intruders slipped in also.

Explosive charges were placed on two ships, and the human torpedoes headed back for the point at which they had entered the harbor. One of the British depth charges killed the two Italians.

Two weeks later, the bodies of Visintini and his companion were found inside Gibraltar Harbor. However, the existence of the top-secret *Olterra* base, located only a stone's throw from one of Britain's most crucial fortresses, had not been compromised.

With Gibraltar defenses on full alert against future penetrations of the harbor, Commander Pierleoni, the director of sabotage operations from his post as a diplomat in Barcelona, realized that a change in human-torpedo tactics was necessary. Ships in the open anchorage around the Rock now would be targeted.

In the weeks ahead, numerous human-torpedoes from the *Olterra* damaged ships at anchor and sunk two of them. Then, on the night of August 3, 1943, a pig with Lieutenant Commander Ernesto Notari and his number-two man, Petty Officer Gino Giannoli astride, were beneath their target, a seven-thousand-ton U.S. cargo ship *Harrison Grey Otis*. Giannoli fixed the five-hundred-pound charge to the vessel and the pig suddenly went berserk. It plunged 110 feet deep (three times the maximum depth in training). Then the pig rushed upward and broke the surface.

Meanwhile, Giannoli had been thrown from his mount and surfaced on the far side of the ship. Thinking that Notari had been killed, the petty officer shivered in the water for nearly two hours. Then he shouted for help and the startled crew of the *Harrison Grey Otis* hauled him aboard.

At the same time, Ernesto Notari, although semiconscious, was still astride the pig. When his head cleared slightly, he saw that, amazingly, the engine was still running. Thinking that Giannoli was dead, he decided to make his getaway on the pig. For more than an hour, his steel mount edged through the water at three miles per hour. He was fearful that the phosphorescent wake would attract the attention of the crew of a British patrol boat.

However, the gods of underwater saboteurs smiled on Notari. A school of frolicking porpoises accompanied him all the way back to the *Olterra*, providing perfect cover for his wake.

Back on the *Harrison Grey Otis*, Gino Giannoli was being interrogated by British officers when the charge he had attached exploded on the other end of the ship. The engine room was badly damaged, putting the cargo vessel out of service for many weeks.

Minutes later, the handiwork of other human-torpedoes that had taken part in that night's operation echoed over the seascape and up towering Gibraltar. A blast broke in two the ten-thousand-ton Norwegian tanker *Thorshovdi*, flooding the bay with a million gallons of oil. The six-thousand-ton British ship *Stanridge* was rocked by a third blast.

Gino Giannoli became a prisoner of war, but all the other Italians got back to the *Olterra* safely. However, the young petty officer would not hold a POW status for long. On September 29, 1943, Italy surrendered and joined the Western Allies, thereby converting Giannoli from a POW to a partner with the British.[15]

# Polish Spies Invade Germany

ANTONI KOCJAN, a mild-mannered Pole of about forty years of age, had spent nine months in the brutal Auschwitz concentration camp. For some mysterious reason, in June 1941, he and fifty other Polish prisoners caught in random roundups by the Gestapo were suddenly released. Unable to believe his good fortune, Kocjan returned to his home in Warsaw. There he joined the underground operation known as ZWZ (Zwiazek Walki Zbronjnej—Union for Armed Struggle).

Before Adolf Hitler launched an invasion of Poland on September 1, 1939, Kocjan had graduated from Warsaw Technical University, after which he got a job at the Experimental Aircraft Workshops helping to design and construct gliders. His engineering achievements were widely known in Europe after he built a motor-glider powered by a very small engine and called a *Bak*. The revolutionary craft set two records for height and distance.

However, Kocjan's modest fame had not reached the Gestapo. It had merely been his bad luck that he had been one of many Poles hauled from their homes and shipped to Auschwitz. Knowing that the Gestapo had nothing on him and that good use could be made of his engineering expertise, ZWZ leaders promptly welcomed Kocjan into their fold.

In an extraordinary feat of intelligence, ZWZ had organized a network of spies within Nazi Germany, at a time when the Western Allies had virtually no means for learning what was going on in Adolf Hitler's domain.

ZWZ spies were planted in the Third Reich by various means and pretexts, mostly by the Germans' recruiting of Poles for work in industry in the Reich. The Polish underground press loudly condemned the volunteers for working in Germany because this helped military production. These volunteers were branded as traitors.

Unbeknownst to the Polish people, however, the volunteer program was permitting ZWZ intelligence to put their agents at key industrial plants because the men and women who went to Germany under their own free will were usually allowed to choose their locales and their workplaces.

ZWZ had another scheme for getting spies into German territory: volunteering for the Organization Todt, a semimilitary agency that was in charge of the German construction industry at home and in occupied countries, building airfields, roads, barracks, and defensive positions.

Yet other Polish agents were slipped into the Reich by using fake identification papers. But this method was used only under special conditions and then for just a few days because personal documents were inspected regularly by local police and the Gestapo.

After a ZWZ agent reached Germany and began to work, he or she remained in peril. As a police state, the Reich had an elaborate system of informers in each factory or outdoor construction project. However, the identities of the informers became known to most workers, so the Polish spies could continue their sleuthing while being careful not to get tripped up by the Gestapo snitchers.

Many agents sent into the Reich by ZWZ had technical backgrounds in various endeavors, and they were able to obtain worthwhile information that was sent to ZWZ in Warsaw by courier. The secret reports contained the types of new Luftwaffe aircraft, technical advances, the speed and range of bombers and fighters, and the levels of production.

These hasty dispatches, of necessity, had only bare facts not supported by analysis or other sources. This type of reporting was known as raw intelligence. These matters needed specialist assessment, so in mid-1941, a Bureau of Economic Studies was established and attached to the intelligence branch of ZWZ. Given the code name Arka, the new bureau was led by an agronomist, Jerzy Chmielewski (code-named Jacek).

Tracking down the many Polish scientists he had known in prewar days, Chmielewski recruited many of them into his secret bureau. Antoni Kocjan had just been released from Auschwitz, so because of his background, he was put in charge of the department concerned with the Luftwaffe and German aircraft production. The engineer was given the code name Korona.

Meanwhile, Great Britain was a lion at bay, standing almost alone against the awesome potential of the mighty German war juggernaut. Moreover, British intelligence was desperate to obtain information from within the Reich because the British espionage network there had been wiped out by the Gestapo within a month of the war's beginning. ZWZ was asked to help.

Consequently, once a month the ZWZ radioed terse information from within Germany to British intelligence in London. The British were especially anxious to receive eyewitness reports on the impact of Royal Air Force bombings. London didn't like what it heard.

Because of problems with night navigation, heavy German fighter attacks, and antiaircraft fire from the ground, most RAF bombs were missing the targets. On occasion, a wrong town was hit. This information from ZWZ permitted British engineers to devise new technical procedures for guiding bomber streams, and the percentage of bombs exploding on Reich targets was vastly increased.

On February 14, 1942, ZWZ was renamed Armia Krajowa (Home Army), and its intelligence network in the Reich continued to expand. Two Polish agents were in a camp for foreign workers on the southern half of an island called Usedom, off northern Germany in the Baltic Sea. On the island was the one-time sleepy fishing village of Peenemünde. Unknown to the British, Usedom had been converted by the Germans into a proving ground for secret weapons with which Adolf Hitler hoped to eventually wipe London off the map—and even bomb New York City, as Germany was now at war with the United States.

Because of widespread German hatred for the Polish nationality, the two Poles at the foreign workers camp were given the dirtiest task there was: cleaning latrines and drains. But as a result of their work, they were assigned a wagon and a team of horses, along with cards that permitted them to roam over a fairly wide area.

The two Poles, whose names would never be learned by the Home Army in Warsaw, grew curious about the engine noises that came from the northern part of Usedom. These were not the sounds of the heaviest airplane engines; these made the ground shake. The Poles could not get any closer, but they made it an objective to be at a vantage point in the early evening.

Gawking northward into the sky, the two spies saw a sight that shocked and puzzled them. What appeared to be a small airplane with short wings and fire blasting out of its tail was flying out to sea. By a circuitous route, this intelligence reached Warsaw.

A coded radio message containing the Usedom sighting was rushed to London, where it reached the desk of Lieutenant Colonel Michel Protasewicz, chief of the VI Bureau of the Polish General Staff. The function of this bureau was secret liaison with Nazi-occupied Poland.

As was the procedure, Protasewicz immediately sent the alarming report to British intelligence, which passed copies on to military and government leaders. It created an enormous flap. Here was the sketchy details of the development of what would come to be known to the Western Allies as a buzz bomb or a doodlebug.

In the meantime, Home Army intelligence had been struck a heavy blow. By happenstance, the Gestapo arrested Jerzy Chmielewski. The Germans did not know of his involvement with the underground. Although he was charged with nothing, the Pole was confined to Pawiak prison for several months, then he was sent to the Auschwitz concentration camp.

Bulwarked by a hefty amount of *zlotys* (money) provided secretly by the Home Army, Chmielewski's family knew which German officials could be bribed, and a few months later, he was released. He promptly resumed his duties in Home Army intelligence.

Soon after Chmielewski was freed, Antoni Kocjan was awakened from a sound night's sleep by a ham-fisted pounding on his door. Two Gestapo agents and a pair of armed soldiers hauled him off to Pawiak prison. The engineer felt he was doomed, that the entire Home Army command apparatus was about to be demolished.

A short time after his interrogation began, however, he felt a tiny ray of hope. His connection to the underground was not under suspicion, rather he was being grilled about a printing press belonging to the Home Army, which the Gestapo had discovered in the basement of the glider factory where he had worked in peacetime. His name and address were also discovered there.

Kocjan was easily able to prove that he had no connection to the printing press, and the Gestapo appeared to be ready to release him. Then he was struck with bad luck. A young woman who had been a courier for the Home Army had been arrested, and she happened to be led past a transit cell where Kocjan was waiting. Tortured to disclose her associates, she could think of no one by name, so she singled out Kocjan.

Instead of gaining his freedom, Kocjan was cruelly treated, burned with hot irons, fingers broken, and beaten so badly that he had to be carried back to his cell on a stretcher. Somehow, he had managed to keep silent about his secret work and was released, a battered and broken man.

Despite his physical infirmities, Kocjan resumed his duties with the Home Army. But later, he was caught with incriminating documents by the Gestapo and shot.[16]

# A Leg Is Parachuted to a British Ace

WING COMMANDER Douglas Bader was leading his Royal Air Force fighter squadrons across the English Channel at 28,000 feet so that they, not the Luftwaffe pilots, would have the height and the sun. Their job was to go after German fighter planes where and when they found them. As the formation knifed past the French coast near Le Touquet, Bader looked down on twelve Messerschmitt 109s about two thousand feet below.

Bader, a scrappy pilot who had twenty-three "kills" and ranked fifth among RAF aces, shouted into his mask: "Dogsbody (code name for his group) attacking! Plenty for all! Take 'em as they come!"

Bader plunged downward in his Spitfire and squirted bullets at the nearest Me 109. Bits and pieces flew off the German fighter, then it burst into flame and fell earthward.

Moments later, the wing commander felt a heavy jolt. His plane had been hit and started to go down in a spiral. *"Get out! Get out!"* he told himself. That would not be easy to accomplish: the thirty-year-old ace had artificial legs.

Bader tore off his helmet and mask. The plane's hood was ripped away. He gripped both sides of the cockpit and managed to get out his top half. Then came a flash of terror. The rigid foot of his right leg was caught in the cockpit. He was stuck and plunging to a seemingly certain death.

Miraculously, Bader managed to break a leather strap that trapped his leg in the cockpit. Moments later, he was sucked out of the cockpit and pulled the ring that opened his parachute. Lady Luck had been his copilot.

*A six-foot metal cannister like these held RAF Squadron
Leader Douglas Bader's artificial leg when it was parachuted to him following a German request. (National Archives)*

Suddenly, he was aware that the earth was rushing toward him, and within seconds, he crashed into the unyielding terrain, instantly losing consciousness. An undetermined amount of time later, he opened his eyes and was aware that three German soldiers were removing his harness. They stared at this curiosity: a fighter pilot with no legs. It was August 9, 1941.

Bader was driven for several miles to a German hospital at St. Omer, a French town twenty miles south of the English Channel coast. His mind slowly cleared and he thought: "I hope the boys saw me bail out and tell [wife] Thelma." That night he was to have gone dancing with Thelma. No one had seen his parachute: he had simply vanished.

Douglas Robert Steuart Bader had been born in London and won a competitive exam to the Royal Air Force College where he was a champion boxer. Commissioned in 1930, he had served only eighteen months when his plane crashed. He survived, but both legs had to be amputated.

Discharged from the RAF, he mastered artificial legs and went to work in London for the Asiatic (later Shell) Petroleum Company. As a civilian, he demonstrated that he could fly an airplane skillfully, but the RAF refused to take him back. When war broke out in Europe in September 1939, however, the RAF brass winked at regulations and commissioned him as a flight officer.

Bader rapidly removed any qualms about his fitness for combat: he shot down an ME 109 and a Heinkel 111 bomber in two missions over the English Channel. One promotion after the other followed and at the time he was shot down, he was leading three Spitfire squadrons.

Now at the St. Omer hospital, Doug Bader's mind was awhirl. He must get word to Thelma that he was alive and he must get a second leg. He could not escape with just one leg.

One day, a young Luftwaffe fighter pilot called on Bader. Speaking flawless English, he identified himself as Count Whomever. The RAF ace seized on the opportunity: "Can you radio England and ask them to send me another leg?" He doubted if such an unprecedented task could be accomplished, but if it could, Thelma would know he was alive.

The German promised that he would do what he could.

Later, the Luftwaffe pilot returned. "I've got news for you," he said cheerfully. "With the permission of Reichsmarschall [Hermann] Goering, we have radioed England on an international waveband." He went on to explain that one RAF airplane had been given unrestricted passage to fly on a specified height, course, and time to drop the leg by parachute over St. Omer.

Pugnacious Bader replied that the RAF didn't need an unrestricted passage and that if the leg was dropped, it would come down with a cascade of bombs. The German grinned amiably. "We'll see," he said. "Let us hope that the next leg will not be shot down."

In London, RAF brass mulled over the contents of the Luftwaffe radio message. After much debate, it was decided to send the leg in a Blenheim bomber. Meanwhile, Bader's comrades hurried to tell Thelma the good news: her husband was alive.

Over St. Omer droned the Blenheim with a Spitfire escort. The bomb-bay doors opened and a cannister, some six feet long and holding the spare leg, dropped out. A parachute billowed above the container and floated earthward. Around it were the angry bursts of black flak from puzzled German gunners on the ground. Inside the leg, Thelma had stuffed tobacco, chocolates, and other scarce wartime goodies.

On the following morning at RAF Fighter Commander headquarters in England, Air Chief Marshal Sholto Douglas received a telephone call from Prime Minister Winston S. Churchill. The British Bulldog, as he was known, said, "I see by the newspapers that you have been fraternizing with the enemy, dropping a leg to a captured pilot."

"Well, sir," Douglas replied, "We [also] managed to shoot down eleven German [airplanes]. I hope you might feel it was worth it."

Churchill grunted and hung up, his curiosity satisfied.

No doubt the Germans regretted the role they had played in getting Bader his spare leg. He proved to be an incorrigible escape artist and finally had to be locked up in Colditz, a massive castle in central Germany that was deemed to be escape proof.[17]

# Sudden Death for the "Blond Beast"

BY THE LIGHT of a half-moon on December 29, 1941, two Czech secret agents—Lieutenant Jan Kubis and Sergeant Josef Gabcik—parachuted from a British bomber into the Bohemian hills five miles south of the major city of

Pilsen, Czechoslovakia. Code-named Anthropoid, the two-man team had a perilous mission: killing Obergruppenführer (SS General) Reinhard Heydrich.

A tall, hawk-nosed man, Heydrich had risen to the top in the Nazi hierarchy when in his late thirties. As chief of the Sicherheitsdienst, the SS security service, he had quickly earned a reputation for brutality and ruthlessness. It was said that even his immediate superior, Reichsführer Heinrich Himmler, was afraid of the steely-eyed general. Behind his back in Berlin, a hotbed of intrigue, Heydrich was known by SS officers as the "Blond Beast."

Eager for yet more power, Heydrich connived to get Adolf Hitler to appoint him Reichsprotektor of Czechoslovakia, which the führer had seized in 1939 in a bloodless power move. Heydrich arrived in Prague in September 1941, hoisted the SS flag over Hradcany Castle, and told his aides: "We will Germanize these Czech vermin."

Soon Czech men, women, and children were rounded up and many were murdered or imprisoned. Heydrich earned a new nickname: the "Butcher of Prague."

Now the Anthropoid team that had landed by parachute to assassinate Heydrich took refuge with the Czech underground, the British-sponsored Central Committee for Internal Resistance (UVOD), where they remained for six months, awaiting an opportunity to strike.

Patiently and stealthily, with the help of the UVOD, the Anthropoids tried to learn the daily route of their target. Then, by an amazing stroke of good luck, the hit men learned precisely where the Butcher of Prague would be on May 27, 1942.

Four days before that date, a prized antique clock on Heydrich's desk in Hradcany Castle broke, and a secretary called in a Czech repairman to fix it. Josef Novatny answered the summons. No one was in Heydrich's ornate office when Novatny took the back off the clock and noticed a piece of paper with the SS general's itinerary for the twenty-seventh typed on it. For whatever his reason, the repairman wadded the sheet into a ball and pitched it into a wastepaper basket.

Soon after Novatny departed, one of the regular cleaning women, a Czech named Marie Rasnerova, emptied the contents of Heydrich's wastebasket into a sack as was her daily routine. Rasnerova was an agent of the UVOD, and a few hours later, the contents—including Heydrich's itinerary—were being studied by Lieutenant Kubis and Sergeant Gabcik. They now knew in detail where Heydrich would be on the twenty-seventh and which route his flashy Mercedes sports-convertible with its SS driver would take.

Shortly after 9:30 on the morning of the twenty-seventh, Kubis and Gabcik took up positions in the Prague suburb of Holesovice, at a point where a hairpin bend in the road leading down to the Troja Bridge would force Heydrich's driver to slow. Kubis and Gabcik had submachine guns concealed under their raincoats. Two armed UVOD agents were posted around the bend.

*SS General Reinhard Heydrich was the only top Nazi assassinated on orders from London. Heydrich's bomb-splintered Mercedes (below). (National Archives)*

At 10:32 A.M., Heydrich's Mercedes reached the ambush site. Gabcik stepped into the road and pulled the trigger. The weapon jammed. Heydrich and his driver both shot at the Czech, but missed. At the same time, Kubis threw a bomb and it exploded near the Mercedes.

Heydrich dropped his pistol, staggered a few yards from the car and collapsed. Kubis had also been hit by shrapnel, but climbed onto a woman's bicycle and got away. The two UVOD gunmen also managed to leave the scene.

Heydrich, bleeding profusely, was rushed a few hundred yards to the Bulkova hospital where he died a week later.

Meanwhile, seven members of the assassination team had gone into hiding in the crypt of the Karel Borromaeus Greek Christian Orthodox Church in the old section of Prague. There they remained while the Czech underground hatched an innovative scheme to evacuate the fugitives.

A mock mass funeral would be staged at the church for victims of German reprisals, at which time the Anthropoids would be spirited away in coffins to the mountains and later taken to England. The Anthropoids radio team was still in contact with London, and June 19 was chosen as the day of the escape from the church.

However, before the Anthropoids could be evacuated, a Czech, Karel Curda, betrayed them when he became covetous of the Gestapo reward of 10 million crowns (125,000 pounds sterling or 600,000 U.S. dollars), a gargantuan sum at the time.

On the appointed day, the Czech resistants drove the funeral cortège into Charles Square, but the "pallbearers" found the area sealed off by SS troops. An hour later, wearing full combat gear, the Germans stormed the church. Inside they were met by a fusillade of small arms fire from the choir loft, where Lieutenant Jan Kubis and some other men were hiding. A hand grenade killed the Anthropoid leader, and two others in the loft shot themselves in the head.

Then the soldiers lifted a heavy flagstone to get into the crypt and were met by a hail of bullets. A fire brigade was called in and, under threat of instant execution, was forced to flood the cellar. Down to their last cartridges, the Czechs shot one another.

German reprisals were savage. The Gestapo unleashed a massive *ratissage* (rat hunt). Over 10,000 Czechs were arrested and some 1,300 were murdered.[18]

# Parachuting in a Boat

EARLY IN THE WAR, the Italians were ahead of the British in the development of weapons and techniques for attacking ships anchored in harbors. Under the prodding of dictator Benito Mussolini, the Italians were experimenting with several other military innovations. Much attention was given to weapons for secret naval missions that would strike at the heart of or behind Allied forces.

Mussolini, who called himself Il Duce (the leader), was ecstatic when Italian frogmen aboard revolutionary two-man torpedoes wreaked havoc on Royal Navy ships in the harbor at Alexandria, Egypt, in 1941.

British intelligence learned about the Italians' most recent naval warfare development—the explosive motorboat. A high-speed launch had five hundred pounds of explosives stashed in its bow. A lone pilot would sneak into an enemy harbor at night, aim his boat at a selected target and open the throttles wide. Then, shortly before the impact, the pilot would pull a lever that triggered his ejection back over the stern. After landing in the water, he would inflate his life jacket and head for the nearest shore.

Near Portland, England, the staff of the Combined Operations Development Center began drafting designs that would add an exotic touch to the Italians' explosive-boat idea. The British version would be dropped by parachute into a hostile harbor or anchorage.

The new development was fraught with danger: a man would be sitting inside the boat when it was dropped. After the prototype was ready for testing, Lieutenant David Cox volunteered to sit in the boat when it was jettisoned from the bomb rack of a four-engine Royal Air Force bomber.

Cox would go down in history. His would be the only parachute drop of a boat. Although known for his courage, he was so terrified from swinging downward through space while strapped helplessly inside the boat that the project was scuttled.[19]

# Part Two

## Freedom's Time
of Crisis

# A Ruse to Spy on Cherbourg

RAIDS BY BRITISH COMMANDOS and paratroopers against the northern coast of France during the early months of 1942 had driven home the threat of invasion from England to Hitler's stolen European empire. Consequently, he signed Directive 40, launching what he considered to be one of the great engineering feats in history.

An Atlantikwall, stretching for more than fifteen hundred miles from the snowy fjords of Norway to the Spanish frontier was to be constructed with "fantastic speed." There were to be fifteen thousand concrete-and-steel structures, immune to bombing or naval gunfire, to protect a continuous, interlocking belt of weapons commanding the major ports and potential landing beaches.

Thousands of slave laborers from all over Europe were rushed to the coast where they would toil around the clock building the massive fortifications.

Soon the Germans established a Zone Interdite (Forbidden Zone) that ran inland for several miles along the entire French coastline. Worried Allied leaders in London urgently requested Centurie, the underground organization in Normandy, to unlock the mystery.

In his directive, Hitler had declared, "If we can keep a major port out of the hands of the [invading] Allies, we can defeat any attempt to gain a foothold on continental Europe."

So the large ports received the highest priorities for manpower and materials. Cherbourg, in Normandy, became one of the most closely guarded cities in France. What Centurie leaders could not be told by London was that the Western Allies would land in Normandy one day, and Cherbourg would be the primary objective.

Failure to seize Cherbourg, some thirty miles northwest of the nearest landing beach, could result in the Allies being bottled up on a slim beachhead and cut to pieces by panzer divisions rushed to Normandy.

Repeated efforts by Centurie agents to penetrate Cherbourg, where in peacetime the luxury ocean liners *Queen Mary*, *Normandie*, and *Queen Elizabeth* had discharged their passengers, seemed to be a hopeless task. Then a bizarre opportunity surfaced.

Outside Caen, a German troop train traveling from Paris to Cherbourg was blown up, and several soldiers were killed. In reprisal, German commanders in Normandy had ten random hostages shot. In addition, the occupiers inaugurated a new procedure to curb the sabotage of troop trains. Just before a train was to depart from Paris for Cherbourg, about thirty French civilians waiting in the station were seized and herded into the coach immediately behind the locomotive.

No Centurie agent in his right mind would voluntarily become a hostage on a German troop train—except for Gilbert Michel of Caen. Michel not only managed to get himself selected as a hostage on one occasion, but he did so repeatedly, knowing that he could be killed or seriously injured should the Paris-Cherbourg train be blown up or derailed.

In Cherbourg—inside the Zone Interdite—the young Frenchman had to wait for four hours each time for the return train to Paris. So armed with a fake permit provided by Centurie craftsmen, he was free to roam around the city.

Through his regular hostage trips, Michel was able to provide a wealth of details on German fortifications being built in Cherbourg. This information was smuggled to London and incorporated onto a huge map of Normandy showing the defenses in the sector where the Allies would eventually invade.[1]

# "Hunting" Germans in Canoes

BRITISH LIEUTENANT Roger Courtney was a large, free-spirited man who had a reputation for drinking any other man in the army under the table. Before the war, he had been an explorer in Africa, and he loved to tell stories about hunting lions from canoes. On one occasion, he paddled a canoe 3,474 miles down the Nile River, from Lake Vitoria to Cairo, Egypt.

In mid-1940, Courtney was a Commando recruit at the Combined Training Center in Scotland. Soon after his arrival, he approached Admiral of the Fleet Roger Keyes, director of Combined Operations, with an innovative idea: Why not "hunt" Germans in canoes?

Keyes and his top aides curtly rejected the "crazy scheme." Canoes were suitable for Boy Scouts, but not soldiers. Courtney was angry, so he maneuvered a personal interview with Admiral Theodore Hallett, commander of the Combined Training Center.

Courtney explained how folding canoes (kayaklike craft known as foldboats) could be used in small raids. Hallett dismissed the junior officer without giving serious thought to the proposal. So Courtney cooked up a scheme to dramatize the fact that his idea would be practical.

Four nights later, Admiral Hallett was holding a meeting of senior Royal Navy officers in a conference room of the Argyll Arms Hotel in nearby Inveraray. Suddenly, the door flew open and in burst Lieutenant Courtney, who had wangled his way past guards although he was wearing only swimming trunks. As the brass looked on in amazement, the Commando pitched a large bundle, dripping water, into the middle of the room.

Courtney explained that he had just paid a visit to the *Glengyle*, a landing ship at anchor in the river Clyde. With mounting anger, the captain of the *Glengyle*, who was present, listened as Courtney said he had paddled out to the ship in a foldboat, got aboard without even being challenged, scrawled his initials on the captain's cabin door, and stole the cover from a deck gun. As proof of his feat, he had brought back the cover with him in the bundle.

Although Courtney might have been court-martialed on a number of charges, he had made a deep impression on Admiral Hallett and the others, presumably including the *Glengyle*'s embarrassed skipper. Foldboats might indeed have a role to play in Commando raids. So Courtney was given permission to begin recruiting and training a small group of Commandos. His outfit would be known as the Special Boat Section (SBS).

This elite band—it would never number more than one hundred men— began reconnaissance missions behind German coastal defenses and ship attacks in the Mediterranean in June 1941. Many of the raids met with disaster. There were drownings when foldboats capsized in turbulent surfs. Paddles were lost, rendering the craft immobile. Some Commandos got ashore in German-held territory and were stalking around inland when they were shot or captured.

There were rumors that Combined Operations was on the brink of scuttling the SBS. Then, almost a year after the inception of combat operations, SBS caught the attention of the British military leaders.

On the night of April 11, 1942, Captain Gerland Montanaro and Sergeant Frederick Preece paddled into the closely-guarded port of Boulogne, on the northern coast of France. Their foldboat had been leaking badly for an hour, but they had refused to turn back.

The two Commandos singled out a large German tanker, sneaked up to it as silently as possible, and attached magnetic mines to its hull. Then they paddled back out to sea to rendezvous with the motor launch that had dropped them off earlier. Just as they reached the launch, the leaking foldboat sank.

There was great elation back at the Commando base in England the next afternoon. Aerial photos revealed that only the superstructure of the tanker remained above water.[2]

# Jewish Raiders in Disguise

BRITISH CAPTAIN Herbert Buck had been taken prisoner by General Erwin Rommel's Afrika Korps while fighting was raging in the vast desert of North Africa in mid-1941. He escaped and set off eastward across the trackless wasteland in the hope of reaching friendly forces. It seemed like an impossible task. One Briton wandering around in the desert would be easily detected.

However, Buck found an Afrika Korps cap and he put it on, mainly to deflect the rays of the torrid sun. Soon he discovered to his amazement—and relief—that he was able to walk freely through German positions and bivouacs. In the desert, the British, the Germans, and the Italians all wore khaki uniforms with short-sleeved shirts and trousers that hit just above the knees. Moreover, Buck spoke fluent German, and he often received directions from men of the Afrika Korps.

When Buck finally reached elements of the British Eighth Army—the Desert Rats, the soldiers called themselves—he approached the brass with an idea. They bought it. He would form and train a new unit that was given a totally meaningless designation—Special Intelligence Group (SIG)—to mask the perilous nature of its task.

The SIG was composed mainly of German Jews from Palestine whose job was to sneak behind German lines masquerading as Afrika Korps soldiers. It virtually would be a suicide outfit. Each Jew knew that capture would mean dying an excruciating death.

Captain Buck was a strict instructor and commander. He knew that a slight slipup could doom an infiltrator. Only German was spoken when the men were training. Each received necessary documents, all of them forged: a phony name, identification tags, and letters from "home."

To reinforce the cover story assigned to each Jew, he carried a photograph of himself with his "girlfriend" in Berlin. Actually, she was a member of the Eighth Army's women's auxiliary who was usually blonde; that is, her features were suitably Aryan. A Berlin background was added in the darkrooms of Eighth Army photographers in Cairo.

Knowing that the slang of all armies often changes, British intelligence officers kept SIG current with the latest words being used by the men of the Afrika Korps.

When Captain Buck felt that his men were ready for desperate missions, he looked around for some action in which they could be involved. That chance came in late May 1942, when twenty-six-year-old Captain David Stirling was ordered to report to Cairo for a meeting with the director of military operations.

Stirling, who stood six feet six, was the founder and leader of a group of desert raiders code-named Special Air Service (SAS). That designation had been invented to make German intelligence believe that a large contingent of British paratroopers had arrived in Egypt.

Stirling was told that a convoy of twenty ships would sail through the Mediterranean bottleneck at Gibraltar in June and try to reach the beleaguered island of Malta, a British crown colony fifty-eight miles south of Sicily. Although it contained only 120 square miles, Malta was crucial to the Allied war effort.

*R.B. "Paddy" Mayne (left) succeeded David Stirling (right) as leader of the Special Air Service after the latter's capture. (National Archives)*

It controlled the vital sea lanes between Italy and Africa, and fighter planes based on the island defended convoys of Allied ships.

Because of its geographic importance, Malta was bombed relentlessly during the war, and its survival depended on getting supplies. Now Captain Stirling was asked to be part of a widespread British effort to thwart or diminish Luftwaffe attacks on the convoy scheduled to reach Malta in three weeks.

Responding with typical alacrity, Stirling produced a plan within twenty-four hours. It called for simultaneous raids on eight Luftwaffe airfields five hundred miles west of Cairo in Libya on the night of June 13. Stirling felt that five of the targets were lightly guarded and would present no real obstacle to the mission. The remaining three airfields, however, were in a region heavily patrolled by motorized units of the Afrika Korps. No one had ever doubted Stirling's courage, so when he mentioned that it might be difficult, or impossible, to penetrate the roving patrols, brass at Eighth Army suggested that a unit about which he had never heard—the Special Intelligence Group—might be able to help.

When Stirling asked Captain Herbert Buck if the SIG could carry out the raiding parties to the three airfields, Buck eagerly replied that he himself would lead his men on the mission far behind German lines.

On the evening of June 12, a convoy of three captured German trucks and a large British truck marked as being property of the Afrika Korps headed for the three airfields in the Derna-Martuba region along the Mediterranean coast of Libya. In the cabs were Buck and his Palestine Jews, all wearing Afrika Korps uniforms and armed with German weapons. In the back of the vehicles hidden under tarpaulins, were Stirling's Special Air Service men.

On the road to Derna, the little convoy came upon a German bivouac. The trucks stopped, the SIG men clambered down from the cabs with their mess kits and casually joined the line at the field kitchen which was serving the evening meal.

Around nine o'clock the next night, about five miles from Derna, the convoy halted and began preparing for the action against the three airports. Only two trucks would be used. One vehicle would head for the lone airfield at Martuba, the other truck for Derna, with its two airports. Each of the three raiding parties would consist of five SAS men who had been recruited by Stirling from the Free French Army that had been created after France had fallen in 1940. Three SIG men would go with each truck. Reluctantly, Captain Buck remained at the rendezvous point to coordinate the recovery of the trucks and raiders.

At about midnight, an SAS lieutenant who had been on the raid stumbled back to where Buck was waiting and told a tale that stunned the SIG leader. The truck going to Derna had developed engine trouble, and the driver stopped only two hundred yards from one of the airfields and climbed out.

From their hiding place under the tarpaulins, the ten Frenchmen heard the alarming sound of many running boots. German soldiers surrounded the truck and one shouted: "All Frenchmen come out!"

The response from the SAS men was a burst of automatic weapons fire and pitched grenades. In the mass confusion, the lieutenant, who would tell Captain Buck the story, leaped out and ran for his life. Moments later, the truck, which had been packed with explosives, erupted into a gigantic ball of fire.

Buck waited at the rendezvous point for a week in the long-shot hope that men from the Martuba missions would return. None did. They had met the same fate as the Derna raiders: all were killed or captured.

British intelligence was convinced that the raiders had been betrayed. Later it was learned that the driver of the Derna truck had been a German prisoner of war recruited by Buck to help SIG perfect its German identity. On the way to Derna, he had invented mechanical problems to turn his SIG comrades and the French raiders over to his own countrymen, the Germans.

Elsewhere, the SAS raids on the five other airfields were resounding successes. Sixteen Luftwaffe planes were blown up, as were hundreds of tons of ammunition and fuel. At an airfield near Benghazi, Captain Stirling and two corporals planted sixty bombs on airplanes, ammunition dumps, and hangars. On their way out, Stirling opened the door to a room in a barracks and saw a German seated at a desk. The Briton pitched a grenade and said, "Here, catch!" By reflex action, the German caught it, and in a voice tinged with terror, he called out, "*Nein, nein!*"

Stirling slammed the door shut and ran. Moments later, an explosion ripped the room into shreds.

Despite the heroics by the men of SIG and SAS, German air and sea attacks devastated the supply convoy bound for Malta. Only two ships made it to port.[3]

# A Conspiracy to Capture Cairo

IT BECAME KNOWN AS "Black Saturday"—June 13, 1942. General Neil Ritchie, a tall, energetic, good-humored man who commanded the British Eighth Army, sent some three hundred tanks to assault Field Marshal Erwin Rommel's vaunted Afrika Korps in eastern Libya. Through wireless intercepts, the famed German commander knew of the attack in advance and laid an ambush of 88-millimeter, high-velocity guns.

In less than a half day, 230 British tanks had been wiped out. Rommel's panzers then charged eastward and crossed the border into Egypt. Before the Desert Fox, as Rommel was called, halted at the village of El Alamein, the Germans had inflicted some 75,000 casualties on Ritchie's army, which had been pulling back in disarray.

With the Afrika Korps only a hundred miles to the west, British military and government offices in Cairo, the capital of Egypt, burned their secret papers in such quantities that the day was called "Ash Wednesday." It seemed only a matter of a week or two before Rommel would be holding a victory parade in the large city.

As great as was the menacing German force poised to await supplies to catch up, behind British lines in Egypt an equally ominous danger was evolving, one of which neither Ritchie nor his successor, General Bernard L. Montgomery, was aware. It was a conspiracy involving the German Abwehr (intelligence agency); the Muslim Brotherhood, a militant Egyptian organization; and the Free Officers Movement, a bitterly anti-British nationalist group within the Egyptian Army.

Heading the Free Officers Movement were two men in their early twenties, Anwar el-Sadat and Gamal Abdel Nasser (both of whom would one day become presidents of Egypt). The key Abwehr figure in the Cairo conspiracy was twenty-seven-year-old Karl-Heinz Kraemer, who was regarded by Berlin as a clever operator.

Kraemer's mission was to overthrow the British government in Egypt and replace it with a pro-German Egyptian regime. If this objective could be realized, the British Eighth Army would find itself confronted by Rommel's Afrika Korps from the west and an Egyptian army from the east. Sadat told the Abwehr agent: "Now is the time to strike. We can turn the [Nile River] Delta into a blood bath if we rise now."

Sadat and Nasser were so confident that Rommel would soon be in Cairo that they found him a residence worthy of a Caesar-like conqueror—an ornate mansion on the Rue des Pyramides.

Kraemer met secretly with a leading light in the conspiracy to free the country from British control, General Aziz-el-Masri, the commander of the Egyptian Army. Masri agreed to cooperate with plans to instigate a jihad (a violent Muslim uprising) when Rommel resumed his offensive.

Masri turned over to Kraemer the British plans for the defense of the Western Desert and Cairo. This move backfired. A British unit overran an Afrika Korps command post and seized a copy of the purloined papers. British intelligence felt there were clues that Masri had been involved, so the general was fired from his key post.

Undaunted, the crafty Karl-Heinz Kraemer plotted to help Masri escape from Cairo so that the ousted general could lead an Egyptian "army of liberation" into the capital side by side with Field Marshal Rommel.

Typically, Kraemer's schemes were innovative. A Luftwaffe airplane disguised with British Royal Air Force markings, landed on the desert outside Cairo. But on the way to the rendezvous, General Masri's automobile broke down, and the fugitive had to return to Cairo.

Fearful that British intelligence had obtained clues to the plan, Kraemer, on a second effort, arranged for an Egyptian pilot, known to be violently anti-British, to fly an Egyptian Air Force plane to an abandoned airfield near Cairo.

Kraemer's qualms had been well founded. Britain's chief of security in Cairo, Major A. W. Sansom, had penetrated the evacuation plot. When Masri was aboard the Egyptian Air Force plane, a squad of British soldiers rushed up just as the pilot was preparing to take off.

Instead of leading an Egyptian Army of liberation, Masri spent the remainder of the war as a guest of the British government—in jail. The planned jihad collapsed.[4]

# Intruders at a Secret Airport

ULTRA, AN INGENIOUS British radio interception and decoding operation at Bletchley Park, forty miles north of London, uncovered fragmented information that the Germans had established a secret airfield in the vast desert east of Tobruk, Libya. The precise site could not be identified, but it was learned that each Saturday near dusk, a convoy of twelve supply trucks left German-held Tobruk and headed for the airfield. It was June 1942.

Tobruk had a population of some four thousand Arabs who existed in a few hundred white houses among a handful of palm trees. However, the tiny port held great military significance. It had the best harbor for a few hundred miles in both directions, and, in fact, was far superior to the Germans' main supply port of Benghazi, more than three hundred miles west of Tobruk.

With the secret airfield intelligence from Ultra, British headquarters to the east at Kabrit, Egypt, laid on a raid to blow up the German facility which would require a long trek westward behind German lines. Captain Douglas M. Smith, a sergeant, and ten privates volunteered for the bold mission.

Climbing into a truck with Captain Smith seated next to the driver, the raiding party set out for the unknown objective. The fierce sun boiled the men, and they were pestered constantly by flies and gripped by thirst. Precious drinking water had to be strictly rationed.

Within a few miles, the truck slipped through one of the many gaps in the lines between the opposing British and German forces. It took three days to reach the initial destination, a curve in the east-west coastal road some thirty miles east of Tobruk. Intelligence had disclosed that the usual Saturday night convoy of German trucks customarily turned southward there into the desert and headed for the airfield.

Smith planned to slip the truck into the German convoy in the blackness and travel with it to the target. The curve in the coastal road, General Erwin Rommel's main line of communications, seemed to be the best place to intermingle with the German trucks.

As night unfolded on the third day, the British raiders parked their truck in a small ravine only fifteen yards from the coastal road, but out of sight of those along it. At about 8:00 P.M., a British sentry who had been placed on a nearby knoll with high-powered field glasses, hurried down to tell Captain Smith that pairs of dim driving lights were approaching from the direction of Tobruk.

Smith rapidly explained his plan. The German trucks, as usual, were traveling about a hundred yards apart. The Tommies (as British soldiers were called) would remain in hiding until eleven of the trucks had passed. Before Number 12 came into sight around the bend, the British truck would swing onto the road and join the convoy.

Smith's men were taken aback. "Wouldn't it be better to let all twelve vehicles go by, then fall in at the rear?" one asked. "No," the captain replied. "The Jerries [Germans] on Number 12 will know that they are the last in line. They'd immediately grow suspicious if another pair of dim lights would suddenly pop up behind them.

"After we sneak into the column, Number 11 will think our vehicle is Number 12 and Number 12 will think our truck is Number 11," Smith explained.

"When the convoy nears the airfield, there is bound to be some indication of that fact," the captain added, "because there will be guards at the entrance. We can't risk their noticing that there are thirteen trucks in the column, instead of the expected dozen."

*A minefield warning is posted along this coastal road traveled by British raiders trying to reach a secret German airfield. (National Archives)*

So a short distance from the entrance, the British truck would have a fake breakdown in the middle of the narrow road, thereby blocking the passage. Number 12 would have to stop and the Germans would come up to find out what was wrong. At that close range, they would see that it was not a Wehrmacht conveyance, so the Tommies would take care of them with knives.

Now the convoy from Tobruk approached the British truck concealed in the ravine. The Germans were driving at about thirty miles per hour, so after Number 11 went past, the British truck sneaked into line.

Moments later, Smith had a haunting thought. What would the driver in Number 12 think when he rounded the curve and suddenly saw that instead of being a hundred yards behind Number 11, he was only forty yards from it? The captain breathed a sigh of relief when the trailing truck dropped back to the required interval.

A half hour later, Number 12 sounded three short honks from its horn. There was no doubt that the German truck intended Smith's vehicle to halt because it raced to close the gap. Then another blast of the horn. Smith told his driver to pull over to the side of the road.

Number 12 stopped about ten yards to the rear, and the German next to the driver hopped out and walked forward. "This is it!" Smith felt. The raiders were trapped in an enemy convoy.

The German, a powerfully built man, came up to the truck. British hands gripped trench knives. "Please, does any of you have a match?" One of the Tommies, Etienne Latour, who spoke flawless German, replied pleasantly, "I'm sorry, friend, but none of us have one."

There was an impatient honk from Number 12, and the German trotted back.

"Step on it!" Captain Smith told the driver. "We've got to get our position back in line."

A half hour later, the convoy turned off the coastal road and headed into the desert. Soon, the British truck came over a low rise and Smith could see pinpoint lights out in the blackness. Obviously, it was the airfield. As planned, his driver halted the truck in the middle of the road, ostensibly with engine trouble.

Moments later, Number 12 pulled to a halt. Two Tommies, standing beside the "disabled" truck, waited for the two Germans to climb out. Both men died without knowing what had hit them. After wiping the blood off and sheathing their knives, the Tommies dragged the corpses into nearby brush.

Then the British truck was parked about fifty yards from the road to serve as a later rallying point. Smith and his men scrambled into Number 12 and took out after the convoy. Two Tommies were left with the getaway truck. In minutes, the raiders were approaching what seemed to be the airfield entrance, a gap in the fence.

The German truck with its British passengers drove past two bored sentries and through the opening, parking near the other trucks in the convoy. The twenty-five or so genuine Germans in the convoy had already departed, presumably into a nearby building for alcoholic refreshments.

Fanning out, the intruders silently placed delayed-action explosives on some twenty aircraft, an ammunition dump, two trucks holding bombs, warehouses loaded with supplies, a tractor, a gasoline dump, and a few small structures. Because the airfield was so far behind Wehrmacht lines, the premises were unguarded except for the two lackadaisical sentries at the entrance.

Their mischief completed, Captain Smith and his men began individually stealing back toward the entrance to return to their own truck in the desert as planned. Suddenly, lights flashed on in several buildings. A siren blew. There were loud shouts: *"Halten!"*

About twelve figures dashed out of the buildings and began chasing after the intruders. It was mass confusion. Although arc lights flooded the area, some of the Germans ran after the fleeing raiders and others chased running Germans. Nearing the entrance, Smith whipped out his revolver, spun around, and fired a shot at a pursuing German who had nearly caught up with him. The chaser collapsed in a heap.

More lights flashed on. More Germans shouted. Now Smith was nearing the entrance. Would the two sentries gun him down? That was a risk he would have to take. Charging toward the gap, he spotted two clumps on the ground: Smith's men had already reached the gate and had silently "dispatched" the guards.

Thirty minutes after the alarm had been given at the airfield, Smith and the other raiders returned to their waiting truck. All were gasping for breath from the long sprint. Three Tommies had been cut down by a burst of machine-gun fire when they tried to scramble over the fence, Smith was told.

Moments later, the British truck and its occupants roared back onto the road and set a course for home—some two hundred miles to the east. All knew it would be a perilous trek because Luftwaffe planes would be scouring the desert for them.

Despite the urgency, the captain ordered the truck to halt on the crest of a slight rise in the terrain about three miles from the airfield. "May as well see some of the show," Smith said. "After all, we paid our admission!"

Soon the raiders saw the dark night pierced with crimson bursts of flame that reached into the heavens. There was a necklace of explosions. The earth shook beneath the Tommies' feet. The pyrotechnics continued for ten minutes; then the sky was black once more except for a faint orange-and-yellow glow hovering above the Luftwaffe airport.

"Let's get the hell out of here!" Smith said.

Three days later, after playing hide-and-seek with German search planes, the nine raiders were back at their base.[5]

# A Special Medal
# for Burma Tribesmen

"VINEGAR JOE" STILWELL was seething with anger as he held a news conference in Delhi, India, in June 1942—six months after Pearl Harbor. Long known for his bluntness, the three-star U.S. general pulled out all the stops.

"I claim we took one hell of a beating!" Stilwell told the reporters. "We got run out of Burma, and it's humiliating as hell!"

Three months earlier, Stilwell had been rushed to the Far East by President Franklin D. Roosevelt, who was concerned that China, with its one billion people, might drop out of the war against Japan. Vinegar Joe's task was to command the small number of U.S. troops in China and to administer the shipment of thousands of tons of American war materials to Generalissimo Chiang Kai-shek, the Chinese strongman.

These accoutrements reached China over the Burma Road which ran from the railroad center at Lashio in Burma for 770 miles eastward to the major city of Kunming, China. The road was little more than a caravan trail which was constantly being washed out by torrential rains.

By the time Stilwell arrived for his new assignment, the veteran Japanese Fifteenth Army had conquered much of Burma. China was isolated. So Stilwell set about to retake the Burma Road.

*The American-organized Kachin Rangers lead their pack ponies along a path in a remote region of Burma behind Japanese lines. (U.S. Army)*

His plan was "crazy," some chairborne army leaders in Washington claimed. It evolved around a tribe called the Kachins who lived in what was known as Upper Burma, a region in the north with mountains towering as high as twelve thousand feet and covered with thick green forests. Through this hostile environment ran the crucial Burma Road.

A contingent of American Rangers, tough fighting men trained for difficult special missions, were brought in to neighboring Assam, a state in India. They had been handed a tall order. Individually, they would parachute into Upper Burma and be irrevocably on their own.

Each Ranger would have to make friends with the Kachin warriors whose language and customs were unfamiliar. Then he must get these natives to accept him as their leader, trusting them not to betray him to the Japanese for a large reward. Once the Ranger was securely established, aircraft flying at night would parachute in weapons, supplies, and food. Now he was ready to lead the Kachins in their own little war far behind Japanese lines and largely isolated from the world.

Stilwell had not launched his plan foolishly. It was known that the Kachins hated the Japanese, who had treated the mountain tribe brutally as inferior human beings. Moreover, the Kachins admired Americans as much as they detested the Japanese.

On parachuting to the ground, the Rangers were given a shock. The Kachins did not fit the Hollywood style of the noble jungle warrior. Most were about five feet tall, had crooked teeth, and their skimpy clothing looked as though it had never been washed lest it disintegrate. What especially worried the Americans on first contact with the Kachins was the tribesmen's shy manner which was mistaken for stupidity. Actually, the Kachins were stupid like a fox is stupid.

The tribe proved to be eager to fight the Japanese and do so under American leaders. Gradually, each Ranger organized his own band of tough little men who were eventually equipped with old, but serviceable machine guns and rifles, then taught how to use them.

About two months after the first Rangers landed, platoon-sized Kachins began to dynamite bridges and blow up Japanese ammunition dumps. The native warriors were particularly joyful over setting up ambushes on remote mountain trails. First they filled the brush on both sides with carefully-hidden, needle-sharp bamboo stakes. When a Japanese patrol neared, it was fired on and by reflex its members dived for cover—and speared themselves with the stakes.

Word of the ambush technique presumably had spread through Japanese ranks in Burma because in future actions, the Japanese stood or crouched in the middle of the trail and were gunned down by the obsolete U.S. army rifles in the hands of the Kachins.

A born jungle fighter, a Kachin liked to shoot a Japanese only to wound him. Then, as his ancestors had done for centuries when hunting wild beasts, he would charge forward and finish off the soldier with a sharp knife.

The Kachins also fought under British officers. At an old frontier post called Fort Hertz, Colonel O'Neill Ford, who had spent many years in Burma, collected a force of some seven hundred Kachins with subunits scattered around villages in the region.

Led by sixteen British officers, the Kachin bands raided, harassed, and deceived the enemy. When the Japanese sent a large force to wipe out the Kachins, the tribesmen melted into the jungle and let the enemy continue marching ever deeper into the wilds before calling off the operation.

A combination of U.S., British, and Chinese forces eventually dislodged the tenacious Japanese from their mountain strongholds in the north and drove them southward to the plains of Lower Burma.

American officers who had fought in the jungles felt that the Kachins deserved a special medal for valor—and they got one. It was designated the CMA award. It came about when an officer misread a radio message from a high headquarters that said his Kachins, for one especially gallant action, would be rewarded with parachute drops of food delicacies and new clothes. After the word "food" appeared the letters CMA, the radio abbreviation for "comma." So the officer told his Kachins that they were going to be decorated with the coveted CMA. The tribesmen were delighted.

But when higher echelons heard of the promise, they were in a quandary. They could not permit an American officer's promise to his men to be broken. But certainly, they couldn't go against army regulations and invent a decoration. Or could they?

Someone in headquarters suggested that the CMA could stand for "Citation for Military Assistance." Days later, a box of shiny new medals was parachuted into the camp of the Kachins. Each decoration was a handsome silver medal bearing the initials CMA which was worn from a green ribbon embroidered with white peacocks. It was a very special recognition for Kachins only.[6]

# American Medics Save Ho Chi Minh

ALTHOUGH IN THE BACKWATERS of a savage global conflict, Vietnam, with a population of some twenty million, was the site of a bloody struggle between occupying Japanese forces and native resistance groups. The Japanese had seized Vietnam to serve as a base for widespread invasions in Southeast Asia when war erupted in the Pacific in December 1941.

Most of the fighting against the Japanese was done behind established lines by the Communist-dominated Viet Minh guerrillas, whose announced goal for the country was independence from France. Although officially not involved with the Viet Minh, members of the cloak-and-dagger U.S. Office of Strategic Services (OSS) helped anyone who was battling the common enemy, the empire of Japan.

At one aid station in the fall of 1942, an OSS doctor tended to a resistance member whose medical tag identified him as Ho Chi Minh. The man was apparently dying from malaria, dysentery, and other debilitating diseases usually spawned in jungles, of which Vietnam had no shortage. The fifty-three-year-old patient was treated with modern drugs and soon made what the physician regarded as a remarkable recovery.

Ho was not without gratitude to the American doctor and his male medical staff. He offered them the company of any of the pretty young Vietnamese women in his large entourage.

Seventeen months earlier in mid-1941, Ho Chi Minh (an adopted name meaning "he who enlightens") had been in China when he founded the Viet Minh (League for the Independence of Vietnam). Chiang Kai-shek, the Chinese Nationalist strongman, had Ho arrested as a Communist agitator, but after the United States was bombed into global war at Pearl Harbor, the prisoner was released—at the request of the OSS—to organize anti-Japanese intelligence throughout Vietnam.

Ho performed his mission for three years, but when it appeared that the war in the Pacific was nearing its end in early 1945, he pulled his sizeable force of guerrillas and secret agents into the highlands to prepare for seizing power once the shooting stopped. Taken into hiding with him were many tons of U.S.-supplied weapons and ammunition.

*Vietnamese guerrilla leader
Ho Chi Minh's life was saved
by American army doctors.
(National Archives)*

When a Japanese delegation signed surrender papers on the U.S. battleship *Missouri* in Tokyo Bay, the Viet Minh were the only organized force in Vietnam. So the guerrilla leader promptly marched into Hanoi, forced Emperor Bao Dai to abdicate (ending a thousand-year monarchy), established the Communist Democratic Republic of Vietnam, and proclaimed himself as president.

Twenty years later, Ho's tough, wily Viet Minh jungle fighters were embroiled in a bitter war with the United States. Would history in Southeast Asia have been different had not the OSS doctor saved the Communist leader's life years earlier?[7]

# A Hoax at Soviet Oil Fields

IN THE EARLY SPRING OF 1942, Adolf Hitler hoped to regain the momentum his armies had lost in Russia during the bitter winter of 1941. He told his generals that he was going to mount a new offensive to capture the rich oil fields at Maikop, Baku, and Grozny in the Caucasus Mountains of southwestern Russia.

Seizing these vast resources would provide the führer's thirsty war machine with fuel to keep driving into Russia. And it would deprive Soviet dictator Josef Stalin of his own badly needed oil. The German offensive would kick off in June 1942.

"If I do not get the oil of the Caucasus," Hitler told General Friedrich von Paulus, commander of the Sixth Army, "then I must end the war."

Stalin could have said the same thing.

When preparations for the all-out attack got underway, Baron Adrian von Fölkersam, who was regarded as one of the German Army's most gifted young officers, was called to a high headquarters and assigned a crucial role for his curious little private army. He called his men the "wild bunch," and with ample reason.

Captain Fölkersam was elated on learning of his mission: he and his men, who officially belonged to an elite Commando-type outfit called the Brandenburgers, were to work their way into the Caucasus and prevent the oil fields at Maikop from being blown up by the Russians before German spearheads arrived.

Fölkersam, the grandson of a Russian admiral, was ideally suited for the daunting task behind enemy lines. He spoke Russian fluently (as well as English and French), and was noted for his coolness in tight situations. Earlier in the year, he had recruited and trained a force of sixty-two Russian-speaking Balts and disillusioned Germans, and he pledged to take them farther behind Russian lines than any Brandenburg unit had ever gone. Now that chance was at hand.

Dressed in the military uniforms of the NKVD, the Russian secret service, Fölkersam and his "wild bunch" sneaked through Red Army lines under the veil of night in July 1942, and headed for the Caucasus in captured Russian vehicles.

A week later, the Brandenburgers tagged on to the rear of a long Russian convoy of trucks on the road to Maikop. On the outskirts of town, they encountered a group of real NKVD men who were trying to sort out a confused traffic jam. Fölkersam, whom his men thought relished perilous situations, halted his truck and approached one of the genuine NKVD officers.

"Well, you finally got here," the Russian exclaimed with a snarl. "Well, we don't need you now!"

"Major" Fölkersam had no idea to what the Russian was referring, but he saluted, got into his truck, and the convoy drove on into Maikop. In the city, the caravan pulled up in front of the NKVD headquarters. Fölkersam went inside and presented himself to a Russian general as "Major Turchin from Stalingrad."

A friendly type, the general seemed to be delighted to have a visitor from where the real war was being fought, apparently disappointed with his assignment in the seeming backwaters of the conflict in Russia. After an amiable conversation with "Major Turchin," the general arranged for comfortable quarters for the newcomers.

For several days, the Brandenburgers meandered around Maikop in their Russian uniforms, sizing up the defenses of the city and those of the nearby oil fields. On the night of August 8, Fölkersam could hear the distant rumble of German artillery firing shells, and the much louder roar of Russian guns emplaced around Maikop. He learned from a genuine Russian officer that the German army was only ten miles from Maikop.

At dawn, Fölkersam called his men together and gave them final instructions. In teams of four or five, they were to stir up mass confusion among the Russians and prevent them from destroying the oil wells.

Lieutenant Franz Koudele and a few men were sent to seize the local telegraph office. When he told the Russian officer in charge that Maikop was being abandoned and that he had better get out while he could, the Russian was not inclined to argue, and he and his staff fled.

Now the Russian-speaking Koudele was in charge of a telegraph system connected to various headquarters and posts throughout much of the northern Caucuses. Messages flooded the office. Soviet commanders demanded to be connected with some officer who knew what was going on at the front. "We cannot connect you, sir," Koudele replied with just the proper tone of anxiety in his voice. "Maikop has been abandoned."

By now, there was a stampede of Russian officers and soldiers heading out of Maikop, away from the front. No one wanted to be left in town to confront the oncoming German army.

Meanwhile, at the Maikop oil fields, army engineers were preparing to blow up the wells, storage tanks, and pumps. Then the counterfeit NKVD men raced up in their Russian trucks and shouted at the engineers to hold up on the demolitions. They quoted Fölkersam's Soviet friend, the general, who had already left for the rear, as the authority for the hold-up order.

As matters turned out, the failure of the Russian engineers to blow up the oil fields played right into the hands of Josef Stalin. Although German panzers reached the outskirts of Maikop, Adolf Hitler's offensive ground to a halt, and Stalin retained his crucial oil source.[8]

# A Woman Heads
# an Escape Apparatus

TWENTY-YEAR-OLD British Flight Officer John Hoskins, pilot of a Wellington bomber, was returning at night with his group from a raid on the Ruhr, a vast industrial region that supplied war accoutrements to the mighty German war machine. Suddenly, the Wellington was jolted, hit by flak, and Hoskins and his crew had to bail out. He came down in the darkness in northeastern Belgium. It was September 1942.

Like all Royal Air Force men, Hoskins had been taught escape and evasion tactics. He hid by day and marched toward the English Channel at night. At dawn on the third day, the pilot was seeking a place to hide when an old man approached on a bicycle. Seeing the RAF uniform, the Belgian took the man to his home and villagers provided the evader with civilian clothes.

After being fed a sumptuous meal, Hoskins was taken to the barn to spend the night, and he fell into an exhausted sleep in a pile of hay.

During the night, the Briton was shaken awake vigorously by a man shouting at him in German. Gestapo agents, his hazy mind told him. "What's going on?" the pilot called out.

The stranger replied: "Take it easy. You're among friends. Come with me."

The newcomer explained that he was a member of the Comet Line, an underground apparatus that rescued downed Allied airmen and arranged to spirit them back to England. Had the pilot responded in German by the rude awakening, the Belgian would have assumed he was a German agent trying to infiltrate Comet and would have killed Hoskins on the spot.

Hoskins was escorted to a Carmelite monastery in Namur, Belgium, where he was concealed for three weeks while forged identity papers were created for him. Almost constantly, the Comet people had him rehearse his cover story: he was a Belgian commercial salesman going to Biarritz, a resort on the Bay of Biscay in the southwestern tip of France and only a few miles from the border of neutral Spain. The evader was supposed to be selling bathroom tile, and he was provided with a number of samples for the kit he would carry.

Time and again Hoskins was instructed how to respond when asked to show his fraudulent work permit, identity card, and travel papers. He was told how to follow the Comet guides, to walk on the other side of the street when going through a town, and to ride in opposite ends of a bus.

The Briton was not a Roman Catholic, so he was informed how to bless himself with holy water and how to genuflect before an altar because he would be hidden in Catholic facilities along the escape line.

A day before Hoskins was to depart, he was introduced to an attractive twenty-four-year-old Belgian nurse, Andrée de Jongh, known to friends as Dédée, the founder of and moving spirit behind the Comet escape line. At first, the pilot doubted that she had played a major role in such a complicated and perilous operation. But others soon convinced him that she was indeed the famous Dédée, who was known quite favorably by MI-9, the Escape and Evasion branch of the British secret intelligence service in London.

Dédée's escape line had its beginning in August 1941, when she turned up at the British consulate in Bilbao on Spain's northern coast. Looking even more girlish than her actual years, she was dressed in a blouse, skirt, and bobby socks. She refused to be brushed off by underlings.

*Belgian nurse Andrée "Dédée" de Jongh, mastermind of the Comet escape line that saved hundreds of Allied lives. (Librairie Academique Francaise)*

Perhaps to get rid of the unwanted pest, aides showed her into the consul's office. He was astonished when she told him that she had brought three fugitives from Brussels with her—a young Belgian wanted by the Gestapo and two British Tommies (soldiers) who had been stranded when most of the British Army had been evacuated from Dunkirk, France, to England more than a year earlier.

The night before, Dédée and her three charges had climbed the towering Pyrenees Mountains along the border of Spain and France. She offered to bring out more stranded British soldiers. Would the consul reimburse her for the railroad tickets and the fee for the Spanish guide who led them over the Pyrenees? Indeed he would.

Dédée returned to Brussels and began organizing her escape line. Headquarters was the house on Avenue Emile Verhaeren where she lived with her father Frédéric, a headmaster of a primary school for boys. Her father was her strongest supporter, but she also was helped by her mother, her aunt, and an older sister.

The shrewd young woman referred to the Allied airmen and soldiers she rescued as "packages," so MI-9 code-named her line "Postman." But in 1942, when she brought an entire Royal Air Force bomber crew across Belgium, France, and into Spain in only one week, the line's code name was changed to Comet. Dédée became a symbol of courage, defiance, and resourcefulness.

Guides to escort the evaders to the Spanish border were mainly young women. They had to be nimble-witted and explain on the spur of the moment the presence of the young men with them who spoke no French.

Now at the Carmelite monastery in the fall of 1942, Flight Officer Hoskins was ready to go, dressed in a gray suit, black homburg, and lugging a case of tile samples. Escorted by Dédée, he linked up in Brussels with two crewmen from his bomber, much to his amazement. The airmen had been collected by the Comet Line.

The little party boarded a train with Dédée in one end of a car and the three evaders at the opposite end. They reached Paris routinely, where they remained in a safe house for three weeks while Dédée made arrangements to continue the trek.

Then the Belgian and her three charges took another train to Biarritz. A sixteen-year-old girl met the party at the train station and escorted the three airmen to a safe house. There Comet Line operatives provided them with new identities. They would masquerade as Basque peasants in berets and threadbare denim work clothes. All were instructed on how to let a lighted cigarette dangle from a corner of the mouth, just as most of the Basque workers did.

Forty-eight hours later, Dédée and the evaders cycled a few miles south to the foothills of the Pyrenees, where they met a Basque named Florentino Giocoechea, who guided the party across the rugged heights to near San Sebastián, Spain. Dédée told the airmen to wait there while she went into town to get transportation. Exhausted, they flopped down in a ditch and almost at once were in deep slumber.

Suddenly, the Britons were jolted awake by the slamming of car doors. Dédée had come back in a taxi.

The Comet leader and the evaders boarded the taxi, and soon they reached a safe house in San Sebastián. There they were met by two men who spoke perfect English: agents of MI-9 who had been sent to meet them.

After a rail journey that took them through Madrid and on to Spain's Mediterranean coast, Hoskins and the other two airmen reached the British bastion of Gibraltar. There they were put aboard an aircraft for England, arriving home just in time for Christmas 1942.

Even as Comet grew much larger, Dédée continued to shun the relative safety of an "office" to work in the field. During thirty-two exhausting trips over the Pyrenees, she escorted some one hundred evaders to safety. Then, in late 1943, she was betrayed. Gestapo agents pounced on a farm in France near the Spanish border that served as a starting point for the trek over the Pyrenees. Dédée and three British evaders were taken into custody.

Handcuffed, Dédée was brought to Paris by train under armed guard. There she was brutally interrogated nearly twenty times, first by the Gestapo and then by the Luftwaffe secret police. These two investigative agencies were bitter enemies, so the Belgian woman's life no doubt had been saved because the Luftwaffe agents sent her to the Ravensbrück concentration camp to spite the Gestapo. She would survive the war.

The teenagers and young persons who belonged to Comet had been inspired by Dédée's plight to carry on her work. Hundreds of evaders who made it to safety during the war owed their lives to the Belgian nurse and her helpers.[9]

## The Ranger Wore Bedroom Slippers

KNOWN AS DARBY'S RANGERS, they had their baptism of fire during the November 1942 Allied invasion of North Africa. Led by thirty-one-year-old Colonel William O. Darby, a West Pointer, the outfit was rough, tough, and resourceful—America's version of the famed British Commandos.

Prior to the landings in North Africa, Darby's Rangers had been handed a daunting task: knock out four big coastal guns which could play havoc with the main body of assault troops. For a green force, the Rangers were spectacular. They destroyed or captured all the big guns and suffered incredibly low casualties: four dead and eleven wounded.

Darby's Rangers had no shortage of free-spirited, gung-ho characters. One in this category was Lieutenant Stanley Farwell, whose boot size was fourteen and a half. When his unit was battling the Afrika Korps in Tunisia in February 1943, his boots wore out on the rough terrain. Then he discovered that the U.S. Army had not contemplated having men with such enormous feet, so there were no spares available. Undaunted, Farwell located a pair of bedroom slippers in an abandoned house, and for weeks he marched and fought wearing the light footgear.

During the fighting in Tunisia, a tire on his jeep was ruined, and there was no replacement. So that night, Farwell infiltrated German lines, crawled and creeped around in his slippers, and finally came upon an unguarded German version of the jeep. Working rapidly in the darkness, he removed one wheel and, lugging the heavy load, sneaked back to friendly lines.[10]

## The Countess and the Commandos

THE NIGHT WAS DARK when the British submarine *Tuna* surfaced eight miles off the mouth of the Gironde River in southwestern France. Silently, twelve Royal Marine Commandos slipped into six canoes and began paddling toward the inland port of Bordeaux, some sixty miles away as the crow flies. Operation Frankton, one of the boldest raids of the war, had been launched. It was December 8, 1942.

Led by Major H. G. "Blondie" Hasler, the Commandos held no illusions: they were on a mission fraught with a potential for disaster. In the event they reached the Bordeaux Harbor without being detected, the raiders were to place limpets on ships aiding the Nazi war effort.

Looking like rectangular chunks of rusty iron, the limpets measured eleven-by-eight-by-three inches and weighed about fourteen pounds each, ten of which were plastic explosives. The ensuing blast could blow a hole five feet square in the hull of the ship. A fuse and time pencil could be set for detonation any time up to six hours. This would permit the Commandos to get a considerable distance before the booms and bangs erupted in Bordeaux Harbor.

There would be only one hope for Hasler and his Commandos to escape capture or death. Planners in London had told them that on completion of their mission, they should walk to the town of Ruffec, where an established escape organization would take charge of them.

Hasler and his men were aware that there was a major flaw in this arrangement. Members of the underground in Ruffec could not be told in advance of the Bordeaux raid, so how could the Commandos link up with the escape organization?

In a canoe named *Catfish*, Hasler led the tiny armada into the mouth of the Gironde and onward for many miles without incident. Then the raiders were hit by a series of disasters. Four canoes were swallowed by the night. In the two surviving craft, were Hasler and John Sparks in *Catfish* and two other Commandos in *Crayfish*.

Hiding in the day and paddling furiously in the darkness, raiders concealed themselves in brush along the bank at dawn after the third night. They were only three miles from Bordeaux. Hasler laid out plans for that night's action. The *Catfish* would head for the western side of the harbor, while the *Crayfish* would strike along the eastern side.

After night had blanketed the region, the two canoes shoved off. Reaching the harbor entrance, Hasler could not believe his eyes. Lined up neatly along the wharf on the *Catfish*'s side of the harbor were seven large vessels. A "row of ducks," he told himself. Hasler paddled along the sides of the ships as silently as possible, pausing briefly at each one while John Sparks attached limpets.

Initially, Hasler was surprised about how lightly the docks were guarded. In fact, the Britons had not spotted a single sentry. Then the major remembered that Bordeaux Harbor was a few hundred miles from the nearest Allied force, so there had been no reason to waste manpower patrolling the docks.

Sparks was placing limpets on the seventh ship when suddenly the bright beam of a flashlight shone down on the *Catfish*. A voice called out: "*Wer ist da?*" (Who is there?)

Hasler and his companion froze. They expected a burst of small arms fire. Strangely, the light was extinguished, and the two Commandos resumed paddling.

Amazingly, the *Catfish* and the *Crayfish* linked up again in the entrance to the large harbor. The Commandos in the *Crayfish* had attached five limpets to two large ships.

The raiders had been in German-controlled waters for five nights, traveling nearly one hundred miles. Together, the two canoes headed back up the river. At dawn, a decision was made for the two teams to separate. Hasler and Sparks would never again see the Commandos in *Crayfish*.

That same morning, a series of explosions rocked Bordeaux as the limpets, one after the other, went off. The targeted ships that did not sink were so badly damaged they would be out of action for a long period of time.

Hasler and Sparks sank their fragile craft and that night headed cross-country toward Ruffec, sixty miles to the northeast. Along the way, farmers provided them with the clothing of French peasants. They marched for five consecutive nights, often having to skirt towns that held German troops. Finally, hungry, thirsty, and nearly exhausted, Hasler and his companion staggered into Ruffec, having covered perhaps one hundred miles on foot.

By happenstance, the two "peasants" went into the restaurant of the small Hôtel de Toques Blanches and ordered soup and vegetables (which did not require food coupons).

Hasler, meanwhile, had been sizing up the *patronne*. Was she a patriotic Frenchwoman? Or would she tip off the Gestapo to collect a small financial bounty? In the latter case, Hasler and Sparks were doomed. Adolf Hitler had ordered that captured British Commandos were to be shot immediately.

Taking out a pencil, Hasler scratched a note: "We are escaping English soldiers. Do you know anyone who can help us?" When the patronne returned, he gave her a five-franc note to pay for the meal, having folded the message inside of it.

When the woman brought back the change, her expression never changed. Tucked inside the currency was her own note: "Stay at your table until I have closed the restaurant." Was this a ploy to gain time for the Gestapo to arrive? Hasler conjectured.

At closing time, the patronne locked the hotel doors and she and her husband, the chef, questioned the Britons. Why had they come to Ruffec? "Because we had been told that friends here would be on the lookout for us," Hasler replied.

"Who were you told to contact?"

"For security reasons, we were given no names."

Hasler and Sparks passed muster. They stayed the night in comfortable hotel beds, and employees washed their filthy clothes. That afternoon, a Frenchman arrived and took the evaders in his bakery van to a farmhouse (code-named "Farm B") a mile out of town. This was the property of Armand Debreuil, a member of the escape organization.

Miraculously, perhaps, the two Commandos had made contact with the resistance members who were to have been on the lookout for them.

Founder of and moving spirit behind the escape line was the Comtesse de Milleville, who, at that moment, was suffering from five fractured ribs, a major head wound, and injuries to her arms and legs in a hospital at Loches, a small town fifty miles from Ruffec.

The countess was a British woman named Mary Lindell who had long lived in France. She combined a passion for adventure and danger with an extremely blunt speech. After serving as an ambulance driver and in field hospitals for the French Red Cross during World War I, she had met and married a wealthy Frenchman, and the couple had lived in Paris with their three children since 1920.

In 1941, the countess was arrested in Paris by the Gestapo for helping British escapers. She was sentenced to nine months in gloomy Fresnes prison, after first giving the trial judge some salty observations concerning his intelligence—or lack of it.

After being released from Fresnes, the forty-six-year-old countess traveled to Lyon, a major city three hundred miles southeast of Paris, to pursue her goal of establishing an escape line from France into Spain. So she wanted to get far away from the Gestapo in Paris.

Mary again became a fugitive on the run. A traitor had informed the Gestapo of her renewed underground activity, and a search was launched for her. Her son Maurice was arrested and savagely interrogated, but he kept silent and was released.

Meanwhile at Lyon, Mary got in touch with an old friend of the French resistance, the U.S. vice counsul, and he issued her the necessary documents: an exit permit from the Nazi-puppet Vichy government that identified her as an "English governess," and visas for her to travel in Spain and Portugal, both officially neutral nations.

Because the countess had earlier established numerous contacts in Ruffec, she decided that town would be headquarters for her escape chain. In the fall of 1942, she was peddling a bicycle outside Ruffec when a car struck her from behind. Knocked unconscious, she was taken by underground members to the hospital in Loches, where she hovered between life and death for many days.

Two weeks later, the local Gestapo came calling. They accused the hospital superintendent and medical staff of harboring "an English agent." After scouring the facility, the Germans left empty-handed. The countess had been taken to the basement when the Gestapo agents entered the hospital. Her stretcher was placed on the floor under a long table and a large pile of wood was stacked around and over her. In their futile search, the Germans had stood less than two feet from where the patient was lying motionless and holding her breath.

Soon after Christmas 1942, Mary, although weak and quite ill, insisted on returning to her base at Lyon, which she reached with the help of her son Maurice. There she found a letter from Armand Debreuil, the owner of Farm B outside Ruffec. It stated that he had "two important parcels of food" awaiting her.

By courier, the countess sent word to Debreuil that the "two parcels" would be picked up on January 6 and escorted to Lyon. Her escape line to Spain through Ruffec had been temporarily stymied because she could not recruit dependable guides for crossing the rugged Pyrenees. So she intended to smuggle the two Commandos across the frontier into neutral Switzerland.

When Major Blondie Hasler and Royal Marine John Sparks were brought to Lyon by Maurice, the fugitives were spirited from house to house during the next two weeks. While the Britons were in hiding, the countess sneaked out of Lyon and headed southward for the Swiss border, even though she remained ill and in pain from the broken bones.

Aided by Swiss intelligence, which leaned heavily toward the Western Allies, Mary crossed the frontier in a fishing boat on Lake Geneva.

On February 23, 1943, London received a message from the British legation in Bern, telling of Mary's arrival there and that two Frankton participants were in hiding in Lyon. She had gone there to arrange for Hasler and Sparks to be smuggled across the border. However, London sent word to Bern that the countess was to remain in Switzerland until her injuries had been healed.

Impatient by nature, the countess ignored the "suggestion" and returned to Lyon. Within a few days, she received word from Farm B outside Ruffec that a reliable guide had been recruited to take the two Commandos over the Pyrenees. At the end of March, the escapers were escorted across the mountains and a week later, they were ensconced in the U.S. embassy in Madrid.

Hasler and Sparks were the only survivors of the Bordeaux raid. Six Commandos had been captured and shot by the Gestapo, and the remainder were presumed to have drowned.

Meanwhile, Mary had returned to Switzerland for badly needed medical treatment, but again, she didn't stay in the hospital long. Changing her name to the Comtesse de Moncy, she established a system for sneaking Allied escapers across the French border into Switzerland.

On November 24, 1943, while in the railroad station at a small French town near the frontier, she was pounced on by the Gestapo and brutally interrogated. On the way to Paris to be "tried" and executed, Mary leaped from the train in a desperate effort to escape, and she was shot twice in the head.

Unconscious and near death, Mary was taken to a hospital at Tours where, ironically, her life was saved by a German surgeon.

For whatever reason, the Gestapo changed its mind about her execution. In early September 1944, after she had recovered sufficiently to survive a trip, Mary was put in the Ravensbrück concentration camp. In April 1945, the countess was liberated by Allied armies. Two weeks later, Adolf Hitler was dead and Germany surrendered.[11]

# "Blow Up Rommel's Railroad!"

COLONEL EDSON D. RAFF, leader of the U.S. 509th Parachute Infantry Battalion battling German forces in Tunisia, summoned Lieutenant Dan E. DeLeo, a twenty-four-year-old native of Chicago. He had yet to see hostile action, having landed in North Africa as a replacement after invasion forces were ashore.

Typically, Raff was terse. "I want you to lead a parachute raiding party to the El Djem bridge, blow it up, and make your way back to friendly lines," the colonel explained.

DeLeo swallowed hard. It was a tall order. Even if the key bridge were destroyed, the Germans and Italians throughout Tunisia would be put on the alert for the saboteurs—and it would be ninety miles to safety through hostile territory. It was December 23, 1942.

Field Marshal Erwin Rommel, the fabled Desert Fox, had pleaded with Adolf Hitler to pull out the remnants of the vaunted Afrika Korps before it was too late, but the führer accused Rommel of cowardice and ordered him to fight to the last man in Tunisia.

As promised, Hitler began pouring troops, weapons, and supplies into the Mediterranean ports of Tunis and Bizerte in northern Tunisia. At these points, the reinforcements and cargoes were loaded onto trains that ran along the north–south coastal track for some three hundred miles to Rommel's heavily fortified Mareth Line at the base of the Tunisian Peninsula.

Seeking to halt this steady flow to Rommel, Allied bombers had tried to destroy a key railroad bridge near the coastal town of El Djem, but the span remained standing. Then a squadron of U.S. fighter planes shot scores of rockets into the bridge. When the smoke had cleared, the trestle remained standing and defiant.

Now Lieutenant DeLeo met with U.S. Air Corps officers who explained that the parachutists would be dropped at night a short distance north of the El Djem bridge, so the raiders would have no problem finding it. All they had to do was to march southward for five miles until they reached the span.

At 10:30 P.M. on Christmas Eve, DeLeo and his raiding party of thirty-three men lifted off in a pair of C-47 transport planes from an airport outside Algiers. Winging through the night in the dark cabins, the men sat in almost total silence, each immersed in his own thoughts.

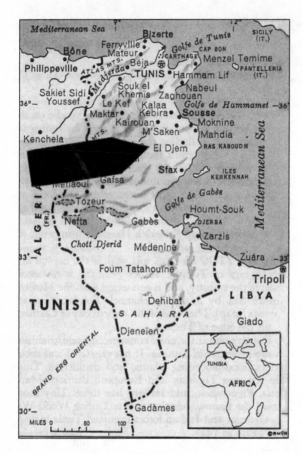

*Large arrow points to El Djem, through which Field Marshal Rommel sent troops to the front in southern Tunisia.*

Suddenly, a glowing red light in the cabin shook them from reveries, and the troopers got to their feet. Each man carried an escape kit containing a small saw blade, a few yards of tough fishing line, a waterproof plastic container holding ten wooden matches, and a tiny magnetic compass.

Moments later, a green light flashed on and the troopers, one at a time, bailed out into the dark unknown. At the same time, the pilots of the two C-47s flipped switches, and a pair of two hundred-pound bundles of explosives, one attached to the belly of each aircraft, were released and parachuted to the ground.

Soon a series of *crump, crump, crump!* could be heard as the parachutists crashed into the unyielding ground. Fortunately, none was injured, although the impact was identical to having jumped off the top of a freight car traveling at forty miles per hour. Lieutenant DeLeo quickly found the tracks and wig-wagged a muted light to assemble his men. Within fifteen minutes, all had gathered. A search turned up the two bundles of explosives.

Because the drop zone was supposed to be north of the El Djem bridge, the group began trudging southward, their baggy pockets bulging with blocks of dynamite. What DeLeo and his men did not know was that they had been misdropped *south* of the target.

DeLeo was gripped by haunting worry. Soon after the raiders had assembled back at the landing site, they had come across two Arabs pushing a handcart. The Americans knew that it was not unusual for natives to pop up in unexpected places at any time of the day or night. Would the two Arabs betray the Americans? DeLeo would get an answer—and soon.

After a grueling five-hour march, DeLeo halted his men at daybreak and pulled a folded map from his pocket. Orienting himself by the contours of a group of hills off in the distance, he took a number of compass readings and said, "Men, we're about twenty miles south of the El Djem bridge!"

Retracing their steps would require perhaps five hours and had to be done in broad daylight. Their discovery would almost be a cinch. Moreover, the troopers were almost near exhaustion from the long, arduous trek loaded with explosives and combat gear. So it was decided to inflict maximum carnage where they were.

The demolition men rapidly went to work planting explosives in a building beside the tracks that held electrical equipment for, a trooper indicated, controlling switching operations for many miles in each direction. At the same time, other raiders were planting dynamite blocks along one hundred yards of tracks. All of the explosives were then joined by a single detonation cord.

When the wiring job was nearly done, DeLeo looked up to see a sentry whom he had sent south of the site running toward him. Nearly out of breath, the trooper blurted, "Lieutenant, there's a platoon of Krauts coming up the tracks toward us!"

Then a sentry posted to the north dashed up. An even larger German force, about a mile away, was marching toward the Americans.

It had been a profitable night for the two Arabs whom the raiders had encountered earlier, DeLeo realized. Not only had the natives collected many valuable parachutes, but no doubt the Germans had also paid them handsomely for squealing on the saboteurs.

The Americans had been caught in a trap. German patrols were scouring the countryside; guards were placed on roads to thwart the intruders' escape. DeLeo quickly decided that they would split into small groups and set out cross-country for the American lines—ninety miles to the west.

A three-minute fuse was lighted; then the troopers raced off to avoid the explosion. Suddenly, an enormous blast rocked the region. Debris from Rommel's railroad track and the building full of electrical equipment spiraled into the sky.

DeLeo, Sergeant John Betters, Private Roland Rondeau, and Private Frank Romero, along with two French soldiers acting as guides, traveled together. They hid out that day, marched all the next night; then holed up at dawn in a thick woods near a well-traveled road. They noticed that numerous

*Disguised in Arab headgear, Lieutenant Dan E. DeLeo sits beside a frightened Italian soldier as they drive through a town filled with Germans. Other raiders peek from beneath tarpaulin. (Author's collection)*

vehicles were randomly heading westward, so DeLeo decided to hijack one of them and drive the raiders hell-bent toward friendly lines.

The men hid at the edge of the woods and waited for just the right vehicle to come along. By fate, the first one was a truck with a canvas over the back—perfect for concealing the escapers.

Without his helmet, DeLeo strolled out into the road holding a pistol behind him. He flagged down the vehicle and when the driver, an Italian soldier, poked his head out through the open window, he found himself staring into the business end of a .45 Colt.

Scrambling from the bushes, the raiders leaped into the covered back of the truck, and DeLeo climbed in beside the petrified driver. In Italian, he told the enemy soldier, "Start driving. And no monkey business or I'll blow your head off!"

DeLeo picked up a white scarf lying on the seat and wrapped it around his head, Arab style. A short time later, he saw a chilling sight: Two long columns of German infantrymen, one on each side of the road, were marching toward the truck. "Krauts!" DeLeo called softly to the hidden troopers. "Keep still and have your weapons ready!"

The vehicle chugged onward and reached the approaching Germans. The Americans felt their hearts beat faster; nerves were taut. Now the truck was moving along slowly between the two columns. DeLeo tried to look casual. He could have reached out and touched the passing enemy soldiers. Few of the Germans even glanced at the "Arab."

After going a considerable distance, the coughing, wheezing old truck broke down along a muddy trail. What to do with the Italian? If he were turned loose, the alarm would be spread. Some of the raiders suggested shooting the quaking man, but he was taken along. It was still more than fifty miles to American lines.

The raiders and their hostage pushed ahead on foot. They halted only when exhausted; then resumed marching. Most of their food was gone, so they haggled with Arabs for something to eat. DeLeo told the natives that he and his men were Germans, and when Arabs balked over giving them food, the lieutenant menacingly fingered his pistol.

Three weeks after their jump at the El Djem bridge, the hungry and nearly exhausted paratroopers came upon a friendly French farmer who told them how to reach a French army outpost. The farmer supplied the Americans with food and coffee; they handed out chewing gum to the children.

After trudging over a mountain range, the Americans felt a surge of elation. Off in the distance was the French outpost. Walking onward, Roland Rondeau noticed that several French soldiers had come out and were waving their arms frantically.

"What in the hell are those crazy Frogs supposed to be doing?" Rondeau asked DeLeo. The lieutenant shrugged. When the Americans reached the Frenchmen, they learned the reason for the wild gesticulating: The raiders had been walking across a minefield. A week later, DeLeo and his five men were back with their outfit.

Meanwhile, two others in the raiding party, teenage Private Charles Doyle and Private Michael Underhill, had jogged from the explosion site for about two hours, then burrowed into a haystack to sleep and await nightfall. A few hours later, they decided to resume their trek before darkness and soon were walking along a path in a thick woods. Minutes later, they bumped into three Italian soldiers who surprised the Americans and took them captive.

After being disarmed and searched, Doyle and Underhill were ordered to climb into the back of an Italian army truck which moved out of the woods and drove through a series of small Arab villages. After traveling for perhaps twenty miles, the truck halted and the two Americans were motioned to climb down and enter a flimsy POW cage. It was merely some barbed wire fastened to tall poles driven into the ground. Now it was quite dark.

About three hours later, another Italian truck drove up and discharged four more Americans involved in the El Djem caper. No sooner were the newcomers in the cage than all of the captives began plotting to escape. Slipping under the loose strands of barbed wire would be simple, they agreed, but the lone Italian soldier on guard would give the alarm—or shoot them.

The six paratroopers laid down and pretended to be sound asleep. In about a half hour, the Italian guard, who had been circling around the cage almost constantly, sat down in a shack at the entrance. When he used a series of matches to light his pipe, thereby diminishing his night vision, the Americans slithered to the fence and sneaked under the barbed wire strand. Outside the enclosure in the darkness, they shook hands solemnly and, splitting into pairs, headed westward toward friendly lines, still some sixty miles away through hostile territory.

Of the thirty-three men who had jumped with Lieutenant DeLeo on the El Djem bridge raid, only eight reached American forces in Tunisia: Doyle and Underhill and the five men with DeLeo.

Sixteen other raiders eventually made it back to Allied forces. Either they had made bold escapes from POW camps or had been liberated by advancing Allied forces.[12]

# Reconnoitering Hostile Beaches

BRITISH LIEUTENANT Commander Norman Teacher and his four teams of Commandos arrived on the island of Malta to launch a highly important secret mission. They were members of the elite Combined Operations Pilotage Parties (COPP), whose perilous task was reconnoitering hostile beaches prior to an Allied invasion. It was late February 1943.

Even though Field Marshal Erwin Rommel and his German and Italian forces were making a last-ditch stand in Tunisia, North Africa, Allied Supreme Commander Dwight Eisenhower already was planning his next step: an invasion of the large, mountainous island of Sicily, eighty miles north of Malta at the toe of the Italian boot.

It was one thing for military planners to pick out invasion beaches from a map, a quite different matter to be certain that the chosen landing sites would be passable to tanks and other heavy vehicles. So the mission of Commander Teacher and his COPP men was for them to swim ashore from light craft known as foldboats to inspect the targeted beaches.

Four submarines carrying the canoeists to the designated beaches stole out of Malta Harbor and took up positions in the darkness off Sicily. At about midnight, Teacher and Lieutenant Noel Cooper scrambled into their foldboat from the submarine *Unbending* and headed for shore. The Mediterranean Sea was kicking up angry waves. Two hundred yards from shore, Teacher, in his rubberized suit, slipped into the icy water and began swimming. He was never seen again.

Despite Teacher's fate, the Sicily mission continued on succeeding nights. One team from the *Unbending* got on the beach, measured gradients and obtained other vital information and got back to the submarine. But other disasters were to follow.

On the fifth and last night, Lieutenant Cooper swam ashore, together with Captain George Burbridge of the Canadian Army. They vanished.

On the northern shore of Sicily, Lieutenant Neville McHarg and a companion left the submarine *Safari* and began paddling. A short distance from shore, they got tangled in fishermen's sardine nets. While struggling to get loose, incendiary flares suddenly turned night into day: Royal Air Force bombers were raiding the harbor at nearby Castellammare. McHarg and his companion eventually disintangled their canoe and paddled back to the *Safari*.

Two nights later, Captain Theodore Parsons reached shore and was crawling along when he became aware of a shadowy figure in front of him. It was an Italian soldier, pointing his rifle at Parsons. An hour later, Parsons's companion, who had been waiting in the canoe offshore, got worried and swam to the beach to contact Parsons. He, too, was captured.

Meanwhile, along the Gulf of Gela in southern Sicily, where the U.S. 1st Infantry Division one day would hit the beaches, Lieutenants David Brand and Robert Smith were reconnoitering a sandbar and overstayed their allotted time. Suddenly, a torrential storm struck. They tried to paddle back to the submarine *United*, but they had to struggle mightily just to stay afloat. For the next few hours, they were tossed about by the violent waves, and with the arrival of dawn, the storm continued to rage.

Every few minutes, the two men had to stop and bail out water with tin cups. They abandoned hope of locating the submarine, and decided to try to paddle to Malta, some eighty miles away. The going was tough. Neither man thought they would make it. One man had to paddle while the other bailed.

Miraculously, Smith and Brand remained afloat as the storm battered them throughout the day. Their tiny canoe was tossed about by the waves. Around midnight, the men were on the verge of exhaustion, but their spirits rose when the violent weather finally broke.

At daybreak, they felt they could not go another yard. Then, off in the distance, was a dim outline of a land mass—Malta!

Soon a patrolling British launch plucked Smith and Brand from the jaws of death.

Back at the COPP base on an island off England's southern coast, the group's leader, Commander Nigel Willmott, was furious. Before the Sicily mission, he had warned Allied brass that his teams had not trained long enough to endure the rigors that they would encounter. Now, at a considerable risk to his career, he "refused" to mount any more COPP missions until he was convinced that his men were ready.

Willmott's obstinacy paid off. With improved spring weather, stronger boats, and intensified training based on lessons learned in the earlier disasters, teams of COPP men reconnoitered all the proposed invasion beaches in Sicily with the loss of only one man.

When the Allies struck at Sicily before dawn on July 10, 1943, COPP teams were offshore in their canoes to guide in the assault boats.[13]

# A Master of Disguises

BRITISH ROYAL NAVY LIEUTENANT David James took a dim view of the Naval Prisoner of War camp near Bremen, Germany. From the first minute he walked through its gates, his primary interest was to escape. It was early March 1943.

For two years, James had been a member of an MTB (motor torpedo boat) flotilla that had been harassing the Germans relentlessly with hit-and-run raids along the English Channel coast. Then his luck ran out. His MTB was sunk just off Holland, and he was fished out of the water by a German ship and taken prisoner.

James, like most escapers, was a free spirit. During the summer at the POW camp, he dug a tunnel under the barbed-wire fence, but only days before it was completed, the Germans discovered the excavation and moved James to another, more secure building.

Undaunted, the lieutenant conceived another innovative scheme for leaving "Adolf Hitler's Guest Resort," as he called the compound. The camp escape committee provided him with expertly forged identity papers, including a photograph, for Lieutenant Ican Buggerov of the Royal Bulgarian Navy. Bulgaria was an ally of Nazi Germany. There was a play on words in James's adopted name: "Ican Buggerov," meaning, "I can bugger off" from the camp.

Wearing a British Royal Navy uniform that had been altered to disguise its true origin, James slipped out of camp through an opening he had discovered in a boathouse. He was relying on the quite accurate premise that German policemen would have no idea what a Bulgarian navy uniform looked like.

On the night of November 1, 1943, "Lieutenant Buggerov" caught a train that took him to the northern port of Lubeck, Germany. While prowling around a forbidden harbor area in search of a neutral-nation ship on which he might stow away, he was recaptured by security guards.

Six weeks later, James again fled the POW camp, this time disguised as Sven Lindholm, a Swedish merchant marine officer who was rejoining his vessel after having been wounded in an Allied air raid. Looking for a ship to Sweden, he drew blanks in Stettin, Rostock, and Gdynia.

At Danzig, however, he sneaked aboard a Danish ship and hid, believing that the vessel was on its way to German-occupied Denmark. There he could catch a neutral ship. He felt a sense of relief when his vessel set sail without his being detected. A day later, his hopes were dashed: the Danish ship tied up in the port of Lubeck where he had been recaptured earlier as "Lieutenant Buggerov."

James's spirits were raised when a Danish officer detected the stowaway but did not turn him over to German authorities. But then the Briton received a shocker: the ship had been commandeered by the German Navy and would be used to prowl the coastline in search of Allied raiding parties.

Under cover of darkness, James slipped away from the Danish vessel, and after considerable probing of the Lubeck Harbor area, he came upon a Finnish ship that was preparing to sail for neutral Stockholm, Sweden. A friendly stoker hid the Briton in a cramped space in the boiler room where he remained for three days and nights until the ship tied up in Sweden.

In Stockholm, James made contact with the British embassy, whose officials arranged to smuggle him out of Sweden. Put in a large diplomatic bag to conceal him from hostile eyes, he was placed aboard a British aircraft that made regular round trips, and was flown to England. Soon James was back in the war.[14]

# Deceiving an Italian General

EARLY ON THE MORNING of June 10, 1943, Supreme Commander Dwight D. Eisenhower stood before a room packed with war correspondents at his headquarters in Algiers, North Africa. Now that the Western Allies had been lying relatively dormant since driving German and Italian forces out of North Africa the previous month, the reporters expected a routine announcement, perhaps an appointment or two to key commands.

What they received instead was a blockbuster, a disclosure possibly unprecedented in warfare. Ike, as he was popularly known, got right to the point.

"We will assault Sicily early in July, with the British Eighth Army under General Montgomery attacking the eastern beaches north of Syracuse and the U.S. Seventh Army under General Patton attacking the southern beaches," he stated.

Mouths fell open. An eerie hush pervaded the room. Eisenhower held back virtually nothing, including the date and hour of the assault, which would be spearheaded by an Anglo-American airborne landing behind the coastal defenses.

Eisenhower left the room as the journalists sat silent and stunned. They realized that should they inadvertently leak the information, the Allies could suffer a bloody debacle in Sicily.

The supreme commander's thunderclap had not been loosed impulsively. It had been debated with key staff officers for many days. Curiously, the purpose of briefing the correspondents in advance was to maintain secrecy.

During the quiet period after the North Africa fighting, to earn their keep, reporters had to continue to send back stories to England and the United States.

Most of the accounts were speculative. Each scribe was seeking a new "angle." Eisenhower feared that a flood of conjectural reports in Allied media could be pieced together by crafty German intelligence agencies to pinpoint Sicily as the next invasion target.

Precisely one month later on July 10, the large Mediterranean island was dark and peaceful at 2:45 A.M. as U.S. and British landing craft disembarked thousands of assault troops along a one-hundred-mile stretch of southern and southeastern Sicily. It appeared that Eisenhower's bizarre gamble to keep the invasion secret had paid off, as the assault elements pushed inland against minimal opposition.

On the left flank of the entire invasion was Major General Lucien K. Truscott's U.S. 3rd Infantry Division, whose initial mission was to seize Licata. Near that small town, a platoon of American dogfaces (as GI foot soldiers proudly called themselves) walked into an Italian command post, whose occupants apparently had fled with the approach of the invaders.

Michael Chinigo, an American correspondent, had just entered the abandoned headquarters when the telephone jangled impatiently. Chinigo, who spoke Italian fluently, picked up the instrument and in an authoritative tone demanded to know "*Chi c'e?*" (Who's there?) The voice on the line identified himself as the general in charge of defending the shoreline in the Licata region.

Was there any truth to reports that Americans had come ashore there? asked the general. "Of course not," Chinigo replied evenly. "Everything's quiet around here."

Indeed it was quiet. The Americans had landed with hardly a shot being fired against them.

"Fine," the general continued, sounding relieved.

Perhaps because he had just been awakened at his comfortable villa some ten miles inland, the general never asked the identity of the "Italian officer" who had answered the telephone in such an unmilitary style.

Chinigo had pulled off a unique hoax on a spur of the moment, deceiving by telephone an Italian general who was located far to the rear of enemy lines.[15]

# The Canal Saboteurs

MOMENTOUS EVENTS were unfolding in the Mediterranean region in mid-1943. A major disaster in Sicily broke the back of an already demoralized Italian military establishment and civilian population. On July 25, mild little King Victor Emmanuel III summarily fired Adolf Hitler's crony Benito Mussolini as Italian premier, a post he had held for twenty-one years. The monarch had Mussolini arrested and locked up.

Now, as much of the civilized world knew, the Anglo-Americans were preparing to invade Italy. To disrupt German efforts to build up defenses in Italy, a French underground network (code-named Armada) sprang into action.

Led by Raymond Basset, Armada began sabotaging the extensive French canal system through which the Germans wanted to move small naval vessels, torpedo boats, and miniature submarines from their ports in the North Sea southward to Italy in anticipation of the Allied invasion there.

On the dark night of July 26, three Armada men blew a huge hole in a dam and lock on a canal at Chalon-sur-Saône, draining a long stretch of the waterway and creating a logjam of barges and other small vessels.

The Germans tried to skirt the blockage at Chalon by using the Briare Canal. A lone saboteur sneaked up to the facility and put it out of action by dynamiting two locks. Armada agents reported that hundreds of barges and vessels bound for Italy were backed up for many miles.

German engineers worked feverishly to restore the dam and lock at Chalon. The canal was in use for only two days when several Armada men returned and blew it up again.[16]

# Strange Places for Secret Radios

DURING THE LONG Nazi occupation of western Europe, citizens were desperate to hear truthful news. Their newspapers and magazines were censored and their radios had been confiscated by German authorities. Consequently, using parts scrounged from many places, many civilians constructed their own radio receivers and tuned to the powerful British Broadcasting Corporation (BBC) transmitter in London.

Because the mere possession of a radio was an offense punishable by fines, jail, or even execution, the makers' ingenuity was focused on camouflage and concealment of the instrument. One of those who turned out several cleverly disguised radios was Alv Bjerklo of Sandnessjoen, Norway, a leader in the underground. Some of his radios were built in vacuum bottles and sofa legs.

Another ingenious Norwegian radio builder was Thorleif Thorgersen of Stavanger. German soldiers often walked within a few feet of a birdhouse that hung on an outside wall, unaware that the seeming refuge for feathered creatures actually contained an illegal radio.

No doubt the most incredibly disguised radio of all was created by a Norwegian soldier, a dental technician in civilian life, who was in a German POW camp near Breslau, Poland, in 1943. Arthur Bergfjord crafted a radio into a fellow inmate's denture plate. To use the receiver, the inmate removed the denture and hooked it to a battery and headset that had been smuggled into camp.

Said the resourceful Bergfjord much later: "The twice-false teeth worked remarkably well. We could hear BBC's news reports loud and clear."

Soon after their French town was liberated by the Allies, inhabitants reclaim their radios that had been confiscated by the Germans. (National Archives)

No doubt the inmate with the radio had been warned to keep his mouth shut when Germans were around—literally.[17]

# Saved from a Firing Squad

FIGHTING ON THE MOUNTAINOUS Mediterranean island of Sicily had been raging for four days. That night, July 14, 1943, the battled-tested men of Brigadier Gerald Lathbury's British 1st Parachute Brigade bailed out near the key Primosole Bridge over the Simento River north of General Bernard Montgomery's Eighth Army invasion beaches in the southeast. Capturing the span was crucial: it would permit the Eighth Army to pour over the bridge and attack northward to seize the invasion's ultimate main objective, the major port of Messina, at the northeast tip of Sicily.

If Montgomery's force, with its path cleared by Lathbury's 1st Parachute Brigade, could reach Messina at an early date, German and Italian forces on Sicily would be cut off from their only route of escape—across the two-mile-wide Strait of Messina which flows between the island and the toe of mainland Italy.

For four days and nights, a savage battle raged for control of Primosole Bridge between the British paratroopers and Lieutenant Colonel Erich Walter's German 4th Parachute Regiment. Although suffering heavy losses, Walter's warriors managed to stall Lathbury's brigade.

Major General Francis "Freddie" de Guingand, Montgomery's able and affable chief of staff, knew why the Eighth Army's advance had ground to a halt short of Primosole Bridge: the German paratroopers had "fought with fanatical savagery." Most of those taken prisoner remained arrogant and hostile in the face of threats by their British interrogators. Spitting in the faces of their captors, some German paratroop officers even refused to give their names, ranks, and serial numbers, as required by articles of the Geneva Convention governing the rules of so-called civilized warfare.

One captured German officer had managed to conceal a small-caliber pistol on his person, and while being grilled by British officers, he jumped to his feet, shouted, *"Heil, Hitler!"* and killed himself with a shot to the head.

During the fighting, Lieutenant Albrecht Günther was cut off alone behind Lathbury's outfit. Putting on an Italian civilian suit, he tried to sneak back to his own unit, but he was captured and brought to General de Guingand at Eighth Army headquarters.

Günther, a veteran of heavy fighting, from the invasion of Holland in mid-1940, in France, and later in Russia, refused to tell de Guingand anything but his rank and name. The general informed him that being caught behind British lines in civilian clothes meant that under international law, he could be shot as a spy—and that was precisely what was going to happen. Günther's face never disclosed the slightest reaction.

"That is quite understood," the German lieutenant responded evenly. "I took the risk and failed; I deserve it." As he was being led away by military police, he gave the Nazi salute and a *"Heil, Hitler!"*

General de Guingand did not have Günther shot; he had the German sent to a prisoner-of-war camp.[18]

# Part Three

## Hitler's Empire under Siege

# Old Popski Invades
# a German Headquarters

DARKNESS VEILED the two-mile-wide Strait of Messina separating Sicily from Italy as a convoy of ships carrying elements of General Bernard L. Montgomery's British Eighth Army prepared to launch the first invasion of Adolf Hitler's vaunted Festung Europa (Fortress Europe). It was September 3, 1943.

In the spearhead of Montgomery's force would be a curious outfit known to the British high command as Popski's Private Army. Its dynamic leader was forty-six-year-old Vladimir Peniakoff, a Belgian citizen of Russian origin. His unit's mission in southern Italy was to infiltrate behind German lines, identify enemy formations, and determine their strengths.

Born to wealth, Peniakoff had been privately tutored until entering St. John's College in Cambridge, England, during World War I as a self-styled "precious intellectual prig with high scientific ambitions, and conscientious objections to the war." However, he left Cambridge, enlisted as an artillery private in the French Army, was badly wounded on the Western Front and invalided out of the service.

Peniakoff trained as an engineer in civilian life, but found no satisfaction in a series of jobs he considered to be boring. In 1924, he settled in Egypt and spent many years manufacturing sugar products. Meanwhile, he became fond of the endless desert and regularly drove around the trackless wasteland in a seemingly indestructible Model A Ford nicknamed Pisspot.

After war broke out and the British army began battling Italian forces in the Libyan desert of North Africa in mid-1940, Peniakoff rushed to the headquarters of the Army of the Nile in Cairo, Egypt, and volunteered to fight. Although desperate for "bodies," as the British military called its soldiers, Peniakoff was rejected: too old, too flabby, too many nagging ailments.

Undaunted, the resourceful Peniakoff located a sympathetic British medical officer who, by adroit "doctoring" of a few records, converted him from a physical reject to a rugged human specimen. Perhaps because Peniakoff spoke Arabic and Italian fluently and had an intimate knowledge of the North African desert, he was commissioned a second lieutenant.

Because British headquarters in Cairo had difficulty spelling his name, he became popularly known there as Popski. His first assignment was to recruit a company of Senussi tribesmen who inhabited the desert, and to harass the enemy. Perhaps the oldest combat officer for his modest rank in the British Army, Popski plunged into his task with typical alacrity and ingenuity. He began to create an intelligence network and, along with twenty-four Senussi and a British sergeant, established a command post behind Italian lines.

Popski's primary source of intelligence was gained from the Arabs who had been given menial jobs in Italian headquarters and messes. These servants were dedicated to the British because they were treated with contempt by Italian officers, who discussed military plans openly, unaware that the Arabs spoke and understood Italian. At various headquarters, secret documents were left lying around in the open; the Arabs read them and relayed their contents to Popski.

Periodically, Popski led nighttime raids across the vast desert to blow up Italian fuel and ammunition dumps. These hazardous excursions were led by the lieutenant in his venerable Pisspot, which eventually broke down and was given burial rites in the desert.

In August 1942, Popski was called back to Cairo and instructed to form a company-sized unit of British personnel. It was called the Number 1 Long Range Demolition Squadron. Soon that designation was changed to Popski's Private Army in official records at Middle East Headquarters in Cairo.

Traveling in jeeps with mounted machine guns and carrying extra containers of food and large amounts of explosives, Popski's raiders roamed behind enemy lines to gain intelligence, blow up enemy installations, and ambush small units.

Now, after General Montgomery's spearheads went ashore in southern Italy against minimal opposition, Popski and his men rapidly infiltrated enemy lines and set up a base in a town that contained a commercial central telephone exchange for the entire region. Giving himself the rank of colonel in the Italian Army and a phony name, Popski used the exchange to telephone various enemy units and spoke to Italian officers in their native tongue. He demanded answers to many questions, and in nearly all instances, he received detailed replies.

Popski was especially eager to pin down the locations and strength of German units in the region, and the Italian officers provided him with that top-secret information on the telephone.

There was a lone exception—and a crucial one. None of the Italian officers knew the whereabouts or strength of the elite German 1st Parachute Division, which Allied intelligence thought was in southern Italy. So Popski was told by his superiors to find the "missing" German airborne outfit.

Popski hatched a wild scheme—and a dangerous one. He removed his British insignia and replaced it with one "borrowed" from an Italian prisoner. Then he pinned an Italian colonel's insignia onto his uniform and put on an

*Vladimir Peniakoff, perhaps history's oldest lieutenant, was the leader of Popski's Private Army. Note his artificial left hand. (National Archives)*

Italian officer's headgear. Hopefully, none of the enemy would notice that the "Italian colonel" was clad in British shirt and trousers, which were roughly similar to those worn by Italian officers.

Leaving his men and jeeps behind, Popski reached the town of Gravina where a German headquarters was located. His scheme would depend on boldness; he had to convey the impression that he actually "belonged." Should his Italian colonel masquerade be penetrated, Popski expected to be shot as a spy.

Assuming the air of purposeful endeavor, Popski bustled into the German headquarters. Because of his senior rank, German officers, who were unaware that at the moment Italian leaders were plotting to defect from their partnership with Adolf Hitler, treated him with a degree of deference. While the Germans went about their duties, the bogus Italian colonel meandered about the building at will.

Suddenly Popski's eyes fell onto a document that sent a shiver of excitement through him: The ration list for the 1st Parachute Division, together with the town where the food was to be delivered. The list reflected the total number of men in the airborne outfit.

Popski cast furtive glances in each direction. No one seemed to be watching. So he quickly snatched up the ration list and stuffed it inside his shirt. Then he strolled as casually as possible toward the door of the building. All the way he felt his heart thumping furiously.

At the door, Popski gave his best imitation of an Italian salute to the two German guards and walked away, fighting off a nagging urge to look back to see if anyone was following him.

A few days later, Eighth Army elements, armed with the secret information they had been provided by Popski, were battling the 1st Parachute Division at Foggia, a major city near the eastern coast of Italy.

In the meantime, Vladimir Popski and his private army were driving northward ahead of Montgomery's advancing force. They reconnoitered routes for British units, gained intelligence from Italian civilians, and launched hit-and-run attacks against German supply convoys.

During a shoot-out with the Germans halfway up the Italian boot, Popski's luck ran out: his left hand was shot off. After a stay in the hospital, he demanded to rejoin his private army, but doctors recommended that he be given a medical discharge.

Popski would have none of that. Rather, he fled from the hospital and was soon back with his men battling the Germans. The steel hook he wore where his hand had been did not handicap him.

"Hell, I can shoot just as good with one hand as I could with two," he said many times."[1]

# The GI with
# the Too-Short Pants

AT A DUSTY, SUN-DRENCHED AIRFIELD near Licata in southern Sicily, men of the veteran U.S. 509th Parachute Infantry Battalion, burdened with heavy combat gear, waddled up short ladders into thirty-nine C-47 transport planes whose engines were running in preparation for a quick takeoff. It was late in the afternoon of September 14, 1943.

Five days earlier, an Allied force led by U.S. Lieutenant General Mark W. Clark had stormed ashore along thirty miles of the Gulf of Salerno, halfway up the boot of Italy on the West Coast.

Field Marshal Albrecht Kesselring, the German supreme commander in the Mediterranean, had rapidly fashioned a steel noose of eight divisions around the beachhead and trapped 140,000 Allied troops. Moreover, the Germans were on the brink of driving the invaders into the Tyrrhenian Sea.

In desperation, General Clark had ordered the 509th Parachute Infantry, which was in reserve in Sicily, to promptly launch a "crash" parachute jump at Avellino, a sleepy, unpretentious town twenty miles north of German lines on the beachhead. German rail and road movements from Rome and northwest Italy had to pass through the town to reach the fighting front. So the paratrooper outfit had been handed the task of sticking a cork in the Avellino bottleneck.

The tough and experienced parachute warriors held no illusions: they had been handed a classic suicide mission. The Allied high command used simple arithmetic: 640 paratroopers would be sacrificed to save 140,000 men at Salerno.

Before takeoff for the long flight to the Avellino DZ (drop zone), a sergeant put into perspective what the paratroopers were thinking: "Our big brass are throwing the Krauts a bone. The 509th is going to be a nice, juicy bone to take Adolf Hitler's mind off our guys on the beachhead!"

Just past two o'clock in the morning, the dark sky in central Italy was awash with billowing white parachutes. Among those smashing heavily into the unyielding ground were Lieutenant Lloyd Wilson and Platoon Sergeant George Fontanesi. Hiding under a poncho to conceal the beam of a small flashlight, they concluded that they were ten miles east of the true DZ outside Avellino.

Along with ten other troopers, Wilson and Fontanesi headed across the dark countryside which was sliced by deep gorges and clogged by thickets. As the sun rose, the little band halted, and the lieutenant pulled out his grimy map. "Bingo!" he called out. They were right on the DZ. But where were the other 628 men of the 509th Parachute outfit?

Wilson and Fontanesi had no way of knowing that the battalion had been scattered over a one-thousand-square-mile region, some as far away as forty miles north of Avellino.

Clearly, the corporation had been dissolved, so the twelve paratroopers went into business for themselves. During daylight hours, they holed up in a cave on a mountainside. Each night, they ventured out to prowl around the region, ambushing German couriers, shooting up truck convoys, planting road mines, blowing up small bridges, and attacking isolated outposts.

Elsewhere far behind German lines, other tiny bands of paratroopers were likewise harassing and tormenting the Germans. Wehrmacht command posts were flooded by reports of "large units" of American paratroopers shooting up the region.

General Heinrich von Vietinghoff, commander of the German Tenth Army, and his intelligence officers concluded that at least a division of ten thousand paratroopers was marauding around the rear areas. Consequently, a large number of German soldiers and vehicles which could have been used at Salerno, were scouring the terrain in search of the parachutists.

On the third morning after bailing out, Lieutenant Wilson, Sergeant Fontanesi, and their men were getting edgy. They were nearly out of rations and were gripped by hunger pains. Emerging from their cave, they saw a farmer toiling in a field in the valley. Fontanesi, born in Italy but an American citizen since boyhood, spoke the native language fluently. So he traipsed down the mountain to talk with the farmer.

Unsure if the man could be trusted, but desperate for food, the sergeant asked if he could provide the Americans with something to eat.

*Platoon Sergeant George Fontanesi daily risked his life by wearing civilian clothes far behind German lines. (Author's collection)*

"My wife and I live in that little town," the Italian replied, pointing into the distance. "But I don't know if we can get food out here to you or not."

"Well, bring me some civilian clothes and I'll help you get the food here," Fontanesi stated.

Early the following morning, as promised, the farmer returned carrying some bread and moldy bacon which the famished paratroopers devoured. The Italian also brought along some old civilian clothes which Fontanesi tried on. Despite the seriousness of their predicament, the sergeant's comrades guffawed at Fontanesi in the bedraggled garments. The pants were five inches too short.

"Your jump boots stick out like a sore thumb!" a trooper called out.

The next day, Fontanesi told his companions that he was going into town dressed in the native garb to seek food. "Like hell you will," Lieutenant Wilson objected adamantly. "If the Krauts catch you in civilian clothes they'll shoot you on the spot."

Wilson added: "And with those boots sticking out like two beacons, the Krauts can hardly miss spotting you!"

An argument erupted. Hunger won out. Fontanesi was given permission to try his luck at obtaining food for the little knot of paratroopers.

The sergeant wore his regulation dog tags and carried no weapon. If captured, a likely possibility, he would plead that he was an escaped prisoner and not an armed soldier in disguise.

Together with his newfound Italian friend, Fontanesi began the trek to the nearby village and reached the square in which there was a fountain. The American had not had a drink of water since the previous day, and he began gulping the liquid from the fountain. He heard a roar behind him and, as casually as possible, turned to see what it was. Chills charged up his spinal column—it was a motorcycle and sidecar carrying two German soldiers.

The cycle screeched to a halt near the fountain and the enemy soldiers walked up alongside Fontanesi. "This is it!" the American thought. "How can they miss seeing my jump boots?" The Germans and Fontanesi exchanged friendly greetings and talked in Italian for several minutes. Then the soldiers, their jackboots clattering on the cobblestoned street, went back to their motorcycle and sped away.

Fontanesi and his Italian friend proceeded to the native's modest home where the man's wife loaded the American with cheese and bread. Feigning a nonchalance he did not feel, Fontanesi began walking through town, passing numerous German soldiers and patrols.

On reaching his comrades, the sergeant was accorded a hero's welcome. "We sure as hell never thought we'd see you again, George!" one called out.

"I don't know if you guys are happy to see I made it back or because I've got a lot of food with me," he conjectured.

"A little of both, George," came an honest reply.

For the next six days, the wife of the Italian benefactor brought a large pot of food consisting mainly of thick soup. She toted the heavy container on her head, and Fontanesi, dressed in his Italian civilian clothes, went into the valley to carry the burden up the mountainside.

Each time Fontanesi ventured forth in daylight to meet the woman, he had to cross a busy road. The American always waved and smiled at the enemy soldiers and tank drivers who passed close enough for him to reach out and touch them. Occasionally, he shook hands with a German.

In the meantime, Fontanesi had been a one-man intelligence agency. Wearing his tattered civilian clothing with the too-short pants, he stalked around the area each day. He struck up conversations with German soldiers who spoke a smattering of Italian and learned from them that a widespread hunt was on to capture and kill the paratroopers.

On one occasion in daylight, Lieutenant Wilson in his jump suit and Fontanesi were in a shack on a mountain near the cave hideout while searching for sabotage targets. Glancing out a small window, they saw a heavily-armed German patrol climbing up the elevation toward them. When only about a hundred yards away, most of the patrol sat down, and one Feldgrau (field gray, the average soldier), continued toward the shack. He was armed with a Schmeisser automatic pistol.

The trapped Americans held a whispered conversation. "Let him in the shack and I'll take care of him with my knife," Wilson said.

"No," Fontanesi replied. "If we stick him, his comrades will come looking for him. I've got a better idea—we'll try to bluff this Kraut."

Wilson concealed himself in a corner. Fontanesi opened the front door to greet the "visitor," and stood casually in front of it. Smiling broadly, he greeted the German warmly, but he felt that the other man was staring at his jump boots that were protruding from below his short pants.

"Who's inside?" the German asked in Italian.

"I'm just hiding an American paratrooper," was the reply.

Fontanesi laughed. The Feldgrau, a friendly type, guffawed.

Bidding the "Italian" a pleasant good-bye, the German returned to his comrades down the mountainside, and they resumed their search for hostile parachutists.

Soon after dawn on September 23—D-Day plus fourteen—the Allies broke out of the beachhead, drove north for thirty miles and captured Naples, the invasion's primary objective.

Meanwhile, men of the 509th Parachute Infantry, alone, in pairs, and in small bands, joined with the advancing American and British outfits. One hundred and nine troopers did not return. Survivors included Sergeant George Fontanesi, who had conducted final rites for his Italian civilian clothes which had served him and his comrades nobly, but could have been his death warrant.[2]

# The New York Subway Connection

TWO DAYS AFTER Anglo-Americans landed along the Gulf of Salerno in Italy on September 9, 1943, U.S. Sergeant Newton H. Fulbright was alone and pinned down by a German machine gun that was angrily spitting bullets across a corn patch. It was soon after dawn. Newton slithered behind a nearby farmhouse and was undecided on what to do next, because he was supposed to cross that corn patch to connect with friendly forces.

It was there that he first came across a strange phenomenon involving the New York subway system some four thousand miles away. When the machine gun was silent, Fulbright heard a shuffling of feet and swung around with his carbine at the ready. Facing him was a small, elderly farmer who spoke adequate English. He said that the German crew had departed.

"Thanks," the American replied. "Where did you learn to speak English?"

"I worked for the New York subway system for many years before returning home to Italy," the farmer answered.

Later that afternoon, Fulbright joined a patrol that plodded up the 3,500-foot slope of Mount Soprana, overlooking the beachhead. From this elevation, German observers had been directing artillery fire at the Americans on the flatland.

As the GIs were cautiously advancing, a farmer came out of a house and said in passable English: "The Germans are no longer here. They gathered up all the bottles of *vino* they could find, then took off to the east."

The Italian had worked for the New York subway system for five years.

Four days later on September 14, Fulbright and five of his men were captured while on reconnaissance behind German lines in the bloody battle of Altavilla. The captives were taken a hundred miles to the north and put in a POW compound. After five days behind barbed wire, the sergeant escaped one night and started the perilous trek back to friendly forces in the south.

German vehicles and troops were using most of the roads, so Fulbright stumbled across country, harassed by barking dogs. When the moon went down, the landscape was pitch black, so he entered a small town in which Feldgrau were meandering about—probably in search of vino, he conjectured.

The American was able to get out of the place, although on several occasions, he collided with German soldiers also stumbling along in the blackness. After these brushes with disaster, Fulbright decided to continue his journey in daylight, even though it might lead to his discovery. So he crawled into a haystack near a farmhouse and fell into a deep sleep.

At dawn, the sergeant crept cautiously out of his concealment, wiping straw from his face and pulling it from his hair. Just then, an elderly woman emerged from the front door of the house and walked into the yard. She saw this bearded, disheveled apparition edging out of her haystack and began screaming at the top of her lungs and calling on the Virgin Mary to spare her.

Moments after the woman had gone back into the house, a large number of family members emerged and invited the stranger inside, where he tried to make friendly conversation without giving away the fact that he was an American soldier who was escaping.

It was a hopeless conversation. The old woman couldn't speak English, neither could her husband nor her sister, nor could three children of a mother who had been killed in the fighting. Fulbright tried to communicate in a mixture of Spanish and English, but the family merely stared at him.

Suddenly, the door flew open and in barged a tall, husky man who, Fulbright thought, had the meanest looking face he had ever seen. Without a word, the newcomer thrust a pistol in the GI's stomach and snarled something in Italian. If this man was pro-Nazi, the American reflected, he was doomed.

Fulbright stood still as the mean-faced man rifled through the sergeant's pockets, pulling out a billfold with three U.S. dollars and a picture of his girlfriend. Finding nothing suspicious, the Italian sat down, apparently uncertain what to do next. Or was he merely awaiting the arrival of German soldiers that he may have summoned earlier?

Then an old Italian with snow-white hair and a handlebar mustache entered through the front door. He spotted the American, beamed, and called out, "Gooda de mornin'!"

Ecstatic to hear English spoken, Fulbright shouted, "Good morning!" Then he leaped up and pumped the old man's arm vigorously.

Now the entire family, their qualms banished, gathered around the GI, slapping him on the back and talking rapidly in the language he didn't comprehend. They provided him with civilian clothes, but it was decided that he should remain holed up and await the arrival of the approaching British Eighth Army.

Five nights later, the flash of artillery could be seen plainly in the south. The British were near, so it was time for Fulbright to depart. He shook hands warmly with the old man with whom he had held many hours of conversation. Had it not been for this Italian, the sergeant could have aroused the fears among members of the farm family and, perhaps, caused them to tip off the Germans.

"By the way," Fulbright said to the old man just before departing. "Where in hell did you learn to speak English?"

The Italian replied: "I worka seventeen years for New York subway system."[3]

# Nose-Thumbing at the Germans

A FORMER FRENCH ARMY COLONEL, Jean Romans-Petit, was the leader of nearly three hundred underground warriors hiding out in the hills of east-central France. In early November 1943, he drew up plans for a scheme that would both permit the Maquis, as the resistants were called, to thumb their noses at the German occupiers, and also to bolster the spirits of underground fighters throughout France.

German commanders forbid any public demonstration in observance of Armistice Day, November 11, the French national holiday that marked the Allies' victory over Germany in the First World War. So Romans-Petit planned a daring celebration of that highly significant milestone in French history.

As the site for the *verboten* (forbidden) festivities, Romans-Petit chose the small town of Oyonnax. A week before the event, he decoyed the Germans through a hoax. Under cover of night, a group of resistants, solo and in pairs, stole into the village of Nantua, twelve miles from Oyonnax, and plastered walls with illegal posters calling for a demonstration there on November 11.

Just as the colonel had expected, the Germans swallowed the bait. They ordered the French *gendarmes* (police) in the region, including those in Oyonnax, to converge on Nantua early on the morning of Armistice Day to prevent or break up the French celebration.

In the darkness of Armistice Day morning, the resistants came down from their hillside lairs into Oyonnax. They posted guards to block traffic from entering or leaving the town. They took over the police station, the town hall, and the telephone exchange. Suddenly, insignificant Oyonnax had been transformed into an oasis in the vastness of German-controlled France.

Surrounded by hundreds of weeping and cheering townspeople, Colonel Romans-Petit and his men gathered around the town's memorial to the French soldiers who had died in the last war. At the foot of the monument, the Maquis commander placed a floral cross of Lorraine inscribed to "the victors of yesterday from those of tomorrow."

Then the emotional crowd, led by the resistants, gave a rousing rendition of the *"Marseillaise,"* the French national anthem, after which the underground warriors formed up and paraded through the town.

Meanwhile, armed German units remained on the alert twelve miles away in Nantua. The hated occupiers had "lost great face." News of the resistants' exploit spread rapidly throughout France, bolstering the spirits of underground members and civilians alike.[4]

# The Chef Had Bombs
# on His Menu

THE NIGHT WAS DARK when two British secret agents parachuted into a pasture near the town of Figeac in southern France. Even while they were rolling up their chutes, several shadowy figures emerged and greeted the new arrivals. They were men of the local underground, headed by the foreman of the Ratier aircraft company which was producing variable-pitch propellers for the German Luftwaffe. It was January 7, 1944.

A few weeks earlier, the Mouvements Unis de Resistance, one of the largest underground networks in France, had radioed London: "If you provide the explosives and indicate the targets, our *réseau* [network] is ready to undertake any form of demolition." As a result, the two British agents had jumped outside Figeac.

Sabotage attacks were referred to as "bangs" by the resistance. Now the Ratier plant had been targeted. The British agents and the resistance men, including the company foremen, went to a cheese shop belonging to one of the conspirators. The shades were drawn, and the men spent the next few hours fashioning bombs, using the explosives that the British had parachuted in earlier.

Meanwhile, the foremen briefed the secret agents on the spots to place the bombs that would result in the most damage to the Ratier plant. By daylight, everything was ready.

One of the Frenchmen, donning a tall, white chef's hat, picked up a tray on which the explosives had been piled and set off across town with it. Masking the true contents were large napkins that covered the bombs. This part of the action had to be done in daylight because of the danger of discovery by German patrols at night.

The "chef" had only two blocks to go to reach his destination, a garage, but he passed close to several German soldiers who paid no attention to him or his large tray.

The bombs were secreted in an automobile, and the saboteurs had to lie low in the garage until nightfall. Then the conspirators drove to the Ratier factory, where they let themselves into the dark building with keys that had been provided by the foremen.

Three hours later, the town of Figeac was rocked by a series of explosions. Several large pieces of equipment that fabricated the propeller blades were destroyed.

Ratier produced no more aircraft components for the Luftwaffe.[5]

# Spying from a Church Steeple

ROBERT DOUIN, the prewar director of a fine arts school in Paris, was considered an eccentric by the people in Caen, known as the cathedral city and located some twelve miles south of the English Channel in Normandy.

German sentries ignored the "nut" with the goatee, weird clothing, and hat with its brim pulled down over his eyes who often bicycled into the countryside north of Caen. Douin always had to halt a few miles short of the Channel because the Germans had established that region as a "forbidden zone."

Douin was a sculptor, and in early 1944, he began to show an interest in examining statues perched high in church towers. That proved he was "touched in the head," Caen natives agreed.

One day, Douin climbed into the steeple of Notre Dame Church near Ranville and he immediately decided that a statue there needed a great amount of restorative work. Actually, the Frenchman was an Allied agent, and from the tall steeple, he could see the flat landscape reaching from Caen to the coast at Quistreham, a sleepy resort town.

Unfolded before him was a beehive of construction activity. Removing his old camera from its case, he began snapping pictures of the new German defenses. Then he scrambled back down and left the church, strolling non-chalantly past two Germans who were standing on a street corner.

Douin had risked his life solely on faith. Neither he nor anyone else in the Normandy underground knew if the Allies would one day land there. Or if an invasion of France would ever take place. So the sculptor was unaware that his clandestine photographs had been smuggled to London where they were eagerly scrutinized by Allied intelligence officers.

At dawn a few months later on June 6, 1944, Commander Philippe Kieffer and his 170 tough French commandos stormed ashore at Quistreham. One of the warriors, Count Guy de Montlaur, who was proud to be a sergeant, led his squad in an assault on Quistreham's gambling casino, a strongly defended German command post.

After Montlaur and his men had captured the objective, the wealthy nobleman quipped to Commander Kieffer: "It was a pleasure. I have lost several fortunes in that place!"

Robert Douin, French patriot, would never know the key role he had played in saving the lives of an untold number of his countrymen in the Quistreham landing. A few weeks before D-Day, he had been caught by the Gestapo carrying film of German defenses and was immediately executed.[6]

# The Black-Hearted Devils

ANZIO HAD SAT QUIETLY for hundreds of years on the Tyrrhenian seacoast of Italy, thirty-three miles south of Rome. Before the war, the charming little town had been a pleasant resort to which Romans would drive on holidays to escape the hustle and bustle of the teeming capital. Late in January 1944, that tranquility was shattered when an Anglo-American force landed and began carving out a beachhead.

Little Anzio had suddenly loomed huge on the strategic landscape. Shingle, as the operation was code-named, had been conceived by British Prime Minister Winston S. Churchill. It called for landing two divisions and attached troops fifty-eight miles behind German lines in Italy. The theory was that the Wehrmacht commander in Italy, Feldmarschall Albrecht Kesselring, would panic and rapidly pull back his army as far as Rome.

Kesselring, regarded by the Allies as one of Germany's top commanders, was not the panicky type. Instead of withdrawing from what was called the Gustav Line, he quickly tied a steel noose around the Anzio beachhead. Soon one hundred thousand Anglo-American soldiers were cooped up on a strip of flat real estate only sixteen miles long and five or six miles deep, hemmed in by a strong German force with heavy artillery support. Enemy observers looked down the throats of the invaders from the heights around the Allied enclave.

*First Special Service Force "courtesy calling card." It reads:
"The worst is yet to come!"*

Dug in along the Mussolini Canal on the right flank of the beachhead was U.S. Brigadier General Robert T. Frederick's elite First Special Service Force of Americans and Canadians. Each of the tough and resourceful fighting men had been hand-picked by Frederick, and all had to qualify as parachutists, skiers, and martial arts experts. There was an informal, loosely-knit relationship between officers and men. As long as the Forcemen were killing Germans, no one bothered too much about the chain of command or rank.

Orders from on high had been for Frederick's men to defend the Mussolini Canal. "Defend, hell!" a Forceman told his comrades. "Let the goddamned Krauts do the defending!"

On most nights, the Forcemen blackened their faces with charcoal, replaced helmets with knit caps, taped loose gear to prevent rattling, and slipped across the canal and behind German lines. They would slash the throats of sleeping Germans, perform similar emergency surgery on enemy sentinels, and return to their own lines just before dawn with a bag of prisoners for intelligence officers to interrogate.

One Forceman came back from a patrol with a diary taken from the body of a German lieutenant who had died unexpectedly from strangulation—by a piano wire. A recent entry stated: "The Black Devils [Forcemen] are all around us at night. They are upon us before we even hear them coming."

General Frederick, who believed in inspiring his men by example and not by dramatic gimmicks, allowed himself a brief departure from that approach. He ordered stickers printed that displayed the insignia of the First Special Service Force: DAS DICKE ENDE KOMMT NOCH! (The worst is yet to come!)

Going on night patrol, each Forceman would pocket a batch of these stickers and after killing a German would paste a sticker on the face or helmet of the corpse. Intelligence reports disclosed that the psychological impact on the Germans by these nefarious antics was devastating.

On one black night, Lieutenant George "the Mustache" Krasevac led a patrol of Forcemen far behind enemy lines and they stole into a presumably abandoned farmhouse for a brief respite. Suddenly, from the front part of the house voices were heard—German voices. The Americans froze. A German-speaking Forceman whispered to Krasevac that the Germans were using the house as an assembly site for a raid on the Mussolini Canal and that they were waiting for more comrades to arrive.

On cue the Forcemen dashed into the front part of the house, brandishing Tommy guns at the startled Germans and shouting, *"Hande hoch!"* (Hands up!) Some twenty enemy soldiers were disarmed and marched back through German positions and over the canal under the guard of two Forcemen.

"The Mustache" decided he had a good thing going and decided to remain with his other men and milk the situation for all it was worth. In pairs and threesomes, new German arrivals walked into the house and were greeted by Tommy guns in the hands of black-faced Forcemen.

German faces turned ashen as they realized they had fallen into the evil clutches of the Black Devils of Anzio. Word had quickly spread through German ranks that the men of General Frederick's outfit were ex-convicts—mostly murderers—who took no prisoners and showed no mercy.

It had been standard procedure for the Forcemen to melt back into friendly lines before dawn, but Krasevac felt that business was thriving. So it would be poor tactics to shut down the shop after daylight when more "customers" might appear.

A total of 108 Germans had been seized at the house and sent back during the night, and by 9:00 A.M., Krasevac believed that no more enemy soldiers were on the way. Just as the remaining Forcemen prepared to depart from their place of business, three more Germans approached. Astonished to see a band of sinister looking Allied soldiers leaving the house in which they were to assemble, the three Germans spun on their heels and fled.

"The Mustache," aware that his capture rate had been perfect so far, did not want the trio of Germans to elude him. "After the bastards!" the lieutenant shouted. Krasevac and two of his men dashed off in pursuit. The Forcemen could have shot the quarries at any time, but that wouldn't have been "sporting." After a long chase through German-held turf, the Americans brought the three men down with flying tackles.

Later, Force intelligence officers found a written message from a high Wehrmacht headquarters on one of the German prisoners:

You are fighting an elite Canadian-American force. They are treacherous, unmerciful, and clever. You cannot afford to relax. The first soldier or group of soldiers capturing one of these black-hearted men will be given a ten-day furlough.

The "black hearts" continued to prowl around behind German lines. On one occasion, Lieutenant Taylor Radcliffe was surprised and captured. By his blackened face, the Germans knew they had seized one of the infamous (to them) Black Devils of Anzio. The Germans bound and gagged Radcliffe, then dragged him off to a house to be interrogated. Only then was the American untied.

A German major demanded that Radcliffe disclose information on Allied dispositions on the beachhead. The Forceman suggested that the interrogator perform an impossible sex act on himself, a response that so infuriated the frustrated German that he struck Radcliffe a heavy blow on the face with a large stick.

Just then the gods of war came to Radcliffe's aid. A heavy Allied barrage sent the Germans scurrying for foxholes in the yard, leaving one unlucky soldier to guard the recalcitrant Forceman. The guard made the tactical blunder of turning his back momentarily, and Radcliffe picked up a board and knocked the German unconscious.

The lieutenant dashed into the next room and freed several bound American prisoners from other outfits, then he fled the building and two days later, returned to friendly lines. A few nights afterward, Radcliffe was back on patrol on German-held real estate.

In the First Special Service Force, where the common denominator was boldness, cunning, ingenuity, and courage, the outfit's leader, thirty-seven-year-old Bob Frederick, had become a living legend among his troops. Before the war would end, he would receive four Distinguished Service Crosses and eight Purple Hearts.

Frederick's personality and appearance were almost precisely opposite that of the Hollywood stereotype of a fire-breathing, rip-snorting, hell-for-leather warrior. He was spare in build, pale in complexion, and a pencil-thin mustache gave him the look of a mild-mannered accountant. However, he spoke rapidly and decisively, was indefatigable, and had an undefinable trait for instilling the warrior spirit among the Forcemen.

Wearing a knit cap and with face blackened, Frederick often went on night patrols into German territory. On one of these sashays, he and his men wandered into a minefield in the inky darkness; then they were raked by automatic weapons fire while trying to get out.

Several Forcemen were cut down, including a stretcher bearer. The surviving bearer was left with a badly wounded man. Frantically, the medic shouted to a dark figure, "Goddamnit, don't just stand there! Grab hold of the other end of the litter!"

After the two Forcemen carried the wounded soldier out of the minefield under a torrent of bullets, the medic caught a glimpse of the comrade he had loudly ordered to lend a hand. It was General Frederick.[7]

# A Scheme to Go under German Lines

ANZIO BEACHHEAD, a month after Allied forces had landed at the site south of Rome, had proved to be a Devil's Inferno where men by the thousands were chewed up in the enormous meat-grinder of violence. Each side had lost about twenty thousand men in the death struggle for the strip of bleak, barren Italian real estate.

In the bomb- and shell-battered town of Anzio on February 22, 1944, U.S. army engineers were digging furiously into a large heap of ancient ruins half buried under a mound of recently pulverized rubble. American officers had heard that Emperor Nero, centuries earlier, had built an underground aqueduct between Rome and his villa at Anzio, then as later a popular summertime resort for the wealthy.

Maybe this was the way to get behind German lines without firing a shot. Some were fascinated by the vision of sending a battalion or a regiment, even a full division of some twelve thousand men, trekking through an ancient and long-forgotten tunnel to surface molelike in the Eternal City thirty miles away.

Those involved in the rubble-clearing mission were ecstatic when they found the underground passage leading from the ruins of Nero's villa. They also discovered that it ended twenty-nine and a half miles short of Rome.[8]

# A New Baby Stymies Normandy Planning

IT WAS A BOLD and hazardous operation. A Lysander, a light aircraft piloted by a member of the Special Operations Executive, the British cloak-and-dagger organization, landed on a dark pasture outside Paris at about midnight. Two passengers scrambled aboard: Pierre Moreau, a slight, bespectacled French railway system official, and his wife, who was heavily pregnant.

Moments later, the Lysander lifted off and set a course for an airport outside London. By daylight, the French couple was ensconced at Brown's Hotel on Picadilly Circus. It was early February 1944.

Moreau was to play a key role in the destruction of the French railway network prior to Operation Overlord, a massive invasion of Normandy scheduled for June. For security reasons, the Frenchman was told nothing about the looming maneuver.

Before Moreau and his wife had been smuggled out of France, Allied Supreme Commander Dwight D. Eisenhower had given his approval to Operation Transportation, a ninety-day bombing attack against eighty rail targets in western Europe. Once the Allies were ashore in Normandy, German panzers and reinforcements would have to move through these rail centers to reach the landing beaches.

Eisenhower and his top commanders felt that the first five or six weeks of the invasion would be the most critical. So it was essential that every measure be taken to ensure that the invaders would seize and hold a large foothold in Normandy.

Now in London, Pierre Moreau, a senior official of the French railway system, the *Société Nationale des Chemins de Fer* (SNCF), knew as much or more than any man about the military capacity of the network and of German plans for its use in the event of Allied invasion. When Moreau had been approached by agents of the British secret service in Paris, he agreed to be exfiltrated to London—provided his wife came along.

Moreau had brought with him a wealth of detailed information other than that in his head: three volumes which constituted the latest operating manual for the French railroads.

Soon after Moreau got to work in a London apartment, a major crisis developed. His wife bore a son and Moreau, a Jew, insisted that the British government finance all expenses regarding the birth, including the circumcision. British bureaucrats agreed to pay the obstetrician's fee, but balked at paying for the circumcision.

With the world involved in a cataclysmic war and history's most crucial invasion on the horizon, Moreau declared that he would no longer work unless all birth fees were paid by His Majesty's government. Incredibly, the subject of the relatively small fee was brought up at a meeting of the Air Council composed of top Royal Air Force leaders.

Air Chief Marshal Charles Portal, the RAF commander, reached into his pocket and tossed a half crown onto the conference table. Others did likewise. The private collection of a small amount of money broke the logjam that had threatened to hold up plans for the most momentous invasion that history had known. Pierre resumed drawing up plans for the railroad-bombing campaign.

Three months later, Nazi-controlled Radio Paris announced that "the French railway system is in complete chaos from the destructive work of Allied pilots."[9]

# Sabotage Campaign by Railway Men

GUSTAV BEILER, a British secret agent stationed at Saint-Quintin, a French city eighty miles south of the English Channel, was on the run from the Gestapo. But he refused to allow that peril to prevent him from carrying out the crucial mission that had been assigned to him in London: orchestrating a sabotage campaign by railway workers to destroy the French network that Feldmarschall Erwin Rommel would be counting on to rush reinforcements to Normandy when Allied forces invaded. It was mid-February 1944.

Aided by detailed information provided by the Railway Research Service (RRS), a secret operation in England, Beiler was able to pinpoint critical facilities in northern France's rail yards: tracks, repair shops, sidings, stations, roundhouse, turntables, storage sheds, locomotives, signals system, switches, and bridges.

Under the constant specter of being caught by the Gestapo, Beiler traveled around the region handing out cans filled with a secret substance to railroad men whom he knew were loyal to the cause of ridding France of the Nazi yoke. The concoction in the cans had been created at a secret laboratory in London.

If a railway man were halted by German sentries or Gestapo agents, the mixture appeared to be ordinary lubricating grease, a product the worker could be expected to carry. Actually, the substance was a highly abrasive compound that quickly wore out parts to which it was applied.

*French railway workers and other underground members destroyed scores of locomotives on the brink of D-Day in Normandy. (National Archives)*

Through use of the diabolical goo, Beiler's clandestine group put ten locomotives out of action for long periods of time.

Moreover, track workers were shown how to jam turntables with a single steel bolt, how to jam the gates at road crossings, and how to keep signals arms at "halt" when they should be at "proceed," thereby stalling trains that were able to make short runs. Switchboard operators were taught how to immobilize a teleprinter circuit solely with a single feather in an armature.

Along with air bombings, the undercover agents in northern France had largely immobilized the rail network and much of its rolling stock by the time the Allies were ready to invade on June 6.[10]

# A Close Encounter
# with Two Jungle Beasts

SOON AFTER DAWN on February 24, 1944, Lieutenant Samuel V. Wilson and his men in the intelligence and reconnaissance (I & R) platoon of Merrill's Marauders rolled out of their ponchos in a thick jungle in Burma. There was apprehension in the air. Wilson's small unit had been given a daunting assignment, one fraught with potential disaster.

Brigadier General Frank D. Merrill, leader of the elite group of volunteers known officially by the jawbreaker designation 5307th Composite Unit (Provisional) planned to swing his several thousand Marauders in a wide arc around the flank of the strong Japanese force to his front. Merrill's mission was to cut the crucial Kamaing Road, down which the Japanese brought supplies and reinforcements.

Thirty-nine-year-old Frank Merrill, a New Hampshire native and West Point graduate, was highly popular with his warriors. He had a pleasant personality, a down-to-earth smile and, most important, when he spoke, he seemed to know what was what in this confused theater of war.

Merrill's current problem was that he didn't know how far his outfit would have to travel sideways to get around the Japanese flank. So Lieutenant Wilson's platoon was tapped to find the answer.

Barely past twenty-one years of age, Wilson had been ordered to recruit and train his I & R platoon. A native of Virginia, he was self-possessed, self-disciplined, and articulate—a natural born leader. He filled out the cadre of experienced soldiers he had started with by going to Merrill's guardhouse, which was well populated. There he picked out his recruits, convinced that men who chafed most under the frustrations of training-camp life would do well in an I & R platoon.

*Merrill's Marauders made extensive use of horses in operations behind Japanese positions in Burma. (U.S. Army)*

Merrill's Marauders and spirited Japanese forces were engaged in some of the bloodiest fighting under brutal terrain and climatic conditions that history had known. Much of the time, the Americans were behind enemy lines—and fighting for their lives.

Malaria dominated the region. Men exhausted by fighting through jungles and up and down steep mountains fell easy victims to its fevers. Casualties were heavy from disease, which included dysentery, swamp fever, and disorders carried by worms, snails, flies, and lice.

Lieutenant Wilson and his forty-seven men set out in the blackness just past midnight. With them were a few mules and horses carrying supplies and ammunition. None of the I & R platoon had any way of knowing that they were embarked on a grueling thirty-mile march.

For the first two days, the platoon had been moving eastward, roughly parallel to the "front." Suddenly, there were heavy bursts of firing. "It's behind us, Sammy!" one man called out. Wilson nodded.

Clearly, there was heavy fighting to their rear, meaning that the Japanese had slipped in between the platoon and the main body of the Marauders. Wilson and his men were alone, isolated.

Although the grating sound of artillery and mortar explosions interspersed by machine-gun fire, could be heard, Wilson kept his platoon moving forward along the trail. Finally, they reached Tanja Ga, a collection of *bashas* (bamboo huts with palm-thatched roofs) in a wide clearing. The village was deserted.

Using Tanja Ga as a base, Wilson and his men probed the region. The lieutenant was convinced that they were now around the right flank of the Japanese force and were, in fact, behind the enemy. This critical information had to be rushed to Colonel Charles N. Hunter, leader of the Marauder regiment, so the platoon's SCR 284 radio was unloaded from a pack mule and set up.

Atmospheric conditions were bad, and contact could not be made. So Wilson decided to ride back on Pride-and-Joy, a magnificent black horse that the lieutenant had selected weeks earlier. He would take one man on another horse with him.

Although nearly exhausted from two days of marching across the rugged terrain, Wilson set out late at night. It would be a thirty-mile trek filled with potential peril. He would follow the same trail back, and it was likely that the Japanese might have closed in on the path.

A few hours along the way, Wilson and his companion, on their horses, were crossing a stream. Pride-and-Joy stretched to climb the far bank and the saddle turned beneath Wilson. His head and shoulders were on the muddy ground with one foot caught in the stirrup. He struggled mightily to free himself lest the horse bolt or fall on him.

Suddenly, Wilson was aware that two large jungle beasts—they may have been tigers or leopards—bounded into the trail some thirty yards to the front, snarling and fighting ferociously. Now the lieutenant felt that his greatest danger was not in getting trampled to death by his horse, but from the vicious beasts. His companion was bringing up the rear and was perhaps a hundred yards away.

The nimble-witted Wilson recalled hearing that wild animals can sometimes be frightened away by the sound of an angry human voice. So he shouted the first words that came to him: "You don't want to tackle me, you crazy cats!" He added: "I'm too damned tough for you!"

Moments later, Wilson managed to free himself, just as the beasts seemed to be eyeing the shouter. He whipped his carbine from the saddle and fired two shots over the big cats' heads. He did not want to madden them by wounds, in which case they might charge him.

Hours later, the lieutenant was back among his own, conveying the crucial intelligence to Colonel Charles Hunter.

Perhaps the I & R platoon leader had a curious thought. Had things turned out differently along the trail a few hours ago, would his loved ones back in Virginia have received the dreaded casualty telegram: "The Secretary of War regrets to inform you that Lieutenant Samuel V. Wilson, serial number, has been eaten in action by two wild beasts."[11]

# "Baby Sergeant York"

U.S. SECRETARY OF WAR Henry L. Stimson, said by many to be one of Washington's more astute minds, made an announcement that stunned many Americans. He said that the U.S. Army would now accept Nisei (second generation Japanese-Americans) as volunteers. It was January 28, 1943.

Stimson apparently had been moved after receiving a letter from Henry Ebihara, a Nisei, who, along with more than one hundred thousand other Americans of Japanese descent, had spent many months in what was called relocation camps, mainly on the West Coast.

"I only ask that I be given a chance to fight to preserve the principles that I have been brought up on and which I will not sacrifice at any cost," Ebihara wrote. "Please give me a chance to serve in your armed forces."

Twelve hundred Nisei immediately signed up from behind the barbed wire in their encampments. Eventually, eight thousand Nisei would serve, and with great distinction, racking up awesome combat records. No Nisei was ever known to have deserted in battle.

In the Pacific, many Nisei were in the middle of heavy fighting—literally—so close that they were shot at by both sides while hearing and translating Japanese commands.

In Burma in early 1944, Sergeant Kenney Yasui earned the nickname "Baby Sergeant York," after the legendary Tennessee mountaineer, Alvin York, who, alone, had captured nearly one hundred Germans during a World War I battle. Yasui earned his moniker because of his diminutive size and a spectacular coup he had pulled off.

Yasui had put on the uniform and insignia of a Japanese colonel, who, the Nisei told comrades with a straight face, had "died suddenly from a cut throat." Then Yasui sneaked behind Japanese lines.

When he encountered thirteen Japanese soldiers, fully armed, he bawled them out for their sloppy demeanor. In an authoritative tone, he ordered them to lay down their weapons. Schooled since boyhood to obey military orders without question, they complied.

Yasui marched the unsuspecting Japanese warriors back to American positions, where they were confined in a hastily built enclosure. No doubt the POWs were puzzled over why a Japanese colonel had put them there.[12]

# A Millionairess Resistance Leader

NANCY WAKE, a beautiful, vivacious young Australian woman, parachuted onto the plateau of Mont Mouchet in central France on the night of March 1, 1944. It was her second tour as a resistance warrior, and she carried with her a

*French resistants in camp clean weapons to prepare for that night's raid. (National Archives)*

large amount of genuine French francs of Special Operations Executive (SOE) cash to finance clandestine operations in the region in preparation for the June invasion of Normandy.

Back in 1939, Wake had been touring Europe when she met and married a French millionaire. Only weeks later, war broke out, France fell to the mighty Wehrmacht in the spring of 1940, and she immediately joined the fledgling resistance movement.

Using her code name, Wake worked for nearly three years as a courier, a perilous task because if stopped by the Gestapo or the Nazi-controlled French Milice (police), she would be carrying incriminating documents.

In early 1943, the Australian was tipped off that the Gestapo was about to arrest her, so she had to flee across France to neutral Spain and then make her way to England. As soon as she arrived in Britain, she sought out the SOE, offered to go back to the Continent, and was trained as a radio operator and as an agent to help instruct the Maquisards (resistance members).

After landing on the Mont Mouchet plateau, Wake was confronted by surly and uncooperative Maquisards. She learned that not all resistance men were warriors on white horses. Later, she eavesdropped outside a meeting from which she had been excluded and, to her astonishment, heard the guerrillas agree to kill her while she was sleeping and steal the SOE money she had brought with her.

Instead of fleeing to save her life, Wake joined a group of raiders who stole into the nearby town of Saint-Flour that night. There they broke into and "borrowed" badly needed boots, blankets, and tents from a sports shop whose owner was a known Nazi collaborator. A note was left thanking him for his "contribution" to the French Maquis.

Wake's courage and willingness to take chances in equal measure with the male Maquisards soon won the respect of the underground cell, and she became a leader in the group. Her main, and crucial, assignment was that of *chef du parachutage*, coordinating by radio with SOE in London the dropping of arms, ammunition, and supplies for some seven thousand resistance men in central France.

Following the Allied invasion of Normandy on June 6, 1944, German commanders in France, outraged and concerned about the heavy concentration of Maquis in their rear areas, launched an assault by some 10,000 troops to wipe out the 3,000 armed resistants on the Mont Mouchet plateau.

Nancy Wake was in the thick of the fighting. While driving a van that was loaded with ammunition and mortar shells, she was strafed by a low-flying Luftwaffe plane. The vehicle was riddled with bullets, but she jumped out just before the van caught fire and exploded.

Confronted by panzers, bombed by warplanes, and outnumbered more than three to one, the Maquis had to pull out of the region. However, they promptly went into business nearby and resumed wreaking havoc on the Germans. Just past noon one day, Wake and thirteen other Maquisards drove straight into the town of Montlucon and screeched to a halt outside a Gestapo headquarters.

As planned, the French resistants leaped from their vehicles, and covered Wake as she charged up the stairs to the second level, threw open a door, and rolled a hand grenade into a room occupied by several Gestapo agents.

Even before the smoke had cleared from the explosion, the Australian woman raced downstairs, scrambled into one of the Maquis vehicles, and the tiny caravan sped out of Montlucon.

Two days later, notices were placed throughout the region, offering a substantial cash reward for anyone who would identify the French "terrorists" who had killed the Gestapo agents. Although natives in the area were quite poor, there were no takers.[13]

# A Woman OSS Agent and "Cuthbert"

EARLY IN MARCH 1944, a submarine surfaced off the dark coast of Britanny, the French Peninsula adjoining Normandy to the east. Several shadowy figures climbed through the hatch, traversed the slippery deck, and dropped into a rubber raft. Minutes later, the dinghy touched the beach. The occupants climbed out and headed inland behind German coastal defenses.

Among these Allied spies was thirty-eight-year-old Virginia Hall, an American who had earlier spent many months in central France organizing and directing underground operations. She had been exfiltrated by a Lysander (short takeoff-and-landing airplane) just before the Gestapo was about to seize her.

Hall was among the Allied secret operatives infiltrated into Britanny with the mission of keeping German forces bottled up and unable to reach the landing beaches rapidly after Allied troops were ashore in Normandy.

Virginia had not only demonstrated exceptional courage and ingenuity in previous undercover missions in France, but her achievements were all the more remarkable because she had an artificial leg. Years earlier, she had an amputation after a severe automobile accident that nearly took her life.

Like many amputees, Hall grew to be indifferent about her physical impairment. This is the way it is, she reasoned, so she made the best of the situation. In fact, she even had a pet nickname for her artificial limb: Cuthbert.

One day after operating under perilous conditions in Britanny for several weeks, she radioed her U.S. Office of Strategic Services (OSS) contact in London: "Cuthbert is giving me a great amount of trouble."

Code names were sprinkled like confetti all over Nazi-controlled Europe. So the London operative apparently thought she was referring to a trouble-making member of her underground unit. He replied: "If Cuthbert is interfering with your mission, terminate him at once!"[14]

# Panzer Watchers
# and Phony Laundries

EARLY IN THE SPRING OF 1944, Allied Supreme Commander Dwight D. Eisenhower and other brass at his London headquarters were showing signs of the jitters. Operation Overlord, the invasion of Normandy, was less than three months away.

Reflecting the anxiety in the high command, Lieutenant General Walter B. "Beetle" Smith, Eisenhower's chief of staff, said in a telephone call to the Pentagon in Washington: "Our chances of holding the beachhead, particularly after the Germans get their buildup, are only fifty-fifty."

It was a frightening analysis: there was a distinct possibility that the assault forces might suffer a bloody debacle.

Eisenhower and his planners felt that the troops could get ashore. But could they stay there? Not if Field Marshal Erwin Rommel, the German commander in northern France, could rush several panzer divisions from inland to the beachhead in the early days of the invasion.

Consequently, the dominant matter confronting Allied planners was to conceive ways and means to delay the German panzer reserves. An extraordinary program of bombing, deception, and underground violence was created. MI-6, the British secret service for foreign operations, and the U.S. Office of Strategic Services (OSS) launched a program code-named Sussex.

More than one hundred teams of two—an observer and a radio operator—were parachuted into France deep behind German positions along the English Channel coast. They had a crucial task: watch crossroads and rail junctions through which German armored outfits would have to travel to reach the Normandy invasion beaches. The American teams were called Ossex while the British were Brissex.

The spies were disguised as farmers, longshoremen, or *gendarmes* (police) and were provided with fake identity cards. For the American teams this task was the responsibility of a highly secret group of men and women belonging to the Cover and Documentation (C & D) branch of the OSS. One tiny mistake by C & D could result in the execution of an OSS agent.

Forged documents had been created by C & D in a building tucked away on a back street in central London. The engraving plant was in the kitchen where water was handy. Heavy presses were located on the concrete floor of the attached garage.

In the attic of the building was a tailor shop. Garments were created with great care. Buttons were sewn with parallel threading rather than the usual American crisscross technique. On such tiny nuances could rest the fate of a secret agent when confronted by Gestapo interrogators.

Some of the Ossex agents wore genuine French clothing from civilian refugees or garments "borrowed" from gendarmes and other officials in France by undercover agents.

C & D operatives even drilled into the very beings of the spies how to look and act like authentic Frenchmen, how to smoke cigarettes until the coal almost burned their mouths. A secret agent could betray himself if a sharp-eyed Gestapo man saw him flip away a half-smoked cigarette because no true Frenchman would waste precious smokes that had cost him a good-sized chunk of his frugal income.

Plausible cover stories were created by C & D, but these had to be reinforced with proof. Fraudulent certificates or a fake letter from a relative about the death of a family member would explain to the Gestapo why the "Frenchman" was far from his own town.

Few if any of the American and British agents snooping on German panzer movements realized that their radioed reports were being studied eagerly in London as time for the Normandy invasion edged closer.

Perhaps the most innovative technique for keeping track of German army units in France was developed by several *réseau* (networks) of the underground whose members opened commercial laundry firms. German officers and soldiers needed clean laundry and, because of low prices and excellent service, these underground firms got a large amount of their business.

Of course, none of the Germans realized that they were dealing with men and women resistants whose primary objective was to provide information that would permit Allied forces one day to wreak havoc on the "customers." These laundry operations were designed to ferret out the deployment of German panzer and infantry units, intelligence that would be radioed to London.

After a German unit received sudden orders to move to a new locale, soldiers who had brought in their laundry earlier would rush into the underground firm to pick up their belongings. However, the "proprietors," sensing an urgency, would lie to the customers that their laundry was not ready, but if the Germans would leave their forwarding addresses, their belongings would soon be mailed to them. This ruse pinpointed the locale where the unit was to be deployed, and the change would be noted in London on a huge wall map of the Normandy area.[15]

# The Supersecret X Troop

DURING THE SPRING OF 1944, the Germans were on full alert along Adolf Hitler's vaunted Atlantikwall, a highly formidable defensive barrier that stretched from Norway to the Spanish border. Across the English Channel, the Western Allies were assembling the most powerful invasion force that history has known.

To obtain current information on German troop deployments and new defenses along the Channel coast of France, the Allied high command called on X Troop, an outfit so secret that many top British and American leaders did not know of its existence.

X Troop consisted of sixty-four men of several nationalities, all of whom spoke colloquial German fluently. Many of them were Jewish refugees who had volunteered for this perilous duty, fully aware of the horrible fate that awaited them if captured. In the hope that their true identities might be concealed if they fell into German hands, the Jews were provided with Gentile names and new identities.

To the Germans manning the Atlantikwall each dawn brought the sight of two or more rickety fishing boats crawling along off the coast of France. On board were X Troop men in civilian disguise. Amazingly, perhaps, with *der Grossinvasion* clearly imminent, the occupying authority permitted French fishermen to continue to pursue their livelihoods.

On occasion, the fraudulent fishing boats, instead of returning to their bases when night fell, edged near the shore at points thought to be unmanned or thinly occupied by the Germans. In rubber rafts, two or three X Troop men would paddle onto a beach and spend several hours prowling behind the Atlantikwall to gather information on new defenses and German troop deployments.[16]

# Miracle at a Normandy Convent

IN APRIL 1944, with D-Day in Normandy two months away, British and U.S. air forces began a massive pounding of German facilities behind the coastal defenses along the English Channel. Designed to inflict maximum confusion within the German armed forces in France when the invasion was about ready to hit, the targets included airfields, fuel dumps, tank parks, communications centers, and German headquarters.

The selection of targets by Allied planners in England was ruthless. It would be impossible to carry out the air campaign without inflicting civilian casualties. Consequently, when Centurie, the underground apparatus in Normandy, and the monitoring of German radio traffic indicated that a huge convent a short distance outside Cherbourg was being used as a corps head-quarters, the magnificent twelfth-century structure was put on the target list.

The convent, which was home to fifty-eight sisters of a French order, had fourteen buildings, including a dormitory, school, novitiate, chapel, and a small hospital. Twenty years earlier, the complex had been destroyed by a raging fire, and it had taken the nuns nearly fifteen years to rebuild it.

Shortly before D-Day, a flight of Allied bombers winged over the convent and dropped tons of bombs, leaving the buildings huge piles of smoking rubble.

During the heavy deluge of earth-shaking explosives, all fifty-eight nuns were huddled in the basement of the main building, reciting the rosary and waiting to be buried under tons of stone or to suffocate from the fires raging above them. But the four-foot-thick walls and ceiling in the eight-hundred-year-old basement held firm.

One by one, the dust-covered sisters emerged from their place of refuge to witness a scene of utter devastation. Although badly shaken, none had received even a scratch.[17]

# A Luftwaffe Pilot Declines to Take Bait

BOTH ALLIED AND GERMAN deception agencies were constantly alert to plant false "evidence" behind the battle lines and into enemy camps. Such an opportunity surfaced for the British in late April 1944 after a Luftwaffe fighter pilot had been shot down and captured.

The German was found to be *führertreu* (loyal to Adolf Hitler) and one of the Luftwaffe's most skilled pilots. As step one in a bizarre scheme, he was taken to the Royal Air Force base at Leuchars in Scotland for more intensive "interrogation."

For nearly an hour, the British intelligence officer grilled the German who was seated in an office with a large window through which the airport runway could be seen. Telling the prisoner that he had to "see a man about a dog," the Briton left the room, leaving the door to the office unlocked.

Moments later, a ground crew brought up the latest model Spitfire reconnaissance airplane and parked it in view of the German and only some thirty yards away. They fueled the sleek Spitfire, turned the propeller, left the cockpit hatch open, and bustled off for a traditional British ritual, afternoon tea.

This was a tailor-made situation for the German pilot. If he were to return to his unit's base and land in a new Spitfire, he would become an instant folk hero in the Third Reich which was in serious need of a morale booster. All the pilot had to do was to walk out of the unlocked door to the office, scramble into the cockpit, and take off.

Inside the cockpit had been placed a set of false maps that would seem to German intelligence to indicate the Allied forces were going to invade France, not in Normandy, but some two hundred miles to the east at the Pas de Calais, which was only twenty miles across the English Channel from Dover, England.

All was in readiness. But the German refused to swallow the bait. He merely sat by the window and casually looked at the Spitfire, waiting patiently for the interrogator to return.

Later, British deception officers concluded that the Luftwaffe pilot, although führertreu, was not stupid. He knew that Germany was going to lose the war, so he would rather sit out the remainder of the conflict in the relative comfort and security of an Allied POW camp.[18]

# Jealousy Thwarts a German Scheme

As preparations for operation overlord, the invasion of Normandy became steadily more hectic, demanding, and nerve-racking in May 1944, Allied Supreme Commander Dwight D. Eisenhower was showing signs of the enormous strain. Reflecting the anxiety that gripped his headquarters, he wrote to his old friend, General Brehon Somervell, chief of the Army Services of Supply, in Washington:

> Everybody here is on edge. Because of the stakes involved, the atmosphere is probably more electric than ever before. . . . We are not risking a tactical defeat—we are putting the whole works on one number.

There was ample reason for London's jitters. British General Frederick Morgan, who had drawn up the original invasion plan, warned, "If the Germans have even a forty-eight-hour advance notice of the time and place of the [Normandy] landings, we could suffer a monstrous catastrophe!"

With D-Day scheduled for the first week in June, chances for a security leak had multiplied many times. Hundreds of U.S. and British officers now were privy to the innermost secrets of Overlord—including the projected D-Day and the locale of the invasion. They were known as Bigots, which took its curious name from the stamp "To Gib" that had been imprinted on the papers of officers traveling to Gibraltar for the Allied invasion of North Africa in November 1942. To confuse the Germans (and Allied personnel not in the know), the "To Gib" letters had been reversed.

At the same time, Adolf Hitler and his generals were trying desperately to discover *der Grossinvasion* secrets. Toward this goal, the Germans were using thousands of Abwehr agents around the world, scores of electronic monitoring posts along the English Channel, and limited Luftwaffe flights over southern England.

Results were mixed. German intelligence was confused by a devious Allied deception plan, code-named Bodyguard, that was designed to coerce the führer into concluding that the invasion would hit at the Pas de Calais, two hundred miles east of the true landing beaches.

In desperation, it was suggested that English-speaking Brandenburgers, an elite commando outfit, don British and American uniforms and sneak ashore at night in southern England. The intruders would push a short distance behind the coastal defenses, kidnap one or more Allied officers, and bring them back across the Channel to be "interrogated" on invasion plans.

Jealousy between the Abwehr, under whose command the Brandenburgers operated, and the Sicherheitsdienst, the security service of the Schutzstaffel (SS), was so intense that the Sicherheitsdienst feared that the Abwehr would be given "credit" by Hitler for ferreting out the time and place of the Allied landings. So the kidnapping machination died from lack of sustenance.

Presumably, no one in the German high command was aware that one of the haunting nightmares of Allied leaders was that a party of German commandos would sneak ashore in southern England in the darkness and abduct one or more Bigots.[19]

# A British POW Saves His Captor's Life

IN JUNE 1944, Lieutenant Colonel Jack Churchill, leader of the British Number Two Commando, was captured while on a secret mission behind German lines in western Yugoslavia.

Captain Hans Thorner of the 118th Division had taken Churchill into custody. When the Briton was identified as a Commando, the German was confronted by a serious dilemma. Should he have Churchill shot immediately, or should he obey the dictates of his own conscience and not kill an unarmed and helpless captive?

Two years earlier, Adolf Hitler had become enraged over British Commando raids across the western European coasts held by the Wehrmacht. Then, when the British struck at Bruneval, a town on the English Channel in France, and stole the Nazi's top-secret Würzburg radar, the führer launched a classic tirade. He demanded to know why the British could make these raids, but the German forces could not. Subsequently, he issued a strict order: captured British Commandos were to be shot on the spot.

Thorner, at great personal risk to his career or even his life, chose to disregard the standing order, and he treated his prisoner, Churchill, correctly. When the Briton was going to be shipped to a POW camp in Germany, Churchill wrote a letter to Thorner thanking him.

Near the end of the war in Europe, Churchill escaped from his guards and rejoined friendly forces then sweeping across the Third Reich. At about the same time, Captain Thorner was captured by U.S. troops near Vienna. Partisan leaders in Yugoslavia demanded that the German be turned over to them for trial as a war criminal—an almost certain death warrant.

Before Thorner could be taken to Yugoslavia, he showed American officers the letter Jack Churchill had written to him almost a year earlier. Back home in Great Britain, the Commando leader learned that Thorner had been taken prisoner, and he volunteered to testify in the German's defense if he were to be court-martialed.

Consequently, Thorner was not turned over to the Yugoslav partisan leaders—who denounced Churchill for his "interference." Instead, Thorner was sent back to Germany and discharged from captivity.[20]

# Part Four

## Beginning
## of the End

# "Hell, We're Halfway to Berlin!"

ON AIRFIELDS in southern England, thousands of U.S. and British paratroopers were preparing to take off for Normandy. They would land behind German coastal defenses to pave the way for an amphibious assault at five designated beaches that would hit soon after dawn. It was the evening of June 5, 1944.

Twenty-three-year-old 1st Sergeant Leonard A. Funk of the veteran U.S. 82nd Airborne Division was among those involved in the tension-racked, seemingly interminable wait.

8:00 P.M. Funk and other troopers check their weapons; then check them again. They test dime store metal crickets that each had been issued for identifiable purposes in the blackness on the ground. One squeeze (*click-clack*) was to be answered by two (*click-clack . . . click-clack*).

8:30 P.M. Seasick pills are taken by each trooper. "Puke bags" are issued in the event the pills do not work. Nervousness is intense. Men get up continuously to relieve themselves.

9:00 P.M. Small, solemn groups sit under plane wings and watch the sun start its downward journey (double daylight savings time).

9:30 P.M. Scores of airplane engines howl. Final checkup: the entire airfield seems to be shaking. Some men feel like vomiting the stew they had eaten for supper. Heavy equipment is put on. Troopers waddle toward C-47 doors.

10:00 P.M. Troopers cram shoulder-to-shoulder in bucket seats. Nobody sings. Nobody cheers. Silence.

11:00 P.M. Hundreds of transport planes knife through dark skies for Normandy. Some troopers doze—or pretend to doze, haunted by the specter of parachutes that fail to open. "Streamers," the troopers call them.

After his C-47 had been flying for more than an hour, Sergeant Leonard Funk peered out one of the small windows and gained the eerie feeling that his plane was all alone. Where were the others? Where was the heavy ack-ack fire that was supposed to greet the intruders over the drop zone?

Suddenly, the red light next to the open door flashed on. A call "stand up and hook up" rang through the cabin. It took an effort to stand. Funk felt huge and bloated in his burdensome combat gear as he and the others staggered into position, one behind the other. Now the waiting stress returned—harder,

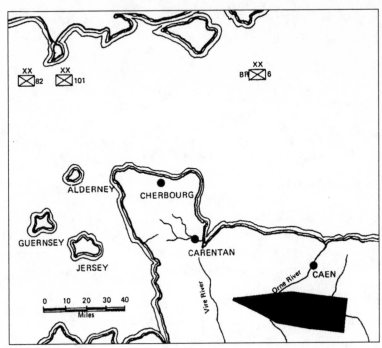

*1st Sergeant Leonard A. Funk and his men parachuted forty miles from their designated drop zone in Normandy (large arrow).*

more nerve-racking than ever. Hearts beat faster—and skipped beats. Stomachs churned. Palms sweat. It would be only seconds.

Now the green light—GO! Funk and his companions began leaping into the eerie, black unknown. Moments later, there were the white flashes of exultation: parachutes had popped open.

Funk and his fourteen men floated earthward. The sergeant was puzzled. He did not recognize a single landmark that he had memorized from studying aerial photos of the drop zone. And, all was peaceful.

Now Funk realized that his C-47 had taken evasive action to escape heavy German flak over Normandy and became disoriented.

"We didn't know where in the hell we were," Funk recalled much later. "All we knew was that we had been flying an extra long time after we'd seen other troopers bailing out."

Piecing together clues from road signs, Funk exclaimed, "Hell, we're halfway to Berlin!"

Actually, he and his men were forty miles inland from German positions along the English Channel coast. An occasional German vehicle drove past with its lights blazing, and German soldiers were seen sauntering around villages unarmed or with only pistols.

Funk recalled: "I told my men that come hell or high water, I would never be taken prisoner, that we were going to fight our way back to friendly forces—even if it took us the rest of the war."

With Funk, toting a Tommy gun, in the lead, the troopers set out northward, marching by night and holing up by day. When possible, they avoided enemy contact, but along the way, they got involved in shoot-outs and scrapes with German soldiers.

"The Krauts seemed to be astonished to bump into American soldiers so far from the battlefront. Three of our scouts were killed," Funk remembered later.

On several occasions during their trek through a countryside thick with Germans, Funk and his men ambushed military vehicles. When they heard a panzer clanking toward them, they rapidly put a land mine in the road and covered it with a thin veil of dirt. Then they hid in a patch of nearby woods and watched in jubilation as the tank blew up.

"That's one damned panzer that won't be shooting at our guys!" Funk declared.

Much of the time, the troopers were hungry and thirsty. Their principal "meals" consisted of apples picked from trees at night. They didn't dare to approach a house for water or food.

Funk could tell when he and his men were getting closer to American lines: Germans were even more numerous. Now it was touch-and-go every yard of the way, and shoot-outs grew in number. Finally, after twenty-one days, the paratroopers reached an outpost of the U.S. 90th Infantry Division.

"We were so filthy and disheveled that the infantrymen thought we were Krauts as we approached them, and they damned near shot us!" Funk recalled.

Funk and the men who survived the arduous trek rejoined their unit. Other 82nd Airborne men were eager to hear details of this amazing odyssey. "When I parachute into battle again," the sergeant quipped, "I want to make certain that an automobile is parachuted in with me."

No one could know that by the time the war in Europe had ended, 1st Sergeant Leonard Funk would be America's most highly decorated paratrooper, including being awarded the Congressional Medal of Honor.[1]

# Alone in a German-Held Town

LIEUTENANT COLONEL August Frieherr Baron von der Heydte, a peacetime university professor and now leader of the crack German 6th Parachute Regiment, was ensconced in his command post in a candlelit basement in the Normandy road and rail center of Carentan. Adolf Hitler had ordered von der Heydte to hold the town at all costs. Its capture by the Americans would link up the invasion beaches code-named Utah and Omaha and give the invaders a continuous beachhead some sixty miles long. It was June 10, 1944.

Von der Heydte's regiment was made up of soldiers whose average age was seventeen and a half years. They were keenly trained and tough, had exceptional spirit, and were willing to die for the führer. Only a week earlier, the teenagers had been singing and laughing and worrying if the war would end before they had a chance to get into it.

Von der Heydte was optimistic because elements of Major General Maxwell D. Taylor's U.S. 101st "Screaming Eagles" Airborne Division, north of Carentan, would have to cross horrendous terrain to reach his German paratroopers dug in a few hundred yards in front of the town. For two miles to the north of Carentan, the ground was a marshland, impassable to tanks and vehicles.

Stretching along this swamp was the asphalt Route Nationale 13, its crown some six to nine feet above the dingy brown water. For the Americans to fight their way into Carentan, they would have to advance on this exposed causeway, which was flat and ran straight as an arrow. There was no place to take cover.

Lieutenant Robert G. Cole's battalion bore the brunt of the causeway attack, and after bloody fighting, it had advanced nearly a mile. But only 132 of Cole's 640 men remained.

It was pitch black during the early morning hours of June 12, the third day of the Screaming Eagles's all-out effort to capture Carentan, when a lone American was driving a horse-drawn cart loaded with mortar shells southward along the causeway. His instructions were to continue to a specified point only about a quarter-mile from German lines. Then he was to make a right turn and deliver the shells to his battalion's frontline position.

The causeway, the scene of bloody violence during the past three days, was now hushed and eerie. The paratrooper was nervous. He had not been on the causeway before, and the absence of any sign of his fellow Screaming Eagles was disconcerting.

In the blackness, the trooper missed the turnoff and continued onward— right into German-held Carentan. Ghostly silhouettes of bomb- and shell-torn buildings loomed starkly around him. The only sound was the horse's hooves and the cart's steel-rimmed wheels on the cobblestones. Here and there, a fire glowed unattended.

Reaching the deserted square in the center of Carentan, the American began to have an uneasy feeling. "I don't think I'm in the right place!" he told himself. Indeed he was not. He was more than a mile behind German lines, and enemy support troops and those in command posts were holed up around him in the dark basements.

At that moment, the intense, ominous silence was shattered. An alarm clock stashed in the trooper's duffel bag and long forgotten picked that time to

*Two nights before this ceremony marking the capture of Carentan, a GI accidentally found himself alone at this spot with Germans on all sides. (U.S. Army)*

begin ringing with the utmost urgency. Its grating noise seemed to the lone American loud enough to wake Adolf Hitler in Berlin.

The Screaming Eagle hurriedly turned his cart around, slapped the horse on the rump, and beat a hasty retreat out of Carentan. In the fog of war, he had never once been halted or even verbally challenged on his journey into and behind German lines.[2]

# Two Admirals
# Go Souvenir Hunting

THICK BLACK CLOUDS OF SMOKE rolled over the ancient Normandy port of Cherbourg, which had been battered and bruised by American warplanes and long-range artillery. Located twenty-five miles north of Utah Beach where the U.S. 4th Infantry Division had gone ashore, Cherbourg had suddenly become the most important port in the world. It was the invasion's primary objective.

Adolf Hitler had proclaimed it Fortress Cherbourg and ordered it "held to the last man and the last bullet." If the city remained in German hands and the Allies could not use it to bring in mountains of supplies, weapons, ammunition, and food, several hundred thousand of the invaders might wither and die on the narrow Normandy beachhead.

Now, on June 27, 1944—D-Day plus twenty-one—American troops battled their way into the city. But skilled German engineers had already followed Hitler's strict order: "If worst comes to worst, leave the enemy not a port but a vast field of devastation."

Hulking Lieutenant General Karl Wilhelm von Schlieben, the commander of the Cherbourg garrison, was trapped in an underground bunker on the outskirts of the city. Wearing the Iron Cross for bravery he had earned on the Eastern Front, he emerged from the fortification and surrendered to GIs of the U.S. 9th Infantry Division. "Goddamn," one astonished soldier called out, "we've nabbed the head Kraut!"

Schlieben was driven to the headquarters of the U.S. VII Corps commander, Major General J. Lawton "Lightning Joe" Collins, who asked the German to surrender the entire Cherbourg garrison. The answer was a quick, emphatic, "*Nein!*"

It had been his experience in Russia that determined groups of soldiers could hold out and cause much damage and delay, Schlieben declared. "For that reason, I will not ask my troops to surrender," he said.

There was much truth to Schlieben's view. At that very moment, Allied news bulletins told of Cherbourg's capture, but a large number of steel-willed Feldgrau (field gray, the average German soldier) was fiercely defending the forty-two thousand acres of harbor facilities, even though it was now a "field of devastation."

Twenty-four hours later, Admiral Alan G. Kirk, commander of U.S. naval invasion forces, sent for Lieutenant Commander John D. Bulkeley, who had been in charge of the PT boats that escorted four groups of minesweepers toward Utah Beach before H-Hour to clear the lanes of explosives for the assault waves. Then Bulkeley and his PT boats had returned to Portland, England, refueled, rearmed, and on the eve of D-Day, the speedy boats were back off Utah Beach preparing to block any German naval effort to disrupt the invasion.

On his flagship, Kirk told Bulkeley that he and Rear Admiral John Wilkes wanted to go into Cherbourg Harbor to inspect the damage done to the port facilities by German demolitions. The two navy leaders apparently had heard the false reports about Cherbourg surrendering.

Bulkeley wasn't too keen about the scheme because the harbor had not been swept for mines and information reaching him was that German soldiers were steadfastly defending the dock area. By taking the two admirals ashore, they would, in essence, be behind German lines and subject to being killed or captured.

Typically, Bulkeley made no protest. He had simply weighed the odds and found them tilted heavily against the survival of Kirk and Wilkes—and himself.

The jig-dog, as PT men called their squadron commanders, was no ordinary warrior. During actions against the Japanese fleet in the western Pacific

*PT-boat squadron skipper Lieutenant Commander John D. Bulkeley would become American history's most decorated warrior. (Courtesy Mrs. John D. Bulkeley)*

early in the war, Bulkeley had earned every medal for valor that his country had to offer, including the Congressional Medal of Honor.

Now Bulkeley kept his own counsel as the two admirals climbed into his PT boat. Soon the seventy-eight-foot vessel bolted into Cherbourg Harbor at high speed, keeping close to the breakwater and not in the middle of the channel. His course proved to be well taken. Acoustic mines in the middle of the channel exploded when ticked off by the noise of the propellers on Bulkeley's boat. Had he barreled into the harbor by the seemingly direct route, two admirals, a legendary war hero, and the boat's crew would have been blown to smithereens.

Bulkeley tied up at the mole, and the admirals leaped out and ran for a nearby fort. Now the PT skipper suspected why they had wanted to get into Cherbourg—to hunt for souvenirs. Bulkeley remained on the boat, telling a crewman, "I'm not going to get wiped out by a booby trap."

About fifteen minutes later, Kirk and Wilkes emerged from the thick-walled fort and were greeted by a burst of machine-gun fire. "What I didn't need was to have to explain how I managed to get two top American admirals killed behind German lines!" Bulkeley recalled much later. So he grabbed the rifle he always kept on his boat and began firing in the direction of the German automatic weapons.

Uncertain if he had hit anyone, he leaped on the inside mole at the waterline, and slipped along it until he found himself behind the two Germans who had been shooting at the admirals. Getting a bead on his target, he squeezed off two quick rounds from his rifle and dropped both of the German machine gunners.

Bulkeley recalled: "With all the shooting going on, Kirk and Wilkes apparently realized that they were behind German lines. They suddenly lost their desire to hunt for souvenirs. So the admirals jumped onto the boat and we got the hell out of there!"[3]

# An American General's
# Strange Odyssey

ART VANAMAN, a young one-star general in the U.S. Eighth Air Force in London, was angry and frustrated. He had been "flying a desk" in England for many months, and, three weeks after D-Day on June 27, 1944, he received orders to rotate back to the United States for another administrative job at Wright-Patterson Field in Dayton, Ohio.

Vanaman had never been on a combat mission, so he promptly asked Lieutenant General Carl A. "Tooey" Spaatz, commander of U.S. Strategic Air Forces in Europe, for permission to go on a bombing raid before departing for home. Spaatz rejected the request: Vanaman knew too much about Allied air strategy and if captured, he might be forced to disclose this crucial intelligence to brutal Gestapo interrogators.

Risking court-martial for disobeying a lawful order, Brigadier General Arthur W. Vanaman was sneaked onto a B-17 Flying Fortress bomber by a pilot who had agreed to take him along as an "observer."

When the flight was high over France, antiaircraft fire damaged two of the bomber's four engines, and the pilot, Vanaman's "coconspirator," gave an order to bail out. Then Dame Fate got into the act in a peculiar manner. Most of those on board, including the general, leaped out of the aircraft. However, the pilot and copilot managed to bring the stricken bomber back to England.

General Vanaman crashed into the unyielding ground, but he was uninjured. Shucking his parachute, he looked up and found himself surrounded by several armed Germans. In keeping with international law, Vanaman gave his true name, rank, and serial number. That was all. Efforts to drag more information from him proved to be futile.

Meanwhile in Berlin, Reichsmarschall Hermann Goering, chief of the Luftwaffe, was advised that Germany had in captivity the highest ranking U.S. POW. For whatever his reasons, the rotund number two man in the Nazi pecking order sent word that Vanaman should be brought to Berlin where he could sit out the war in a luxury apartment.

Suspecting a Nazi machination and knowing that he could never escape from Berlin, Vanaman turned down the offer. Consequently, he was taken to

Stalag Luft III, a POW compound for Allied air officers. There he linked up with Colonel Delmar T. Spivey, whose Eighth Air Force bomber had been shot down over Germany.

A few weeks later, POWs in the camp heard alarming reports from guards and German workmen. With the war going badly for the Third Reich, Reichsführer Heinrich Himmler, head of the Gestapo and Schutzstaffel (SS), told Adolf Hitler that the thousands of Allied POWs in Germany were a burden to the war effort. Himmler urged that he be given control of the camps and that the POWs be "liquidated" (that is, murdered).

Vanaman asked Lieutenant David Bowling, who spoke German fluently, to make a one-man escape and inform top Allied leaders of the mass murder threat. It would be a long shot at best. Even if Bowling were to get out of the barbed-wire enclosed compound, he would probably be apprehended—and executed. But Bowling accepted that risk.

The camp escape committee provided Bowling with money, civilian clothes, a compass, and an identity as a French worker being transferred to a new job for the Third Reich. When the lights were extinguished at the customary 10:00 P.M., Bowling crawled out from under the barracks where he had been hiding, slithered to the wire barrier, and cut his way through with the cutters that had been given to him for the escape. Then he headed for a rail station a mile away and caught an early morning train heading toward the border of neutral Switzerland.

Only weeks later would a few POW leaders learn that Bowling had defied the long odds against him and reached Switzerland. He had hit a home run, in prison camp jargon. That feat may well have saved many POW lives because Allied intelligence, through a contact in neutral Sweden who was in regular touch with the Nazi hierarchy in Berlin, informed Himmler that the Allies were going to hold him personally responsible for any vengeance murdering of POWs.

Meanwhile, Hitler's bold gamble to snatch victory from the jaws of defeat in what became known as the Battle of the Bulge had been smashed and the punch-drunk Wehrmacht was sent reeling back into Germany. At the same time, the Soviet army was driving westward in the direction of Berlin.

Late on the night of January 27, 1945, the POWs at Stalag Luft III were told they were to be evacuated. The Red Army was only fifteen miles away, and the Germans presumably wanted to hold on to the two thousand British and American airmen as bargaining chips.

The weather was horrible: about zero degrees and a foot of snow was on the ground. With General Vanaman and Colonel Spivey at the head of the long column, the POWs marched through the main gate to begin a one hundred-mile trek to the southwest. Five days later, the hungry and nearly exhausted Americans and Britons staggered into the bleak town of Spremberg.

Then a curious episode took place. Vanaman and Spivey were brought to Berlin by a German officer for immediate repatriation. The German capital, hammered by Allied bombers for nearly three years, was a pile of rubble. Spivey and Vanaman were taken to quarters for Polish officers in a small POW camp. In the mass confusion, the German commandant did not know why the two American officers had been brought to his domain.

A week passed. Vanaman and Spivey were moved to a German army barracks outside the camp. No one there knew why. Now the two Americans demanded to know why they were in Berlin. Their request finally reached General Gottlob Berger, who was in charge of all Allied POWs.

Berger's reply was a blockbuster. In a highly secretive manner, he informed the two Americans that there was a plot among high ranking Wehrmacht officers to kill Adolf Hitler, after which the German armed forces would surrender to the British and American armies on the Western Front. Berger was proposing that Vanaman and Spivey carry back a personal letter from him to American leaders, outlining the surrender proposal.

There was one glaring hitch to Berger's proposal: the two Western Allies would have to agree in advance to join the Third Reich in fighting the Soviet Army. Spivey and Vanaman knew that President Franklin D. Roosevelt and Prime Minister Winston S. Churchill would never agree to such a grotesque deal—even though both Allied leaders were already looking on the Soviet colossus as an enemy.

Vanaman and Spivey did agree to deliver Berger's letter, which contained a code that would permit German radio monitors to pick up the Anglo-American reply.

The next day, the two POWs set out for Switzerland in a military automobile driven by a lieutenant who carried with him a letter signed by General Berger ordering the German troops to allow the safe passage of the party. Several times along the way, the vehicle was attacked by Allied fighter-bombers, but on the third day, Vanaman and Spivey crossed the border into Switzerland.

In Zurich, the secret letter was presented to the U.S. consul, who radioed its contents to Washington. No reply was ever received. With the Third Reich in shambles, teetering on the brink of a gargantuan defeat, German generals were in no position to be proposing "deals."

Only later would Spivey and Vanaman learn why they had been detained in Berlin for several weeks. Hitler had issued orders for all POWs to be murdered, but Gottlob Berger, at great risk to his own life, had ignored the order. In the chaos of the Third Reich in these final days of the war, the führer had not checked to determine if his mass killing order had been carried out.

After General Vanaman and Colonel Spivey had departed from Berlin, General Berger personally escorted a large number of Allied prisoners across the border into Switzerland.[4]

# Mission: Kidnap
# Field Marshal Rommel

A MONTH AFTER D-Day in Normandy, nearly a million and a half U.S., British, and French troops were ashore and engaged in savage fighting against tough and motivated German soldiers. Adolf Hitler had ordered them to stand fast, not to give up one foot of ground. Allied gains, if any, were measured in yards.

Consequently, British General Bernard L. Montgomery, commander of Allied ground forces for the invasion, gave his approval to a scheme which, he hoped, would help break the deadlock. Field Marshal Erwin Rommel, whose popularity on the homefront in Germany rivaled that of Adolf Hitler, was to be kidnapped or killed.

Code-named Gaff, the clandestine operation had its origin on June 8, 1944, a few days after D-Day, when Lieutenant Colonel William Fraser, a member of the elite British outfit called the Special Air Service (SAS), parachuted deep behind German lines in France. Fraser's orders were to make contact with an underground operative code-named Louis, who would take him to the headquarters of a resistant group known as Camille.

As previously arranged, Fraser met Louis at a certain bridge. After the Briton had established his bona fides, the two men, along with the SAS radio operator, marched for nearly forty-eight hours and arrived at the farmhouse headquarters of Camille.

While waiting for radioed instructions from London, Fraser met an older Frenchman who was living in a nearby château. He said his name was Defors, and that he owned an estate near La Roche-Guyon, a village that had rested undisturbed for twelve centuries in a large loop of the Seine River roughly midway between Paris and Normandy.

Then, Defors made a remark that electrified Fraser. On the edge of the village of 543 people was a castle that had been home for a succession of Dukes de La Rochefoucauld. This imposing edifice was headquarters for Field Marshal Rommel.

La Roche-Guyon was the most occupied community in all of occupied France. There were sentries everywhere. Clad in camouflage capes and coal-bucket-shaped helmets, they stood inside both gates of the castle, at roadblocks at each end of the village, and in pillboxes built flush into the outcropping of the hill above the castle.

Now Defors asked Colonel Fraser a seemingly simple question. Rommel's presence was causing the inhabitants to fear that Allied bombers might demolish La Roche-Guyon, so could Fraser go there and kill the field marshal?

Fraser was struck by the irony of the situation. Since the previous March, the British secret service had been planning to kidnap or kill the man who was a symbol of German military skill and heroism. However, despite searching by the French underground and electronic and aircraft surveillance, Rommel's headquarters remained unknown in London.

Clearly Defors had been giving considerable thought to killing Rommel. He told Fraser that the castle could be approached through a forest on the other side of the Seine. Each evening that he was at home, the field marshal strolled in the gardens of the castle. A sniper could pick him off from about three hundred yards away, the Frenchman said.

On June 14, Fraser radioed London about his discovery and asked for maps of the La Roche-Guyon area—and two sniper rifles. "Would prefer you not to send another party for this job as consider it is my pigeon," he added.

At a country estate outside London that was an SAS headquarters, Fraser's blockbuster message was closely studied by Brigadier R. W. McLeod, the SAS commander, and his intelligence officers. The obstacles to the proposed mission were promptly evident. Fraser was some two hundred miles from the castle, and he would have to travel through areas swarming with German soldiers and field police. Even if he were to get through, Rommel might not be present.

Brigadier McLeod radioed his reply: Fraser was forbidden to make a personal effort; the job would be done by an SAS team.

On July 20, with the Allies still bogged down in Normandy, McLeod issued an operation instruction. One passage stated: "If it should be possible to kidnap Rommel and bring him to [England] the propaganda value would be immense . . . such a plan would involve finding and being prepared to hold for a short time, if necessary, a suitable landing ground [near La Roche-Guyon]."

McLeod added that "to kill Rommel would obviously be easier than to kidnap him."

A specially trained party of SAS troopers—an officer whose *nom de guerre* (war name) was Raymond Lee and six men—was assigned to carry out Gaff. Lee was something of a mystery man. He was a captain in the International Squadron of the SAS, a unit composed of men of several nationalities— Bulgarians, Corsicans, Algerians, Yugoslavians, and the like. Lee's squad had been formed much earlier to commit special acts of violence, including the murder of enemy generals.

In the days ahead, SAS collected a wealth of information about Rommel and his headquarters. On July 10, Captain Lee and his band of assassins were ensconced in a London apartment awaiting orders to launch the operation.

Ironically, at the time the SAS was preparing to kidnap or murder Rommel, the field marshal was scheming to eliminate Adolf Hitler. He invited the führer to the castle in La Roche-Guyon, at which time he would try to convince him that the war was lost and that he, Hitler, should seek a negotiated peace with the Western Allies while Germany still had something with which to bargain.

If the führer rejected Rommel's proposal, he would have Hitler arrested by soldiers fanatically loyal to the field marshal. Hitler accepted the invitation—but he chose to hold the conference at a command bunker near Soissons, far to the east of La Roche-Guyon. The führer was too wily a fox to be trapped in Rommel's lair.

Rommel and his superior, Field Marshal Karl Rudolf Gerd von Rundstedt, the aging supreme commander in the West, confronted Hitler in the bunker, which had been built four years earlier for the führer to direct the planned invasion of England. Fireworks erupted almost immediately. No one ever talked to Hitler in the tone used by Rommel and survived.

Rommel said that the German front in Normandy was about to collapse, even though the Feldgrau were fighting with "unbelievable courage and tenacity." The field marshal concluded his briefing with a bold question: Did Hitler really believe that this war could be won?

Unknowingly, Rommel had signed his own death warrant.

Furious and frustrated, Rommel returned to La Roche-Guyon, firm in his belief that Germany could survive only if he could secretly negotiate with the Western Allies to halt the conflict.

Meanwhile in London, Captain Lee and his SAS assassins had a long wait for the weather to clear over the drop zone near Orleans. Then, on July 18, the team parachuted into France at night and made ready to head for the castle at La Roche-Guyon.

Then fate intervened. Rommel was on an inspection trip when his command car was strafed by a pair of low-flying British Typhoons. The Mercedes overturned and Rommel, unconscious, was pulled from the wreckage by his driver.

Rommel was recovering from his grievous wounds at his home near Ulm in southern Germany on October 14, 1944, when he received a visit from two of the führer's staff generals. Hitler had learned of the field marshal's role in the Schwarze Kapelle, the conspiracy to eliminate the Nazi regime and its leader.

If Rommel agreed to die by taking poison (the generals had brought it with them), the field marshal's wife and fifteen-year-old son Manfred would not be executed.

A half hour later, the hero of the Fatherland was dead. Hitler gave him an elaborate funeral and ordered a large statue of Rommel to be sculpted.[5]

# A Soviet Spying Mission Fizzles

THROUGH HIS AMBASSADOR TO ENGLAND, Soviet Premier Josef Stalin learned that the Germans had successfully test-fired a revolutionary new weapon, the V-2 missile. It was forty-six-feet long, had a range of more than two hundred miles, and contained a one-ton warhead. Being supersonic, it was impossible to intercept it.

The Soviets had no missile research and development program, so Stalin and other leaders in the Kremlin were deeply disturbed by this electrifying intelligence. In July 1944, Stalin set up a special technical committee headed by Georgi Malenkov, chairman of the Council of People's Commissars, a sort of supreme political overseer.

Malenkov was perhaps Stalin's most trusted aide. For twenty-five years, he had been at the elbow of the Soviet dictator in one capacity or another. A man of mental toughness and ability who had a formidable memory, Malenkov was the guiding force behind Stalin's massive purge of Russian leaders suspected of being threats to Stalin's total power. In the late 1930s, millions of Russians were murdered or imprisoned.

Now, in light of his directive from the supreme Soviet leader, Malenkov set his sights on Peenemünde, a town on the island of Usedom, just off the German mainland on the Baltic coast in the north. This secluded locale was the home of the Heeresversuchstelle (Army Experiment Station), where hundreds of physicists, scientists, engineers, and technicians were putting the finishing touches on the V-2.

Peenemünde was one of the most tightly guarded facilities in the world. Abwehr agents and picked men of the SS seemed to be everywhere, keeping sharp eyes for any sign of intruders.

With Soviet tank-tipped spearheads charging westward across Poland toward the border of the Third Reich, Malenkov, bent on gaining an enormous scientific edge over the Americans, British, and French, targeted Peenemünde for a cloak-and-dagger mission. Nine German prisoners of war, who agreed to work for Malenkov's secret committee, would be parachuted at night into the Peenemünde region, about 150 miles behind German lines on the Eastern Front.

The German POWs were taken to an airfield in Poland on an especially dark night. They were provided with genuine Reich money, bogus identification papers, and shortwave radios. Their task was to penetrate the top-secret German facility and radio back information on missile development.

As soon as the POWs parachuted to earth, they shucked their parachutes and buried their radios. Then all but one headed for their families' homes in the Fatherland.

Only Lieutenant Erwin Brandt radioed back to Moscow brief items of minor interest about Peenemünde. After his seventh message, Brandt was tracked down by the highly efficient *Funkabwehr* (radio intelligence) and was executed by the Gestapo.[6]

# A "Dead" GI Returns

A BROILING MEDITERRANEAN SUN was beating down on the encampment of the U.S. 509th Parachute Infantry Battalion outside Naples, Italy, on the afternoon of July 14, 1944, when a rough looking, oddly dressed man walked up to the guard at the gate. Sporting a full beard and shoulder-length hair, the disheveled stranger wore British army shoes, mustard-colored cotton pants, a torn American paratrooper jacket, and an Italian civilian straw hat with an orange band.

Corporal Milo Peck, the sentry, eyed the man curiously, convinced that he was some sort of a nut, of which there was no shortage in a nation torn apart by four years of war. "Don't you remember me?" the newcomer asked.

"Am I supposed to?" was the reply.

"I'm Manuel Serrano."

"Sergeant Serrano! You've been dead for two years, since back in Tunisia! Where the hell have you been all this time?"

"Well, I've been all over Italy, fighting with the Eytie [Italian] partisans up in the mountains."

Born in Puerto Rico, the twenty-four-year-old Serrano had lived in Brooklyn, New York, since the age of five, and in early 1942, he had volunteered for the paratroops.

A month after Operation Torch, the Anglo-American invasion of North Africa in November 1942, Serrano had participated on a crucial mission to blow up a key railroad bridge at El Djem, ninety miles behind German lines in Tunisia. The paratroopers then split to infiltrate back to friendly lines and Serrano was captured by Italian soldiers.

Serrano was ensconced in Number 59, an Italian POW camp at Servigliano on the Adriatic Sea coast, where he remained for nine months. Then, on September 8, 1943, an electrifying report raced through the compound: Italy had surrendered and gone over to the Allies. So Serrano and many other prisoners broke out of the enclosure and headed for the hills.

A day later, Serrano came upon three Italian partisans (guerrillas) who took him on a grueling sixty-mile hike to their hideout buried in mountain underbrush. Once the American's bona fides were established, he was chosen to go on his first raid. Only later did he learn that the partisan chief, a tough taskmaster who had been a captain in the Italian Army, was testing the newcomer's courage and resourcefulness.

The objective was Penna, about fifteen miles to the east, where the raiders were to kidnap several of the town's most notorious pro-Nazi leaders and bring them back to camp for "a fair trial and a hanging."

Night had fallen by the time Serrano and twenty partisans reached Penna, and they sneaked into town one by one. The streets were dark and deserted. As he was edging along, Serrano suddenly heard the sound of hobnailed boots. There was no time to hide. So he stood stone-still. The three-man German patrol marched past him so closely that he could have reached out and touched one of them. Soon he resumed breathing and continued onward stealthily.

The raid went off with clockwork precision. Partisan sympathizers in Penna had earlier provided the raiders with the five men on that night's calling list. Each of the pro-Nazis was bound and gagged, spirited out of town, and by morning, they were in the partisan camp. Two hours later, the prisoners were hanged.

The band of partisans to which Serrano belonged was one of several operating behind German lines in northern Italy. The units received instructions through a clandestine radio station known as Italia Combatte (Italy Fights).

Huddled inside a cave on a mountainside or in a thick forest grove, Serrano and the others would tune in the radio to listen for their code signal, *Sole tra monte* ("The sun is between the mountains"). Then they would write down the instructions for the next mission.

These orders were also in code. "Pietro's beard is white" might mean to blow up a certain railroad bridge. "The snow in Russia is cold" could indicate a German warehouse was to be destroyed. "The mule is on the moon" might mean a certain German motorcycle courier was to be shot while en route to a headquarters.

One of the most crucial partisan functions was helping downed U.S. and British airmen to escape from Italy. In Serrano's band, three young Italian women collected the names, ranks, and serial numbers of airmen hiding in area farmhouses. This information was radioed to Allied headquarters at Bari, on the Adriatic coast, for confirmation and to make sure that the Gestapo had not sneaked in a bogus Allied airman to locate the partisans' hideout.

Most of the downed British and American airmen were escorted at night to the Tyrrhenian Sea coast in the west where the escapers were picked up by submarines or small vessels.

Serrano had his share of close shaves. One day he was sent into the town of Porto San Giorgio dressed in civilian clothes to reconnoiter conditions prior to a planned raid. The American blended with the population; he was dark-complexioned and spoke Italian with the accent of the people of the region.

Serrano's heart skipped a beat when two German soldiers on foot walked up to him. He felt a huge surge of relief when the Feldgrau, thinking the American was a native, asked for directions to a local saloon. Later, another German soldier stopped him and wanted to know the way to a certain road. In appreciation, the Feldgrau pulled out a package of cigarettes and offered one to the helpful "civilian." The smokes were a popular American brand—Chesterfields.

When General Bernard L. Montgomery's British Eighth Army rolled northward through the partisan band's region, Serrano hitched a ride southward and he came upon an American paratroop major who directed him to where the 509th Parachute Infantry Battalion was camped.

After being greeted warmly by the comrades he had not seen for twenty months, Serrano, whose first-sergeant rating had come through soon after he had been captured in Tunisia, was asked what he would like to do now.

"I tell you what I'd like to do," he exclaimed. "I'd like to parachute back behind Kraut lines again with a Tommy gun—and take about twenty of these fellows with me!"

Sergeant Serrano's wish became reality. A month after his return from the "dead," he and his parachute battalion bailed out behind German lines along the Riviera coast to spearhead the Allied invasion of southern France.[7]

# Operation Sauerkraut

SHORTLY AFTER DAWN ON JULY 21, 1944, Supreme Commander Dwight D. Eisenhower was in Normandy calling on his combat leaders. An excited aide rushed up to him and blurted, "The Krauts set off a bomb to kill Hitler!"

"Holy smoke!" Eisenhower exclaimed. "There seems to be a revolt going on!"

For the past three weeks, British secret agents had been in periodic contact with leaders of the Schwarze Kapelle, the conspiracy of German military and government leaders bent on eliminating the führer and the Nazi regime. So the looming assassination attempt was not a total surprise to MI-6, the British secret service.

But only later would Eisenhower learn details of the plot. A decorated German count, Colonel Klaus von Stauffenberg, had been the "hit man" for the conspirators. Tall, lean, and handsome, he had lost an arm, part of the other hand, an eye, and a piece of his scalp when strafed by American fighter-bombers during the fighting in North Africa.

Colonel Stauffenberg had brought with him from Berlin a British-made time bomb in a briefcase to Wolfsschanze, Hitler's headquarters in a sprawling complex of buildings and underground bunkers set among thick woods outside Rastenberg, East Prussia.

While Hitler and his generals were gathered around a long conference table, thirty-eight-year-old Stauffenberg covertly shoved the bomb-loaded briefcase under the table. Miraculously, the führer survived the blast that virtually destroyed the conference room and killed or maimed several officers.

Although the murder effort had been a failure, the episode triggered a scheme in the fertile minds of the men and women at the U.S. Office of Strategic Services (OSS) in Rome. They hatched Operation Sauerkraut, which was designed to undermine or even destroy the will of the German Army to fight in Italy.

Barbara Lauwers, a Czechoslovak by birth and a lawyer who was fluent in five languages, rushed from the OSS base in Rome to a POW compound near

Naples. After carefully interviewing German prisoners, she selected sixteen Feldgrau who seemed to be genuinely anti-Nazi.

Housed in a secluded mansion outside Rome, the POWs were provided with new identities painstakingly created by Lauwers. Each had to memorize his cover story that fit his true background and the region in Germany from where he had actually lived. On occasion, the prisoners were shaken awake at night and OSS operatives loudly demanded to know their adopted name, rank, and unit.

Fewer than four days after Operation Sauerkraut was hatched, the "turned" Germans were ready to infiltrate the front line along the east-west Arno River. Loaded with the customary combat gear provided by OSS scroungers, each man carried a few thousand sheets of propaganda which he had been instructed to nail on trees and buildings, stick in unmanned German vehicles, and scatter in the streets of small towns.

At midnight, the Sauerkraut recruits, one at a time, passed through German lines, crossed the Arno, and walked miles behind the front. One recruit was suddenly challenged by a sentry who demanded to look into his knapsack which was crammed with the bogus OSS propaganda. Just as the sentry was reaching into the bag, the quick-witted Sauerkraut man whipped out a package of American cigarettes that had been provided by his OSS handlers for just such a crisis.

The sentry eagerly took a cigarette and lighted it. Both men talked for a few minutes before the OSS operative warily walked on.

At several points, the intruders posted bogus proclamations painstakingly crafted by the OSS and carrying the counterfeit signature of Field Marshal Albrecht Kesselring, the Oberbefehlshaber Süd (Supreme Commander, South).

In the proclamation, Kesselring stated that the "war is lost to Germany," and that the "senseless slaughter" was continuing only because Adolf Hitler decreed that the army would fight to the last man. Therefore, the field marshal "announced" that he was resigning.

Rumors spread like wildfire in combat areas, and soon thousands of German soldiers in Italy heard that their commander was deserting them (false) and that a major revolt of generals had erupted back home against Hitler (true).

At first, Kesselring chose to ignore the uproar Sauerkraut had generated. But on September 13, a month after the phony proclamations had been posted, he felt it necessary to officially deny his involvement.

OSS leaders in Italy were delighted. Their scheme had forced one of Hitler's most capable field marshals to take note of the proclamations to his troops. Because of the success of Sauerkraut, several more groups of German POWs were sent behind Kesselring's lines on similar missions.[8]

# A POW Haul in a Saloon

SEVEN WEEKS AFTER Allied troops had hit the beaches in Normandy, a million and a half soldiers were bottled up on a relatively small bridgehead. But on July 25, 1944, Operation Cobra, a plan to end the stalemate, struck the German defenders along the American sector in the West.

After a massive air and artillery bombardment near St. Lô, Cobra punched a wide hole in German lines and tank-tipped spearheads charged through the beach and headed southward.

On the morning of July 30, Field Marshal Hans Günther von Kluge, Oberbefehlshaber Westen (Supreme Commander, West), was on the telephone to German General Alfred Jodl, Adolf Hitler's closest military confidant, at Wolfsschanze, the führer's battle headquarters on the Eastern Front.

"Herr Jodl," Kluge cried. "Everything here is *eine Riesensauerei* (one gigantic mess)!"

Now it was a wild melee between bands of mostly disorganized German units and surging American task forces of tanks and infantry that were fanning out in several directions. Some spearheads were barreling westward into the neighboring province of Britanny, and others were rolling in the opposite direction, eastward toward Paris.

Night was falling when Colonel George H. Barth, leader of a spearheading regiment of the U.S. 90th Infantry Division, knew that his dust-covered men were nearly exhausted from what would be called the rat race for Paris, so he set up his command post (CP) in an old saloon on the edge of Mayenne, a quiet town eighty miles south of the Normandy invasion beaches. Barth's men who were not assigned to the CP bivouacked around the building.

Although Colonel Barth and the GIs knew that they had rolled many miles that day in trucks, jeeps, and weapons carriers, they had no inkling that they were far behind German lines.

About two hours after their arrival, the Americans heard the sound of vehicle engines. Soon two camouflaged trucks halted in front of the saloon. Out hopped twenty-nine German soldiers, who were laughing and chattering. Perhaps they were delighted to be at least thirty miles from the closest American combat outfit—or so they thought.

Eager to quench their thirsts, the Germans left most of their weapons in the trucks and hurried toward the front door. They never made it. A swarm of Americans brandishing Tommy guns and rifles suddenly leaped from the shadows and shouted: "*Hande hoch!*" (Hands up!)

Startled to be confronted by American soldiers so far from what they had thought to be the front lines, the Germans complied.

During the night, six more vehicles carrying Germans with parched throats stopped in front of the saloon with similar results.

The total haul of POWs for the night was seventy-eight.[9]

# "The Madman of St. Malo"

COLONEL ANDREAS VON AULOCK, commander of the German-held port of St. Malo on the northern coast of the Britanny Peninsula, was a disappointed warrior. A veteran of bloody battle in Russia, he told his staff: "I was placed in charge of this port. I did not request it. Now the führer has given me orders to hold out to the last man and the last bullet. I will carry out those orders, even if I am the last German alive in St. Malo!" It was August 5, 1944.

Eleven days earlier, armored spearheads of the just-activated U.S. Third Army, under Lieutenant General George S. Patton Jr., had turned the corner from Normandy, bypassed St. Malo and charged westward for the major port of Brest, two hundred miles away at the tip of the Britanny Peninsula. Now St. Malo was an isolated fortress deep behind American lines.

Meanwhile, Allied commanders in France had grown uneasy about leaving intact the strong German force in their rear area, so Major General Robert L. Macon's U.S. 83rd Infantry Division was ordered to capture the port, which bristled with bunkers and guns.

Knowing that St. Malo would be destroyed in heavy fighting, Colonel von Aulock requested to his superiors that the historic old port be declared an "open city," a term used to convey to an enemy that there would be no armed resistance.

Aulock's "defeatism" angered Adolf Hitler. "In warfare, there is no such thing as an historic city," the führer replied testily. "You will fight to the end."

Consequently, Aulock forced each of his officers to sign a pledge:

It is my duty to hold this position to the last, even though we are encircled and lack food and ammunition. Should I not fulfill my duty and surrender, I shall be court-martialed on my return to Germany and punished severely.

Before the Americans assaulted the port, 83rd Infantry Division intelligence officers grilled a few Germans captured during skirmishes outside St. Malo. "He's a madman," one POW exclaimed about Colonel von Aulock. Another said that Aulock's wife and children had been killed in Berlin during an Allied bombing and that "he has nothing to lose and will fight to the death."

Based on the remarks by the POWs, newspapers in the United States began referring to Colonel von Aulock as "The Madman of St. Malo."

*"The Madman of St. Malo" held out in the Citadel
(background) until his men ran out of ammunition and
food. (U.S. Army)*

On August 6, elements of the 83rd Infantry Division launched assaults against the city, but were beaten back by heavy German artillery fire. American big guns roared in response. One of the shells struck the imposing St. Malo cathedral, toppling the steeple into the street. "A bad omen," frightened civilians told one another.

Outside the beleaguered city, the Americans inadvertently added to the woes of citizens inside the port. The mayor of nearby St. Servan-sur-Mer volunteered to point out the location of valves, and St. Malo's water supply was cut off to encourage the German defenders to give up.

Colonel von Aulock's response was to announce to his command that "anyone trying to surrender will be shot immediately."

That night, Aulock issued an order for the port facilities to be destroyed. For miles around, the countryside shook as enormous blasts erupted. Quays, breakwaters, locks, cranes, harbor machinery, offices—all were blown up. A thick pall of smoke and dust would hover over the area for a week as St. Malo burned.

Fifty feet underground in the granite of the Citadel, Aulock knew his situation was hopeless. But he would fight on. He refused to even see an American officer carrying a surrender ultimatum from General Macon. A French woman who had been the mistress of Aulock was sent into the town by the Americans with a plea for "honorable capitulation to avoid more senseless killing." She, too, was summarily rebuffed.

Medical supplies for German wounded were taken into the city by the Americans under a flag of truce. A captured German chaplain was sent in to relay an ultimatum. Aulock's reply: "Surrender to an American is not compatible with the honor of a German soldier."

After Aulock and his men held out for two weeks against insurmountable odds, the final curtain was coming down on the drama of St. Malo. The town had been battered relentlessly, day and night, by Allied bombers, large-caliber guns, the point-blank fire of tanks, and assaulted repeatedly by the 83rd Infantry Division.

Out of food, water, and ammunition, Aulock put out the white flag of surrender. Begrimed (but with boots shined), proud of their defiant stand (but badly hung over after losing a farewell bout with Calvados), the Germans marched out of their fortifications with hands in the air.

The Madman of St. Malo was the only hero Adolf Hitler had during the disastrous Normandy-Britanny campaigns. So he made the most of it in propaganda value. Radio Berlin repeatedly broadcast Aulock's final message to his führer: "Further resistance had to come to an end only because of lack of food." Hitler's reply was trumpeted: "Your name will go down in German history forever." A funeral dirge was played and a solemn-voiced announcer said that "the Hero of St. Malo perished among the ruins with his men."

No doubt that pronouncement came as a surprise to Colonel von Aulock. At the time, he was drinking wine and residing comfortably with his American captors.[10]

# The "Terrorist" Was a Lady

MARIE-MADELEINE FOURCADE, a petite homemaker in her early forties, was peeling potatoes in the kitchen of her modest home in Aix-en-Provence, a picturesque town twenty miles north of the major port of Marseilles along the Côte d'Azur (Blue Coast) of southern France. It was the hot afternoon of August 2, 1944.

French civilians in the region had been living in an almost constant state of anxiety for many months under the heel of the Nazis. Almost daily, there were reports of savage reprisals taken against French "terrorists."

Suddenly, ham-fisted pounding shook Madame Fourcade's front door. Her heart beat faster. Moments later, a squad of German soldiers broke down the door and barged inside the house. With the intruders were four civilians; she could tell by their trademark felt hats that they were Gestapo agents.

"Where's the man?" one Gestapo man barked. "Where's the man?"

White-faced with fright, Fourcade dropped her peeling knife. In a shaky voice, she protested that there was no man, that she lived alone.

"You lie, whore!" another German shouted. "A man was seen in your yard!"

The German glared icily at the woman. "He's tall, fair-haired, and you French swine call him the *grand-duc*" he snapped.

"No, no, there must be some mistake," Fourcade exclaimed. "I am a woman alone, I tell you."

As casually as possible, Marie-Madeleine sauntered over to a sofa and sat down. One Gestapo agent bolted across the room, kneeled, and swept his hand under the sofa. Removing a sheath of papers, he called out triumphantly, "Well, well, what have we here?"

These were copies of secret messages she had sent to London. Marie-Madeleine was a spy, the founder and moving spirit behind a highly effective espionage network known as the Alliance of Animals.

Indeed there had been a man at her house the previous day. He was the grand-duc, one of the key leaders in the spy apparatus, who had met with Fourcade to discuss the distribution of tons of ammunition, guns, grenades, explosives, and other supplies that had been parachuted onto a pasture near Aix two nights earlier. These accoutrements were intended for use behind German positions along the Mediterranean coast when Allied forces would land.

Having found the secret messages, the Gestapo agents pounced on Fourcade, slugging and slapping her repeatedly while shouting threats. "Confess you're a terrorist!" they yelled. "Where's the grand-duc? Talk! Talk!"

Fortunately for Marie-Madeleine, the Germans thought she was only a minor cog in the underground network. Bleeding profusely from the nose and mouth, the leader of the Alliance of Animals was roughly pulled upright by the hair and hustled outside and into a car. She was driven to Gestapo headquarters for the region and thrown brutally onto the concrete floor of a cell.

That same night, Marie-Madeleine stripped naked, covered her wet body with soap found in the cell, squeezed between two bars, and dropped to the ground from the second level. Crouching for several moments to assess the situation, she slipped off into the night and took refuge in the home of a comrade.

In the eleven days before the Allies invaded southern France on August 15, 1944, Fourcade directed her widespread network in collecting last-minute information on German defenses, no doubt saving many Allied soldiers from being killed and smoothing the way for a rapid push inland.[11]

# Jeds behind the French Riviera

A ROSY SUN was beating on the airport at Algiers in North Africa as a transport plane lifted off and set a course northward. On board were Captain Aaron Bank, who belonged to America's cloak-and-dagger agency, the Office of

Strategic Services (OSS), and two members of French General Charles de
Gaulle's secret service branch, the Bureau Central de Renseignement et d'Action (BCRA). It was early July 1944.

Bank was leader of the three-man Allied guerrilla and sabotage team
known as a Jedburgh, named after their quarters during training: Jedburgh, a
royal burgh on the Jed River in the Scots border country of Roxburghshire, a
place infamous in earlier times for "Jeddart Justice," in which a man was
hanged first and tried in court afterward.

The two Frenchmen were a lieutenant whose *nom de guerre* (war name)
was Henri and a radio operator known as Jean. None of the French Jeds used
their real names because most had families in France.

Prior to D-Day in Normandy a month earlier, the Allied brain trust had
known that there were some sixty French underground *réseau* (networks). But
if they were to be fully effective, the resistance groups would have to be heavily reinforced with parachute drops of weapons, ammunition, and supplies.
Allied soldiers of great judgment, courage, leadership qualities, and skill in
guerrilla tactics would have to jump into France to supervise these drops and
to train and direct the fighting of the underground warriors (known as Maquis)
in accordance with Allied operations. As a result of these needs in the shadow
war behind German lines, the Jedburgh teams had been created.

A few hours after Captain Bank, a wiry, five-foot-eight bundle of energy,
and his two companions flew off from Algiers, they parachuted into the dark
unknown fifty miles inland from the coast of southern France. The Jed team's
mission was to organize, coordinate, and direct the French underground réseau
behind German lines prior to and during Operation Dragoon, the invasion of
southern France.

Allied forces would storm ashore along the fabled Riviera in an operation
second in scope only to the landings in Normandy. Dragoon would involve a
thousand vessels, three thousand airplanes, and a force of three hundred thousand men. The invasion was designed to seize the badly needed French ports
of Marseilles and Toulon, to liberate the southern two-thirds of France, and to
drive up the Rhône River valley to link up with Allied forces that were to break
out of Normandy.

After Aaron Bank and his two companions landed and shucked their
parachutes, they rapidly located Commandant Raymond, code name for the
underground leader in southern France. The Jeds were taken to a "safe house"
in a small village near where Bank planned to set up his command post (CP).
Commandant Raymond assured Bank that there was no danger that the Germans would discover them there.

The OSS man and his two comrades fell into exhausted sleep in a room
on the ground floor. They slept in their underwear and with boots on—just in
case. During the night, the Jeds were jolted awake. Someone in the house was
yelling, "Les Boches! Les Boches!" (Germans! Germans!) Grabbing uniforms

*French resistants collecting weapons and supplies parachuted by Allied aircraft. (National Archives)*

and weapons, the Jeds leaped out the window and followed Commandant Raymond along a path leading into a forest. Bank had forgotten that he was wearing only his underwear until Raymond quipped, "Captain, you're out of uniform!"

Minutes after the guerrillas had fled, the Germans broke into the house — apparently they had been tipped off by a French informer. After daybreak, the Jeds' precious radio, which had been hidden within a basement coal pile, was retrieved.

In the days that followed, Bank and his Jeds led Maquis bands in the ambush of German convoys, attacked enemy posts and installations, and organized and formed reception committees for the recovery of parachuted arms and explosives.

One day, through an informant, Bank learned that the Gestapo had built up a dossier on him and Henri, classifying the two Jeds as the region's "leading terrorists." Commandant Raymond's pride had been bruised — the Gestapo had labeled him "only" as an underground leader, not as a terrorist.

Bank remained close to his CP, waiting for the invasion alert. He and his comrades were deeply concerned. Operation Dragoon was possibly the war's worst-kept secret. The Germans knew that the invasion was about to strike. Finally the anticipated alert reached Bank: the Allies would land along the Riviera on August 15.

Bank had organized his resistants into a paramilitary regiment of three battalions, a task made easy by the fact that most of the Maquisards were former soldiers. Now this entire force was deployed into blocking positions on secondary roads so that the Germans retreating northward up the Rhône Valley would have to travel on main roads where they could be cut to pieces by Allied fighter-bombers and long-range artillery.

On D-Day, Bank and his guerrillas cheered wildly as they heard the distant rumble of big navy guns and the dull thud of bombs. The Allies were coming ashore.

At his headquarters in far-off East Prussia, Adolf Hitler knew that his army in excess of one hundred thousand men in southern France was in immediate danger of being cut off from Germany by Allied spearheads that had broken out of the Normandy beachhead and were racing eastward across France toward the Third Reich. Reluctantly, the führer ordered his force along the Riviera to pull back several hundred miles to the German border.

During the German retreat up the Rhône Valley, Captain Bank, Napoleon-like, directed operations of his three guerrilla battalions from a CP in the telephone exchange in the town of Alès. Fleeing German units and convoys were pinpointed with incredible accuracy. Motorcycle couriers from Maquis reconnaissance teams regularly sped up to Bank's CP with urgent intelligence messages. With the entire regional telephone system at his disposal (there was no longer fear from Gestapo wiretappers, as they were also fleeing), Bank was able to give instant orders over the telephone to his widely dispersed underground warriors.

Bank's personal situation was not without peril. The main roads leading northward passed through Alès, and the OSS officer could see long columns of German infantry, vehicles, and tanks moving past under his window.

Seeking frantically to escape from the gauntlet of bombs and bullets from swarming *Jabos* (as the Germans called Allied fighter-bombers) and the deluge of shells from long-range artillery, the Germans occasionally tried to reach the mountains to either side. Forewarned by telephone from Bank's CP, the Maquis set ambushes and inflicted heavy casualties on the Germans. Within three weeks from D-Day for Dragoon, all of southern France had been liberated.[12]

# The Mysterious Lady in Red

JUST BEFORE DAWN began to break over the Mediterranean on August 15, 1944, three haggard, bloody prisoners were silently awaiting their fate in a stifling cell at a Gestapo building in Digne, a town twenty-five miles inland from the fabled French Riviera. All were Allied secret agents who had been captured by eagle-eyed Gestapo men three days earlier when, disguised as French businessmen, their car had been halted at a roadblock. They had been sentenced to death by a firing squad.

One of the captives was Lieutenant Colonel Francis Cammaerts (code-named, Roger), who was the master spy along the coast for the Special Opera-

*British Lieutenant Colonel Francis Cammaerts, underground leader in southern France, was saved from execution at the last moment. (National Archives)*

tions Executive (SOE), the British cloak-and-dagger agency. In recent months, Roger had been directing the activities of scores of secret agents parachuted into the Riviera region.

With Roger in the suffocating lockup were another British officer, Major Xan Fielding (code-named, Cathedrale), and Major André Sorensen, a Frenchman.

Five months earlier, in preparation for an invasion of Normandy, SOE had launched an operation code-named Ratweek. Its goal was to murder as many German secret service agents as possible in western Europe. Nowhere did Ratweek meet with the exceptional success than it had in southeastern France under the direction of Francis Cammaerts, an unlikely espionage leader.

He was the son of Emile Cammaerts, a Belgian writer and poet, who had moved his family to England and had become a professor at London University. His son Francis was attending St. Catherine's College when war broke out in Europe in September 1939. A confirmed pacifist, he vowed to have no part of the conflict. So he left college and began farming.

For whatever his reason, Cammaerts's view did a flip-flop in August 1942, and he offered his services to the SOE. Given the code name Roger, he became one of the agency's boldest and more successful leaders.

Now, two years from the time he had volunteered, Cammaerts and his two companions were in the filthy Digne jail awaiting execution. When the door to their cell clanked open and a Gestapo agent beckoned them, each spy thought, "This is the end!"

Moments later, the captives felt a fleeting surge of elation. From far to the south could be heard the faint rumble of a massive bombardment of the Riviera that told them Operation Dragoon, an invasion of southern France, had been launched. This was the event for which the captives had risked their lives for months to help pave the way for Allied forces. But it apparently had come too late to save them.

Roger, Cathedrale, and the French officer marched along the corridor with the Gestapo man behind them. They were puzzled. Why had the normally cautious Germans sent only one man to escort three presumably dangerous "terrorists" to the firing squad? And the German was armed with only a Luger pistol, and it was in its black leather holster.

Then the captives grew more astonished. They were ordered to head for the front door instead of turning in the direction of a courtyard where several rifle volleys had been heard a day earlier. At the door, two SS guards remained motionless as the tiny procession walked outside.

There the condemned men were told to get into a car in which a stone-faced male civilian was seated on the passenger side of the front seat. The Gestapo agent got behind the steering wheel and drove out of town and into the countryside.

Roger and his companions were flabbergasted. What was going on? Were they to be shot in some remote area? Their bewilderment heightened when the Gestapo agent halted the car next to an automobile parked on the side of the road. A shapely young woman was standing next to the car. Roger immediately recognized her—she was the Lady in Red, a mysterious figure whose background was unknown, but who had been working undercover with Roger for many weeks.

"Get out!" the Gestapo man told his three captives. They wasted no time. Moments later, the spies scrambled into the backseat of the second vehicle. The Lady in Red climbed into the front seat beside a driver, and the car sped away.

Only when they were several miles down the road did the Lady in Red unfold the story of the miraculous escape. The Gestapo officer was not a Gestapo officer, but rather a Belgian who had been serving as an interpreter for the dreaded police agency. He was known only as Max. The secretive civilian who had been seated in the Gestapo car was known only as Captain X. He was a member of the hated Milice, the French police force that worked hand-in-glove with the Nazis.

When the Lady in Red, whom Roger thought to be of Spanish birth, had learned that her chief and his two lieutenants had been seized by the Gestapo in Digne, she knew there was only one remote hope for saving them: bribery. She immediately contacted her superiors in North Africa, told them of the plight of Roger and the other two spies, and asked for money for the payoff. That same night the equivalent to some $250,000 was parachuted to her.

Utilizing her keen intellect and feminine wiles, the Lady in Red singled out Max and Captain X as the targets for her bribery. If she guessed wrong as to their loyalty—or lack of loyalty—to the Nazi cause, she herself would be doomed. After a series of tense and secretive negotiations in which the $250,000 carrot was dangled from a figurative stick in front of their greedy faces, Max and Captain X agreed to cooperate.

Now, as the escape car sped away, Roger called out, "Head for the beaches, I want to meet the Allies!"

A few days later, Captain X was found dead in a field outside Digne under mysterious circumstances. The fate of the $250,000 was never learned.[13]

# An Escape by Eight "Policemen"

EIGHTEEN-YEAR-OLD Private Stephen J. Weiss was walking point for his U.S. 36th Infantry Division company on the late afternoon of August 25, 1944, ten days after the Allies invaded southern France. Now the German Nineteenth Army that had been defending the region was pulling back rapidly toward the Third Reich and American units were nipping at the Germans' heels.

Weiss's outfit had been ordered to attack and seize Valence, a town on the Rhône River more than two hundred miles north of the invasion beaches. The situation was "fluid," meaning that there was considerable confusion on both sides because of the rapid movements.

Weiss's job as first scout was not conducive to longevity. Marching about a hundred yards ahead of the main body of his company, he was a prime candidate to be shot first, thereby alerting those following that there were Germans ahead.

On the road to Valence, the Brooklyn teenager was earnestly scanning the landscape to his front when a burst of machine-gun fire sent bullets hissing past his head. He flopped to the ground, and a brief shoot-out erupted. Then the Germans withdrew.

With Weiss still at the point, the Americans continued the advance, moving across open fields. Night fell. While trying to pierce the blackness with his eyes, he suddenly heard a German shout: "*Halten!*" Moments later, a torrent of small-arms fire broke out. Weiss could see the yellowish muzzle flashes as he hit the earth.

Knowing that he was in a perilous predicament, the teenager scrambled to his feet during a short lull and began to zigzag back toward his comrades. Grenades exploded around him and streams of tracer bullets split the night. Eventually, he leaped into a ditch next to Captain Allen E. Simmons, his company commander.

After taking stock of the muddled situation, Simmons ordered Weiss and a seven-man squad to cross a large open field and attack the unseen enemy. Soon after moving out, the patrol was illuminated by a flare that burst above them. The GIs were raked by machine-gun bullets, but no one was hit.

By now, it became starkly clear to Weiss that his tiny band was confronting a much larger enemy force than had been anticipated. Knowing that they would soon be dead if they remained exposed in the field, Weiss and the others began to creep and crawl to an irrigation ditch some fifty yards to the rear.

Throughout the night, shells—German and American—exploded around them. At dawn, one of the isolated men slipped back to make contact with Captain Simmons and request the company to move forward. Simmons couldn't be found—nor could any of his men.

What Weiss and his squad members did not know was that during the night, his company's mission had been suddenly altered. It was ordered to abandon its attack on Valence and move without delay to join in the battle to seize Montelimer, an even more important objective thirty miles to the south.

Now Weiss and his companions knew that they were marooned behind German lines. Aware that they would be killed or captured if they remained in the ditch, the GIs agreed to a plan. Sergeant William K. Scruby would make a dash for a farmhouse a few hundred yards in the distance. If he reached his destination, the men would leave the ditch one at a time and follow him.

There was one nagging uncertainty: the isolated Americans did not know if the farmhouse was closer to friendly or German positions. However, the die was cast.

Scruby slithered out of the ditch, crouched, and dashed across the field. No one fired at him. Now he stood up and ran as fast as he could. His comrades in the ditch were spurring him along: "Come on, Scruby! Keep going, Scruby!"

Only minutes had elapsed since Scruby began his mad dash, but it seemed like hours to Weiss and the others. Finally, the sergeant reached the farmhouse and waved at his comrades from an upstairs window. One by one, the GIs in the ditch took out across the field and reached the structure safely.

Now complications surfaced. Gaston Reynaud, a farmer, his wife, Madeline, and daughter Claudette lived in the house. Could they be trusted? Weiss explained the Americans' plight and hoped the residents would not tip off the Germans.

Two days after the GI squad took refuge at the Reynaud farm, in German-held Valence an urgent conversation was being held between Chief of Police Henri Gerard, an underground leader who had been masquerading as a Nazi collaborator, and Policeman Louis Salamon, also a resistance member. Word had reached the two patriots about the eight Americans, and it was decided that Salamon would investigate the situation.

To get through German roadblocks from Valence, Gerard created an "official" pass printed in French and German, "ordering" Salamon to go to the Reynaud farm on urgent police business.

After his car had been halted several times by the Germans, Salamon was allowed to drive on after the phony pass had been inspected. Salamon reached the Reynaud farm and walked toward the house.

Steve Weiss was standing guard on the first level of the barn while his comrades were resting in the loose piles of hay above him. Spotting the French policeman strolling toward the house, the teenager felt a surge of alarm. Had the Reynauds alerted policemen who were loyal to the Germans?

Weiss lifted his rifle to drill the visitor, but he held back when Gaston Reynaud came around the side of the house to talk with the new arrival, whom he had long known. Reynaud, too, was a resistance warrior, but he had kept that secret from his visitors.

Salamon was briefed by Reynaud, who vouched that his "guests" were genuine Americans, and the policeman headed back to Valence to see Chief Gerard. Again his car was halted numerous times at German roadblocks. On arriving at the police station, Salamon and Gerard hurried to call on Michel Ferdinand, head of Coty, the region's resistance network. A bold plan of action was promptly conceived, one that could mean the execution of the Frenchmen involved should things go awry.

Chief Gerard provided an official Citroën automobile for the machination, and Ferdinand, Salamon, and two other underground men drove off. They brought with them four genuine French police uniforms. Throughout their trip to the Reynaud farm, the resistance men kept the blue light revolving atop the Citroën, hopefully causing the Germans to believe that these indomitable enforcers of the law were on an emergency call. The ploy worked. Sentries at several roadblocks waved the Citroën on through while Salamon, in his police uniform, saluted them as the four Frenchmen sped past.

At the farm, the Americans were handed the four police uniforms. Salamon explained that they could conceal only that number of garments, and that they would make another trip to Valence and bring four more uniforms.

Within an hour after the French resistance men had returned from Valence with four more uniforms and departed, a squad of SS soldiers came to the Reynaud farm. They were in a foul mood. Holding a pistol muzzle to Reynaud's head, they demanded to know where the Amis (derogatory term for Americans) were. Badly frightened, the farmer lied that they had departed two days earlier.

Actually, the refugees were huddled in the hayloft of the barn, weapons at the ready. The SS men searched the house, but left quickly and soon were out of sight. They had not even glanced toward the barn.

Now the Americans prepared to escape to friendly forces. They donned the police uniforms—few of which fit. But they had to make do. The men would leave in groups of four. Steve Weiss, a tall man whose pants were far too short, went with the first batch. For a fleeting moment, he wondered if they would be shot as spies for wearing French police uniforms if captured.

Driving a dilapidated automobile—a not unusual sight in war-torn France—Weiss and his three companions left the Reynaud farm. Some fifteen minutes later, they drove slowly through a town crowded with Germans, who showed total disinterest in four French policemen.

Continuing onward and out of town, the escapers came upon a French shepherd tending his flock and seeming to be half asleep. Actually, he was a resistance man who had been placed along the road the GIs were to take. He signaled for the car to stop and gave directions to a house a mile away. When Weiss and his pals drove into the farmyard, they were greeted by their four comrades, who had arrived only minutes earlier.

It may well have been the first escape from behind enemy lines by soldiers disguised as policemen.[14]

# An Endangered Pilot Is Saved

EARLY IN THE MORNING, a flight of U.S. carrier-based fighter planes zoomed low over Halmahera, a large island in the southwest Pacific that was held by 37,000 Japanese troops. After completing their strafing runs, the pilots were headed back to their carrier when Ensign Harold A. Thompson's plane was struck by antiaircraft fire over Wasile Bay in northern Halmahera. It was September 16, 1944.

Thompson was painfully wounded by shrapnel, but he managed to throw open his canopy and bail out, parachuting into Wasile Bay a few hundred yards from the beach. As he floundered about, a Catalina flying boat winged low and dropped a rubber raft. The ensign managed to inflate the raft and climb into it.

Almost at once, the raft began drifting toward shore, and when it nestled up to an unmanned Japanese cargo ship some two hundred yards from the beach, he tied the raft to the vessel's anchor chain to ponder his next move.

Thompson could not have picked a worse place anywhere in the vast Pacific to get shot down. Wasile Bay has a narrow entrance, and the approach was protected by several shore batteries and heavy mine fields. Moreover, Japanese troops were on three sides of him. In essence, he was some thirty miles deep into an enemy-held region.

The downed pilot took hope from the fact that his squadron mates, working in relays when fuel ran low, continually circled menacingly overhead, dropping down on occasion to strafe the shore when it appeared that Japanese soldiers were trying to reach Thompson. They could have killed him easily from the beach, but apparently, they were under orders to take Thompson alive, because he would be an invaluable intelligence gold mine.

Although suffering greatly from his wounds, Thompson's thought processes remained clear. He knew that night would arrive in a few hours, and with it he would be doomed—killed, drowned, or captured.

Meanwhile, Thompson's plight had been radioed to Vice Admiral Daniel "Uncle Dan" Barbey, commander of the amphibious forces that had a day earlier put U.S. troops ashore on Morotai, sixty miles north of Wasile Bay. Barbey promptly sent for Commander Selman "Biff" Bowling, leader of all PT boats in the southwest Pacific.

"Can your PTs get the pilot out of there?" Barbey asked. Bowling and the three PT-boat skippers he had brought with him held no illusions about the task. If ever there was a suicide mission, this was it. Charging in broad daylight into the narrow bay entrance guarded by many guns and minefields held little promise for survival of a rescue party. Knowing that an effort would be made to pluck Thompson out of Wasile Bay, the Japanese there would be on full alert, primed and waiting for the quarry to enter the trap.

Bowling, known for his great courage, told Barbey, "I'd hate to have to *order* my boys to go in after the pilot."

"I agree," the admiral replied evenly. "I have no intention of *ordering* your boats to go in."

There were moments of silence. Bowling glanced at his skippers. Their faces were grim. But he could tell by the looks in their eyes that each was thinking: We can't stand by idly and let this pilot die, even though none of the PT men knew Hal Thompson.

"Well, Admiral," Bowling finally said, "I feel confident that with air cover I can find two boat crews that will *volunteer* to give it a try."

With that, his three skippers blurted out in unison: "I'll go!"

Bowling rejected one skipper because his squadron was scheduled to go on patrol that night. He selected Lieutenant Murray Preston for the mission. Then Lieutenant Donald Seaman, Bowling's intelligence officer, spoke up. Pointing out that he had studied the Wasile Bay region and could be of great help, he insisted on going along. Reluctantly, Bowling approved the request.

Rushing back to his base, thirty-one-year-old Murray Preston, a Washington, D.C., lawyer in peacetime, quickly assembled the officers and crews of Eight Ball, nickname of the boat skippered by Lieutenant Wilfred B. Tatro, and Ace's Avenger, under Lieutenant Hershel F. Boyd. Preston explained the Wasile Bay mission, omitting none of the perils, and asked for volunteers. Both officers and every bluejacket raised their hands.

Preston, friendly, courteous, and well liked by his men, climbed into Eight Ball with Wilfred Tatro and, with Ace's Avenger following astern, the swift, eighty-foot-long boats raced off southward at full throttle. An hour later, nearing the entrance to Wasile Bay, the PT men caught their first glimpse of the mountain masses on both sides. No doubt Japanese guns were positioned on those heights. Another haunting specter emerged. "Where in the hell is our

*A U.S. Navy pilot, Ensign Harold A. Thompson, downed behind Japanese positions near this pier in Wasile Bay, was rescued by men in two PT boats. (U.S. Navy)*

goddamned air cover!" a voice rang out on Eight Ball. Navy planes from the carrier *Santee* had not arrived.

As the rescuers had expected, the Japanese were alert and waiting. When the Devil Boats, as they were called by the Japanese, were two miles from the Wasile Bay entrance, three heavy guns began dropping shells around the zigzagging craft. Preston gave orders to pull back and await air cover.

Minutes later, planes from the *Santee* roared in and Preston gave the order, "Head for the entrance!"

Now the Navy aircraft were swooping down on both sides of the entrance, much like gigantic hawks pouncing on prairie chickens. Bombs exploded, machine guns chattered. The approaching PT-boat men felt like cheering. The euphoria was short lived. Japanese shells continued to explode around the two boats.

As the two craft charged into the Japanese noose, scores of guns ringing the bay joined in an all-out effort to demolish the impudent Devil Boats. All the while, machine gunners on Eight Ball and Ace's Avenger were blasting away at unseen targets on shore. "At least we're making the bastards keep their heads down!" one gunner shouted above the cacophony of noise.

Despite the heavy fire from the shore, the two boats charged deeper into the bay. "There he is!" someone aboard Eight Ball called out above the roar.

Those on board could see the downed American pilot, huddled in his raft tied to the anchor chain of a cargo ship only about the length of a football field from Japanese soldiers on the shore.

A plane from the *Santee* zoomed in to lay a smoke screen to blind the Japanese there. Eight Ball then edged up to Ensign Thompson, while the men on Ace's Avenger were firing automatic weapons at the beaches.

Murray Preston and his men knew they would have to act quickly, or all of them, plus the pilot, would die. The smoke screen was rapidly dissipating. The rescuers could see that Thompson was wounded and was unable to cast his raft loose from the cargo ship's anchor chain.

Sizing up the situation, Lieutenant Don Seaman and Motor Machinist's Mate 1st Class Charles D. "Happy" Day plunged into the water, swam to the raft, and towed the nearly unconscious pilot back to Eight Ball.

Thompson was hauled aboard and Murray Preston declared, "Let's get the hell out of here!" No one needed any urging.

Aware that an American pilot had been snatched from under their noses, Japanese gunners around the bay fired scores of shells at the racing Devil Boats.

Finally, Eight Ball and Ace's Avenger were out of range. "You know," a teenager muttered to a comrade, "I ought to have my head examined for volunteering for something like this!"[15]

# Shooting Up an "Iron Kraut"

FOR NINETY MINUTES, the sky parade roared over London en route to Holland for the largest airborne operation of the war. More than fifteen hundred Allied transport planes crammed with 35,000 U.S. and British paratroopers, along with towed gliders that hauled artillery, jeeps, munitions, and soldiers, were to lay down a slender carpet northward for sixty miles along a single road, all the way from Eindhoven in the south to Arnhem on the Rhine River (known in that region as the Neder Rijn). It was September 17, 1944.

Code-named Market-Garden, the audacious operation had been conceived by the customarily cautious British Field Marshal Bernard L. Montgomery. Designed to bring the war in western Europe to a rapid end, Market-Garden would permit the Allies to skirt the vaunted Siegfried Line and avoid the heavy bloodshed that would occur if that concrete-and-steel fortified belt had to be pierced by frontal assaults.

Two hours after the aerial train passed over London, where huge numbers of Sunday worshipers emerged from churches to gawk at and to cheer for the awesome scenario in the sky, men of the U.S. 82nd and 101st Airborne Divisions and the British 1st Airborne Division began jumping and landing among the Dutch windmills.

Like a well-oiled machine, the invaders began seizing bridges over Holland's maze of waterways and other objectives with astonishing speed. When night fell, elements of Major General James M. Gavin's 82nd Airborne were dug in just south of the key town of Groesbeek. Only two miles to the east was the Reichswald (German forest), said by Allied intelligence to conceal panzers and SS troops. Through Groesbeek ran railroad tracks that led to Nijmegen, a large town six miles to the north.

The paratroopers outside Groesbeek were edgy. Like other airborne outfits in Holland, they were isolated. Suddenly, the men heard a train approaching from the rear. They could not believe that one would be operating with Allied troops having landed.

With the 82nd Airborne men gawking, the train loaded with German troops chugged through their position without a shot being fired at it and escaped to German-held Nijmegen.

Two hours later, the chagrined paratroopers at Groesbeek got their revenge. Another train came through bound for Nijmegen. A bazooka rocket from the darkness ripped into the locomotive, disabling it in a cloud of steam. Then a fusillade of machine-gun bullets raked the passenger cars. Scores of German soldiers bolted out the doors. Those not cut down scattered in all directions.

An elated lieutenant reported to 82nd Airborne headquarters over the radio: "We just shot the hell out of an iron Kraut!"[16]

# Hiding a "Pregnant" Glider Pilot

ON SEPTEMBER 19, 1944—D-Day plus two—for the invasion of Holland, 380 Waco gliders towed by transport planes lifted off from England to bring more than two thousand soldiers, jeeps, and artillery pieces to the U.S. 101st "Screaming Eagles" Airborne Division, which had been engaged in heavy fighting.

Low clouds and thick fog turned the reinforcement flight into a near disaster. Seventeen gliders had to ditch in the English Channel, and thirty-one others broke loose from or were released prematurely by their C-47 tugs over Belgium.

Glider pilots were a breed apart. They had a perilous and sparsely recognized job. A successful landing, the pilots declared only half in jest, was when they escaped with only two broken legs.

A landing zone (LZ) was merely a dot on the map, even though it was a rectangle of reasonably flat ground about two miles long and a mile wide. It often took all the skill that a glider pilot could muster—plus luck and divine intervention—to locate an LZ while ack-ack shells were bursting around him.

After being cut loose from its tug, a glider would pancake onto the ground at eighty miles per hour and skid on its belly for more than two hundred yards. If the glider encountered a tree stump, ditch, or some other obstacle, the craft usually became a pile of twisted scrap, killing all on board.

At the controls of one of the Wacos in the 101st Airborne Division reinforcement armada was Flight Officer George F. Brennan, a veteran of D-Day in Normandy. Beside him was his copilot, Sergeant Basil Thompson. Two soldiers were in the rear where a jeep and many artillery rounds were lashed down.

Soon after Brennan's craft began winging over Holland, German gunners on the ground opened fire. Bullets ripped through the glider's thin fuselage, and shell fragments struck the pilot's foot. Another round hit Brennan in the hand. Copilot Thompson had a bullet smash into his leg.

Although the C-47 tug had been hit by flak and was smoking, it flew onward. Then fragments from another flak burst peppered Brennan in the chest, leg, arm, and buttocks. Despite great loss of blood and enormous pain, he was determined to reach his designated LZ.

Moments later, a bullet hit a gasoline line in the jeep and fuel poured onto the floor. An incendiary round then set the gasoline on fire, and Brennan and Thompson were singed by the flame before it could be extinguished.

When the Waco was released from the C-47, it drifted toward the ground when yet another exploding shell sent white-hot fragments into Brennan's jaw. By superhuman effort, despite a useless hand and foot, he managed to crash-land the glider.

With the help of two uninjured passengers, the bloody Brennan and Thompson reached a nearby ditch. After bandaging the two seriously wounded men, the soldiers took off cross-country for the true LZ ten miles away.

Soon Brennan and Thompson were aware that they had landed behind German lines. In pairs and small groups, curious Feldgrau showed up to inspect the Waco and exercise a soldier's penchant to loot.

Knowing that they would be discovered—and possibly shot—if they remained in the ditch, Brennan and Thompson later limped away and finally reached a barn. Exhausted by their physical and mental ordeal, they flopped down in piles of straw and soon lost consciousness.

Presumably tipped off by the farmer, members of the Dutch underground stole into the barn later that night. After awakening the two Americans, the Dutchmen hid them under straw and manure in a horse-drawn farm wagon and delivered them to a maternity hospital in the town of Schijdel, which was rife with German troops.

The facility was distinctive, one of kind. It was indeed a genuine maternity hospital with a staff of Dutch doctors and Catholic nuns serving as nurses. The building also was headquarters for the region's Dutch resistance group which had been harassing the occupying Wehrmacht for four years. On the first floor was a command post for a German infantry outfit.

Throughout the night, Dutch surgeons and physicians tended to the many wounds of the two Americans. Outside the operating room, Catholic nuns were stationed to warn of the approach of German officers, who, on occasion, came upstairs.

Sergeant Thompson was deemed to be the least seriously wounded, and he was ambulatory, so he was concealed in a locked storage room where the medical staff could look in on him. Flight Officer Brennan was transferred to a ward filled with Dutch women in advanced stages of pregnancy.

The hospital staff converted the glider pilot into a "pregnant woman" by strapping a large pillow around his waist. A female wig was put on him, and white gauze wrapped around his head concealed most of his face. The "cover story" for Brennan was that "she" was on the verge of delivery and had been wounded in the fighting around the area.

For two long months, Brennan remained "pregnant" in the maternity ward. Finally, he was rescued when British forces drove the Germans out of Schijdel.[17]

# The "Lone Raider" on the Prowl

AMONG THE PARATROOPERS jumping into Holland in Operation Market-Garden in September 1944, was twenty-one-year-old Private Ted Bachenheimer of the U.S. 82nd Airborne Division. Soft-spoken, friendly, and with the face of a choir boy, he had become a legend as the "Lone Raider of Anzio" for his regular jaunts behind German lines on that bloody Italian beachhead earlier in 1944.

Tall and curly-haired, Bachenheimer spoke flawless German and hoped to be an opera singer after the war. Held in awe by his comrades, he was something of a mystery man. It was known only that Ted had been about ten years old when his parents had fled their native Germany to escape Nazi oppression, eventually settling in California. The father, a skilled pianist and director of opera, died a few years after coming to the United States.

Bachenheimer made no outward display of his hatred for Nazi Germany, but the few troopers close to the thin youngster knew that he was pledged to conducting a one-man war against Hitler. His specialty was solo raids into and behind German lines; before long, his foes at Anzio knew Bachenheimer by name. He had become an irritating—and often deadly—menace.

Bachenheimer's battalion commander, Colonel Warren Williams, a resolute fighting man himself, remembered the Lone Raider of Anzio:

"Watching Ted apply soot and dirt to his face before departing for a trek behind German lines one night, I asked, 'Tell the truth, Ted, aren't you sort of scared on these missions?' He pondered that question, then replied softly, 'Well, Colonel, I'm a little nervous when I leave friendly lines, and I have to take a leak a few times out in no-man's land. But after that, I'm not bothered.'"

One night on Anzio, Bachenheimer was persuaded to take comrades on a particularly perilous mission. Out between the lines, a flare shot into the sky and the patrol was raked with machine-gun fire. Three of the troopers, reasoning that their task of locating German positions had been achieved, headed back toward friendly lines. Bachenheimer continued onward.

Minutes later, automatic weapons chattered angrily in the direction that Bachenheimer had taken. Then silence. Ted's three comrades speculated that the Lone Raider had been killed. But after the troopers returned, an outpost telephoned the 82nd Airborne lines: "Bachenheimer just passed here on the way back. He's got a Kraut sergeant in tow."

When Bachenheimer and his captive reached the light of battalion headquarters, the German sergeant was horrified to see that he had been taken prisoner by, as he termed it, "a kid ten years younger than me."

The Feldgrau insisted on telling intelligence officers how it had happened. He said that his men had become nervous because American paratroopers had been infiltrating German lines almost nightly, and that one of his outposts had opened fire at a "movement." The sergeant went forward to investigate and heard a voice call out in German: "Here are the Amis [Americans]. We've got them!" So when he walked toward the voice, an American [Bachenheimer] with a pistol pointed at the German's stomach, instructed him to "come with me or you're dead."

On another dark night, Bachenheimer was prowling behind German lines when he came upon an enemy soldier in a slit trench. The paratrooper sat down nearby and the two engaged in casual conversation; men on outpost duty get lonely. Ted told the German that he was from an adjacent Wehrmacht unit. Finally, tired of the cat-and-mouse game, the American shoved a pistol in the startled Feldgrau's stomach and ordered him to come along quietly.

A German who had been lying quietly nearby overheard the conversation, raised up and shot Bachenheimer through the left hand. The paratrooper killed both Germans; then returned to his own lines, disappointed that his prisoner-for-the-night had eluded him via a sudden case of lead poisoning.

On the way back, Bachenheimer stuffed dirt into his hand wound to stem the bleeding. Reaching battalion headquarters, the Lone Raider was told by Lieutenant Colonel Williams that he would be evacuated out of the beachhead to Naples, but the youth protested so vigorously that the commander reluctantly changed his mind.

Lieutenant Virgil F. Carmichael, intelligence officer in Bachenheimer's battalion, recalled years later: "We used to joke that we couldn't tell whose side Ted was on because he seemed to spend as much time behind German lines

*U.S. paratrooper Ted Bachenheimer got across this bridge at Nijmegen while it was in German control. (U.S. Army)*

as he did with us. But we decided he belonged to the U.S. Army because he killed or scared hell out of so many Germans."

Now, on D-Day in Holland, Private Bachenheimer parachuted close to the 82nd Airborne's drop zone south of Nijmegen, a city of one hundred thousand people. One of the division's objectives was seizing the huge bridge over the Waal River in the heart of Nijmegen, eleven miles south of Arnhem. The tactical plan was for the crack British Guards Armored Division to dash along the airborne corridor, cross the bridge to Nijmegen, and rush on to Arnhem and link up with the 1st Airborne Division.

Although Nijmegen was in German hands, Bachenheimer somehow got across the bridge, explaining later that he had done so to "draw German fire and cause them to disclose their positions."

While prowling around, a lone American in the enemy-held city, he entered the railroad station and got into a shoot-out with eight or nine German soldiers. During a brief lull, a call to surrender was made through the loudspeaker, which announced the arrival and departure of trains.

"We have all of you surrounded," the voice in cracked English declared. Apparently, the Germans did not believe that only one man was creating such havoc. While the ultimatum was being "broadcast" several times, the American slipped out of the station.

Bachenheimer returned to his comrades south of the Waal and was asked why he had gotten himself involved in the train station shoot-out, knowing that the odds for survival had been heavily stacked against him.

"Well, this was the first time any of those Dutch people saw an American soldier," he explained in his soft, slightly accented voice. "So it wouldn't look right for an American to run off just because he saw a few Germans."

Hours later, the Lone Raider's comrades saw him start to peddle an old bicycle toward the Waal. Clearly, he was going back into Nijmegen, and they cautioned him that it was still "thick with Krauts." Ted shrugged and replied: "Aw, I'm just going to go over there to see what the score is."

Bachenheimer took with him two of his best friends, known as Bill One and Bill Two. After sneaking into Nijmegen at night, Ted, Bill One (Willard Strunk), and Bill Two (Bill Sellars) made contact with the Dutch underground, and its leaders urged Bachenheimer to take charge of their operations in the city.

The Lone Raider and his two pals set up their headquarters in the candlelit basement of an old school. Much like a field marshal directing his army, Ted sent out his "troops"—a motley but eager band of Dutchmen wearing orange armbands and armed with a curious assortment of weapons—to ambush German patrols and attack isolated posts and sentries. Other underground bands were dispatched to collect information on German positions around the Nijmegen Bridge, intelligence which he sent back to his regiment by a Dutch courier who sneaked across the Waal in a small boat at night.

Armed with this information, a battalion of the 82nd Airborne captured the north end of the Nijmegen Bridge with a bold crossing of the Waal in assault boats. Soon British tanks rumbled over the span and continued northward to relieve major elements of the 1st Airborne Division that were trapped on the far side of the Rhine at Arnhem. Just short of the Arnhem Bridge, Operation Market-Garden ground to a halt.

In October, the 82nd and 101st Airborne Divisions leapfrogged northward and took up defensive positions between the Waal at Nijmegen and the Rhine at Arnhem. Fighting in the Island (as the troopers named it) was savage and costly. Freezing weather. Torrential rains. Foxholes half-filled with icy water. Shells screaming in.

It was during this period that Ted Bachenheimer vanished while behind German lines. Later, his body would be recovered. A pall of gloom was cast over the men of the 82nd Airborne. Only a few days earlier, his battlefield commission as a second lieutenant had come through, and he had agreed to accept it.

Ted, who had a unique talent for war, had actually been a man of peace. "I am against war in principle," he had said. "I just can't hate anybody."[18]

# A Secret Mission in the Alps

"Sure, i'll volunteer. Sounds like fun!"

Twenty-year-old Corporal Duffield W. Matson, a husky American paratrooper, was responding to a call from an Office of Strategic Services (OSS) detachment in southern France for six men to parachute deep behind German lines in the rugged Maritime Alps along the French-Italian border. The team was to make contact with an Italian who reported he had crucial information that would be of help to the Allies. It was late September 1944.

Six weeks earlier, Duff Matson had parachuted behind German lines along the Riviera to help spearhead Operation Dragoon, the invasion of southern France. Now he and the other five men on the secret mission would again be jumping behind German lines, only much deeper than he had in Dragoon.

Soon after the Allies had stormed ashore in southern France, most of the German Army began pulling back for nearly three hundred miles to establish defensive positions on the border of the Third Reich. However, two German divisions along the Riviera had been conducting a fighting withdrawal eastward to the Maritime Alps and were being pursued by elements of the 1st Airborne Task Force.

Duff Matson, by his own admission, was "one mean son-of-a-bitch," a vivid description not challenged by comrades. He had been one of Brigadier General Robert Frederick's human reclamation projects. Frederick, the thirty-seven-year-old leader of the 1st Airborne Task Force, was not overly concerned with a man's past, only demanding that he be a fierce and resourceful fighter and loyal to his comrades and his unit.

A few weeks before Frederick's paratroopers had launched Dragoon, Matson was in a military prison outside Rome for perpetrating mayhem on a U.S. military police lieutenant and assorted other acts of violence. Earlier, Matson had been court-martialed three times for attempted murder.

One morning, after serving forty-five days, Matson was escorted from the prison by two of General Frederick's paratroopers, Captain George Pysienski and Sergeant Leonard "Wahoo" Cheek, who had been a star athlete in a Georgia high school. Both escorts were toting Tommy guns, no doubt in deference to Matson's reputation for violence.

Pysienski told Matson firmly, "The general wants to see you. He knows about you and thinks you'll make a damned good fighter." Then came a word of caution to Matson: "Don't try to escape from us or I'll blow your goddamned head off!"

Reaching 1st Airborne Task Force headquarters outside Rome, Matson was briefly interviewed by Frederick. "I need a bodyguard," the general said. "I think you'll do if you want to join us."

*Corporal Duffield W. Matson was "bailed out" of a prison and became a spy behind enemy lines. (Courtesy Jim Phillips)*

Stunned by the sudden dramatic turn of events in his life, Matson eagerly accepted. Turning to others in the office, Captain Pysienski called out, "This is Matson. He's got a lot of talent. He's one of us now."

Behind the French Riviera in the blackness of D-Day morning, Frederick had bailed out wearing a white scarf made of parachute silk and carrying a blue-lensed flashlight for signaling on the ground. Duff Matson, carrying a Tommy gun, a dagger, three razor-sharp combat knives, and four hand grenades, crashed to earth near where his boss had landed.

Peering through the darkness, the general's bodyguard detected a parachute draped over a pole in a vineyard and concluded that it had to be Frederick, whose blue-beamed flashlight was glowing faintly. Matson, who had landed on a tree stump and "messed up" his leg, hobbled toward Frederick, recalling the words of an officer, "You are to protect the general from harm— even if it costs you your life!"

Nearing Frederick, the bodyguard felt a surge of concern. Five or six dark figures were moving toward the general. Moments later, Matson detected the dim outlines of their distinctive helmets—they were Germans!

Matson squeezed off a burst from his Tommy gun and two of the Germans toppled over. The others fled into the night. Frederick, who was studying a map by the blue flashlight, casually looked up, then returned to his task.

Now, a month and a half after Matson had saved the general's life, he and the five other volunteers climbed into a C-47 at an airport outside Nice, on the French Riviera, and lifted off for the Maritime Alps to rendezvous with the mysterious Italian at a specified locale.

The secret mission got off to a haunting start. When the paratroopers bailed out, two of them were killed when crashing into the craggy, boulder-strewn ground.

In those inhospitable mountains, a person could walk for days without seeing another human. So perhaps it was not strange that the Italian never showed up at the rendezvous site: he might well have gotten lost in the trackless landscape.

After waiting for two freezing, miserable days, Matson and his three companions had no choice but to begin the long and arduous march westward to friendly lines. For several days, they saw no other person. Then one day, a noise was heard nearby. Matson edged up to a precipice and looked down to see a group of Germans digging a gun emplacement. This disclosure meant that the Americans were getting close to the front lines and in much more danger.

Mountain goats would have had a hard time keeping their footing in the rugged terrain, so Matson slipped on loose rocks and tumbled down the embankment right at the feet of a German who was wielding a pick. He was a huge man, even larger than the tall, muscular Matson, who lay momentarily stunned. Surprised at suddenly having an American soldier plunge into the gun emplacement, the German paused for several moments, a fact that no doubt saved the paratrooper's life. Then the German raised his pick and swung it downward. Matson rolled to one side, and the lethal end of the pick gouged into the ground inches from his head.

Matson whipped out his dagger and plunged it into the giant—three times. Meanwhile, the other paratroopers unloosed a fusillade of bullets and killed the bleeding German and his comrades, except for a major, who, for some reason, was with this gun crew. Like many Germans, the officer spoke fluent English. When Matson said, "You're coming with us, Kraut, and no funny stuff or you're a dead man," the captive nodded his head.

After slipping through German frontline positions at night, the four Americans and their prisoner reached friendly troops. Except for bringing back the German major, who could provide intelligence officers with a wealth of information, the secret mission had been a failure.

"That's the way it goes in these things," Matson told his comrades. "You wins some, and you loses some."[19]

# Part Five

## Peace at Last

# "League of Lonely War Women"

AFTER LIEUTENANT GENERAL Mark W. Clark's U.S. Fifth Army captured Rome on June 6, 1944, Field Marshal Albrecht Kesselring, the German commander in the Mediterranean, pulled back his forces and established a heavily fortified belt across Italy. Typically, the German soldiers fought tenaciously.

In Rome that fall, the twenty-two men and one woman assigned to the Morale Operations (MO) branch of the U.S. Office of Strategic Services hatched an innovative scheme to dent the morale of the Germans in northern Italy. The machination focused on the "League of Lonely War Women," and it was aimed mostly at the Germans who had wives or girlfriends in the Fatherland.

German language experts in the MO carefully created a document announcing that a "League of Lonely War Women" had been formed in Germany to make furloughs at home more pleasant for the fighting men. To withstand later scrutiny by German technicians, an old printing press that had actually been used in the Third Reich ran off thousands of copies.

All a war-weary German soldier had to do when he arrived in the Fatherland for a brief respite was to pin a small replica of a heart on his lapel, the fake document stated. Then he would quickly find a woman most anxious to fulfill his every desire, because there were members of the league throughout the Reich.

"We German women realize it is our duty to our fighting men to help however we can," the printed piece stated. "Your wife, sweetheart, or mother is one of us, doing her duty for the Fatherland and bolstering its birth rate."

Members of the Italian underground surreptitiously distributed thousands of the printed pieces behind German lines.[1]

# Curious Doings in a POW Camp

PLATOON SERGEANT James W. Collins was one of five thousand Americans in Stalag III-B, a prisoner-of-war camp near Frankfurt, in western Germany. Collins had been regarded as one of the fiercest fighters in his outfit when he was taken by surprise and captured by the Germans in Tunisia, North Africa, in the spring of 1943.

Unlike most young American draftees, Collins had found the strict, often harsh discipline and regimentation of army life to be easy. The sergeant had grown up in the hills of rural Kentucky, one of thirteen children in a family that had to scramble almost constantly just to exist.

For many months, the German colonel commanding the POW command had been frustrated. He could never figure out the "crazy Americans" and had regularly employed subtle and not-so-subtle tactics to cow the prisoners, to crush their spirits and pulverize their morale. But he had failed.

One reason the Americans' morale had remained relatively high was that they had established a unique intelligence system that kept them informed on the progress of the war and also about schemes to be utilized against the POWs by the German commandant.

The key component of the camp's intelligence apparatus was an anti-Hitler guard, an elderly man who risked his life almost daily to pass along tidbits. Now, in October 1944, the mole told the Americans that Allied armies were pushing up against the western frontier of the Reich. He added that the German Army was preparing to do something peculiar to stem the Allied tide in the West.

Sergeant Collins recalled much later: "Our Kraut, as we called him with a degree of affection, informed us that German officers would soon enter our barracks and demand that we give them our uniforms. We stayed awake most of the night conjecturing about the means of such an extraordinary action." As was forecast, a Nazi officer entered Collins's barracks two days later and ordered the Americans to remove their uniforms and deposit them in a pile in the center of the floor. Noncommissioned officers stripes and any unit insignia were to be left intact. This clothing would be used for an American infantry unit that had just been captured and did not have uniforms, it was explained.

"What a crock," Collins whispered to a comrade. "I guess our generals are sending our guys into battle these days stark naked!"

The German officer said that he would go to another barracks, then return in an hour to pick up the uniforms. When the German came back, the uniforms had been placed as ordered. But each POW had taken a razor and slashed his garments to ribbons.

Red-faced with anger, the German stared at the stack of mutilated garments, then he spun around and barged out of the barracks. Collins and his comrades broke out in wide smiles and launched a blizzard of mock Nazi salutes and "*Heil, Hitler!*" calls.

Only much later would the POWs learn that Adolf Hitler had ordered the collection of one thousand U.S. army uniforms from various camps in the

Third Reich. These garments would play a key role in an ingenious scheme hatched by the führer to snatch victory from the jaws of defeat on the Western Front.[2]

# POWs Parachute into the Reich

LIEUTENANT GENERAL Alexander M. Patch, leader of the U.S. Seventh Army, was both sad and frustrated. A few weeks earlier, his son, Alexander Jr., an infantry captain, had been killed while fighting in Normandy. Now, in November 1944, after a heady six weeks in which the Seventh Army had raced from the beaches of southern France for 280 miles to the borders of the Third Reich, German resistance had stiffened and a stalemate had set in.

Known to his colleagues as Sandy, Patch called in Captain Henry Hyde (thirty years of age), who was head of the Office of Strategic Services (OSS) detachment assigned to the Seventh Army. Scion of a wealthy family, he had graduated from Harvard Law School when he was only twenty-three.

Hyde was held in high regard by Patch, a reputation earned before and during the southern France invasion for spying out Nazi defenses prior to the Seventh Army landing. Hyde's image gained more luster when he sent agents ahead of Patch's army to smooth the way for the rapid drive to the Reich border.

Because of the great success of his OSS detachment, Patch presumably had become "spoiled." So when Hyde reported to the general's headquarters, Patch wanted to know why the steady flow of OSS intelligence from behind German lines had largely dried up.

Hyde explained that the Frenchmen he had used to report on German activities in southern France were unsuited for infiltrating German lines near the border of the Reich. Then the OSS officer suggested a plan that was both highly hazardous for the would-be agents and against international law. "We could 'recruit' some German POWs, furnish them with false papers, and send them behind the lines," Hyde explained.

Moreover, as both Hyde and Patch knew, Supreme Commander Dwight Eisenhower had a strict rule against using POWs as spies. Patch, however, was a realistic man. With a wink, he told the younger man, "I expressly forbid you to use prisoners of war." That was Hyde's signal to move ahead at full speed.

Hyde sent three of his German-speaking American agents into the cages where newly captured Feldgrau were confined. The camp staff had been told to watch for any overt or covert indication from a POW that he was disillusioned with the Nazi regime.

Once a potential agent was identified, Hyde's officers would deliberately provoke him in a private interview, seeking to gain the German's true outlook.

If the candidate quickly agreed that Adolf Hitler had destroyed the Fatherland, he was immediately tapped for espionage duty.

Turning on their own country was an agonizing decision to many POWs. So the OSS sales pitch was sweetened with promises of a lucrative job in Germany after the war—whose conclusion seemed to be only a matter of a few weeks—or even a chance to emigrate to the United States.

Soon Hyde had his German espionage candidates. Following the "cue" handed down by General Patch, Seventh Army officers turned blind eyes to doctoring POW records, or even to erasing any indication that the candidate had ever been a prisoner.

Those selected were blindfolded and taken for a final scrutiny to Henry Hyde. The Harvard Law School graduate had drawn up a standard contract that the German had to sign. It was a binding pact between "Oberleutnant _____" and the "government of the United States." To avoid misunderstandings, as with any contract, terms of the agreement were spelled out.

The final clause no doubt sealed the new allegiance of the German espionage candidate. If he were to betray the Americans, he would be tracked down after the war no matter how long the effort took, and his wife and children would be arrested.

Hyde took his plan to General Patch. Not the bombastic, two-fisted, hell-for-leather-type combat leader so often portrayed in Hollywood movies, he was soft-spoken, but brought out the best in those serving under him. He was not too picky about flaunting Eisenhower's headquarters and international law if it saved his men's lives and shortened the war, so he quickly gave his approval to Hyde's project.

Forged papers were painstakingly crafted for each POW agent. So that he would have freedom to travel behind German lines, it would be indicated that he was on a short leave because of a death in his family or that he was to be treated at a hospital for a disease.

Hyde's OSS operatives in charge of plausible cover stories and fraudulent papers had an unqualified expert, a peacetime lawyer from Dresden whose job in the German Army prior to being captured had been to make certain that a soldier's papers were in order.

The POW agents were instructed to infiltrate German lines for a few miles, then report back with the location of ammunition dumps, artillery batteries, reserve units, and headquarters. Only about half of the POWs made a return trip. Most of the others were blown up by mines or cut down by German or American machine guns. A few presumably took off for their homes. However, the POWs that did return brought back a wealth of high-grade intelligence.

Aware that he would run out of agents at this rate, Henry Hyde and his aides hatched a scheme for greatly reducing the casualties from line crossings.

The POWs would parachute forty to fifty miles behind German lines (most leaping from airplanes for the first time). They had carefully memorized a trek that would take them to points that General Sandy Patch was especially interested in. Within about two weeks, the agents would slip back through American lines. Two-thirds of these missions were successful.

Once the returning POW agent was debriefed (that is, OSS officers questioned him on what he had done, seen, and heard), the information was passed along the Seventh Army chain of command. Also getting copies were intelligence officers of the U.S. Army Air Corps for use in deciding how many bombs could be dropped on what troop assembly area or gun batteries or aircraft to perpetrate the most carnage.[3]

# The Good Samaritan
# of Leyte Gulf

A BORED SOLDIER of the U.S. 728th Amphibious Tractor Battalion was manning a lonely post along the Leyte Gulf shoreline, where a powerful army under General Douglas MacArthur had stormed ashore four weeks earlier in his heralded return to the Philippines. As with most soldiers overseas at quiet times, the sentry's thoughts were 9,047 miles away (the distance he had calculated to his hometown in the United States). It was November 27, 1944.

The guard felt he had no real reason to be nervous or even concerned about danger. His outfit was far behind the front where U.S. and Japanese troops had been slugging it out in bloody encounters.

Suddenly, the soldier's reverie was shattered when he heard a swishing sound similar to that given off by an airplane as it came in for a landing. Then he caught a glimpse of the shadowy silhouette of an aircraft splashing onto the water only a short distance offshore. Presuming that it was a friendly plane in distress, perhaps forced down by engine trouble or lack of fuel, the sentry hurriedly removed his shoes, jacket, and helmet before going to offer assistance. What the GI did not know was that the downed aircraft was filled with Japanese troops.

Earlier in the evening, the Japanese had launched Operation Wa, in which a large contingent of paratroopers bailed out over three airstrips behind American lines and a short distance inland from Leyte Gulf. After these airstrips were seized and U.S. planes destroyed, transport planes loaded with soldiers were to land on the sites, wipe out the Americans there, and secure the key facilities.

Almost at once, Wa went awry. Although the Japanese parachutists landed near their targets, they were killed or driven off by men of the U.S. 11th Airborne Division. The inexperienced pilots on several transport planes, including the one the American sentry saw crash-land in Leyte Gulf, missed their designated objectives.

Now the GI sentry plunged into the water, swam to the floating aircraft offshore, and climbed onto a wing. The occupants were decidedly ungrateful: they tossed hand grenades at the puzzled Good Samaritan. He leaped back into the water and swam back to shore, being peppered by bullets all the way.

The rifle fire and grenade explosions awakened the Good Samaritan's nearby comrades, and there was a mad scramble for weapons. When the Japanese on the floating transport plane reached land, they were greeted by a fusillade of small-arms fire. In the shoot-out, several Japanese were killed and the remainder of the intruders fled into the dark countryside.[4]

# "Scarface Otto" Creates Mass Hysteria

IN THE FREEZING DAWN, the eerie stillness along the Ghost Front, a seventy-mile sector in the Ardennes Forest in Belgium and Luxembourg, was shattered by a mighty cacophony of sound and fury. Nineteen hundred German artillery pieces and mortars joined in showering death and destruction on mostly green American troops.

After forty minutes, the thunderous bombardment lifted and tens of thousands of German assault troops, supported by hundreds of panzers, plunged through the thin and disoriented American positions and raced deep into Belgium. It was December 16, 1944.

The offensive was Adolf Hitler's final roll of the dice to snatch victory from defeat in the West, and he had taken the Allies by total surprise. Code-named Wacht am Rein (Watch on the Rhine), the operation's main objective was the port of Antwerp, eighty miles to the northwest, through which flowed most of the supplies for the Allied armies.

On the heels of the spearheads, seventy-five Germans, wearing American uniforms, carrying American weapons, and using authentic dog tags taken from prisoners, fanned out in Belgium riding in genuine American jeeps, trucks, halftracks, and two Sherman tanks.

They spoke fluent to passable English and had been formed and trained by 6-foot-5, 250-pound Obersturmbannführer (Lieutenant Colonel) Otto Skorzeny.

A year earlier, Skorzeny had become world famous when he led a small band of German paratroopers in a daring rescue of recently ousted Italian premier Benito Mussolini, who was being held prior to execution in a tightly guarded prison atop a towering mountain in the Alps. Skorzeny became a folk hero in the Third Reich, a villain in the Allied camp.

*Hulking SS Lieutenant Colonel Otto Skorzeny (left) was assigned a bizarre mission by Adolph Hitler. (National Archives)*

Now the role of the German imposters was to create panic and confusion behind American lines by ambushing vehicles, shooting couriers, spreading false rumors, turning around road signs, and cutting telephone lines.

Two days after the massive German breakthrough, a military policeman at Aywaille, eleven miles south of the major city of Liege, Belgium, halted a jeep with three men in American uniforms. Their manner was suspicious. They were nervous and said virtually nothing. Their dog tags identified them as Privates Charles W. Lawrence, George Sensenbach, and Clarence Werth.

Pointing his rifle at them, the MP yelled, "Hands up!" Other MPs rushed up and took the three men into custody. Concealed in the jeep were two American Colt .45s, two British submachine guns, and six American grenades. On their persons were German military paybooks (an incredible security lapse), one thousand U.S. dollars (counterfeit), and one thousand English pounds sterling (also phony). Three days later, the captives were tied to poles, blindfolded, and shot to death by a firing squad.

On the same day that the bogus Americans were executed, U.S. soldiers manning a checkpoint near Namur, Belgium, took into custody three of Skorzeny's men. They freely confessed to their role. One of them, Lieutenant Günther Schulz, knowing that he would soon be facing a firing squad, concocted a fanciful tale for his interrogators. There were two thousand German soldiers in

U.S. uniforms roaming about in American rear areas, Schulz declared. (Actually, there were now less than fifty.)

Then Schulz's fertile mind loosed a bombshell. Colonel Skorzeny's main objective, he lied, was to murder General Dwight Eisenhower. The doomed lieutenant even spontaneously invented details of the nonexistent assassination plot.

Forty-eight hours later, Schulz was shot, never knowing the gargantuan turmoil and hysteria that would result from the phantom scenarios he had concocted on the spur of the moment.

In the wake of the Skorzeny's "killers on the loose" fairy tale, tensions bordering on paranoia permeated American rear areas. No one trusted another unless he recognized his face.

Hysteria spread rapidly into the civilian populations. The "notorious" Skorzeny was clearly not only dedicated to killing American soldiers, but he also was bent on murdering any civilian man, woman, or child he could get his bloody hands on—or so thought the frightened citizens of Belgium, Luxembourg, and France.

The mass paranoia among civilians intensified after French newspapers tagged Skorzeny with the sinister sobriquet, "The Most Dangerous Man in Europe." Other blaring headlines called him "Scarface Otto," alluding to the blemish on his cheek from a fencing duel while a university student in Vienna.

A nervous police chief at Valenciennes, France, informed the natives that "Scarface Otto" and his "band of cutthroats," dressed as priests and nuns, had parachuted just outside the town. For several days, doors and windows were kept shut and locked. Few civilians dared to venture into the streets. Genuine priests and nuns remained secluded for more than a week, fearful that mayhem would be committed on them by panicky civilians who might mistake them for Skorzeny's killers.

At Meaux, east of Paris, a man in civilian clothes was collared by *gendarmes* (police) and hustled off to jail after an excited woman had identified him as Otto Skorzeny. He even had the telltale facial scar, she exclaimed. The suspect was grilled vigorously, even though he protested that he was a longtime resident of Meaux. Eventually, the man was released. He stood five feet six (nearly a foot shorter than Skorzeny) and his "dueling scar" was a nick received while shaving that morning.

Rumors and outrageous media reports kept the hysteria pot boiling among the Allied civilians. The German-language "black radio," a British propaganda subterfuge aimed at the German people, broadcast that three hundred of Skorzeny's men in American uniforms had been captured (only three had been apprehended at that time), but seven hundred more remained on the loose.

A newspaper in Nice, on the French Riviera hundreds of miles from the Ardennes, reported that Scarface Otto's men had robbed a Nice bank (no doubt taking the heat off the real perpetrators of the heist).

*About eighteen of the Germans in American uniforms were caught and executed during the Battle of the Bulge. (U.S. Army)*

A customarily staid London newspaper solemnly published a story that stated beautiful, English-speaking young German women, armed with sharp knives, had been recruited by Skorzeny to parachute behind American lines. Their mission was to seduce unwary GIs and stab them in their backs while torrid romantic interludes were in progress. Seven of these Teutonic Mata Haris already had been arrested, the London newspaper added.

Paris police distributed tens of thousands of pictures of "The Most Dangerous Man in Europe." Then the gendarmes in the French capital announced that a large number of German paratroopers had landed near to the Trianon Palace in Versailles. That imposing structure housed SHAEF (Supreme Headquarters, Allied Expeditionary Force). The closest German paratrooper was in distant Belgium.

SHAEF was turned into an armed fortress. The guard was doubled, then quadrupled, as reports arrived that Skorzeny and his men were nearing Paris to murder General Dwight Eisenhower. The supreme commander was one of the few at SHAEF who refused to succumb to Skorzeny mania. He railed against the elaborate security precautions being taken to protect him.

Colonel Gordon Sheen, SHAEF security chief, briefed Eisenhower on details of the "Skorzeny plot." Sheen said that the SS colonel and fifty of his men were to rendezvous in Paris at the Café de la Paix on the Place de l'Opera and proceed from there to the Trianon Palace. Sheen, who was hardly eager to have the supreme commander murdered on his watch, proposed a masquerade to foil the German commandos. Eisenhower grunted, then agreed to it, "but only so you people will let me get back to running the war."

As a first step, Eisenhower moved from his villa in Saint-Germain-en-Laye, a suburb of Paris some distance from SHAEF, to a house close to the Trianon Palace. Then an officer who bore a remarkable resemblance to the supreme commander, Lieutenant Colonel Baldwin B. Smith, was instantly "promoted" to five-star general. He moved into the Saint-Germain-en-Laye villa, and each day, the clay pigeon was chauffeured to headquarters and back in Eisenhower's Packard with its five-star flag.

Meanwhile, American counterintelligence officers set up an ambush (including the use of two tanks) around the Café de la Paix. But neither Skorzeny nor his men showed up. Scarface Otto, in fact, had never gotten within two hundred miles of Paris, nor had any of his men. Throughout what came to be known as the Battle of the Bulge, Skorzeny wore only his regular SS uniform and insignia.[5]

# A POW Colonel Takes Command

"COLONEL, I've got some bad news for you. We're going to shoot you."

In the little room in a schoolhouse in Luxembourg, the intelligence captain of the 2nd Panzer Division stared at his prisoner, Colonel Hurley Fuller, leader of the 110th Regiment of the U.S. 28th Infantry Division, a Pennsylvania National Guard outfit.

"Why shoot me?" asked the American, who pretended to be nonchalant about the quite real threat.

This was not the reaction the German was seeking. He was trying to frighten Fuller into disclosing the site of the 28th Infantry Division headquarters and other military secrets.

"We're going to kill you because you ordered German prisoners killed," the captain replied. "We found their bodies."

"Baloney!" the colonel barked.

Fuller knew that the Germans might murder him, but he felt that the captain was bluffing. As far as Fuller knew, no German POWs had been killed, with or without his orders.

Now the frustrated German sat silently, smoked American cigarettes, and glared at Fuller, waiting for him to crack. Fuller glared back—and won the standoff. A German sergeant was called in and told to take the colonel to a POW enclosure.

Three days earlier, in the morning of December 16, 1944, Colonel Fuller began receiving conflicting reports by messengers at his command post (CP) in the Claravallis Hotel in picturesque Clervaux, Luxembourg. Although Nazi Germany had been declared as good as defeated by the Western Allies, it appeared that the German Army had launched some sort of attack to his front.

Fuller was mildly concerned. The 28th Infantry Division, led by Major General Norman "Dutch" Cota, had been badly chewed up in bloody fighting in the Huertgen Forest north of Luxembourg in Germany, and had been brought to what was called the Ghost Front of the Ardennes in Belgium and Luxembourg for rest and refitting. Fuller's regiment was stretched along a seven-mile sector, three times the distance recommended for a unit that size in a defensive mission.

At dawn that day, the Germans had unleashed a massive bombardment that destroyed telephone communications with his battalions on the line and his radio network had been jammed. So the colonel could only surmise that his regiment might be in big trouble.

Alarm spread rapidly through Fuller's CP, but the colonel remained typically calm. Panic was headed off when word spread that the "old man" was in routine form, barking out orders.

Fuller had never gone out of his way to be popular with his soldiers, so most of them respected rather than liked him. Over the years, he had been too frank with high-ranking officers to gain a general's star. But he was a fighting man, an impeccable professional, and now the burden of halting a major German offensive rested on his shoulders.

As the day wore on, Fuller knew that his regiment was in serious trouble. After nightfall, an officer burst into the Claravallis Hotel and called out, "Colonel, six Kraut tanks are coming down the street!"

Moments later, there were loud explosions below Fuller's second-floor office. The panzers were firing at point-blank range. The hotel shook and was filled with smoke. Then a machine gun stitched bullets into the wall just over the colonel. Plaster fell on his head.

Fuller went into the hall and his operations officer said, "Colonel, we're trapped!" Fuller had already reached that obvious conclusion.

"Well, let's get the hell out of here," the colonel said evenly. "We can assemble what's left of the regiment behind Clervaux."

Chaos erupted in the dark building. German voices were heard on the first floor. In the basement, some fifty wounded GIs cringed in terror.

Grabbing his carbine, Fuller rushed up to the third floor and headed for a window at the rear of the hotel. An officer who had been blinded by a shell explosion minutes earlier held on to Fuller's belt and followed him out the window. Along with some fifteen others, the colonel and the blind man, one by one, crawled across a horizontal iron ladder for several feet to a cliff, then made their way up steps carved into the elevation and flopped exhausted to the ground.

When they regained their breaths, Fuller told his men to follow him, and he set off to establish a new command post to continue the fight.

Two days later, Fuller and four of his men were trudging through a thick forest when they suddenly heard voices calling out in German. The Americans

*Colonel Hurley Fuller survived beatings, bayoneting, captivity, and lengthy marches. (U.S. Army)*

had stumbled into an enemy bivouac. Then the colonel felt a heavy blow on the head. An undetermined amount of time later, he regained consciousness, and was vaguely aware that four of his men and a German soldier were standing over him.

Fuller felt a sharp pain in his groin, and realized that he had been bayoneted, apparently while unconscious. Biting off his words through clenched teeth, the colonel told his four soldiers, "Don't tell the bastards anything!"

A German officer came up and struck Fuller a mighty blow on the head with the butt of a pistol. Again, the colonel lost consciousness. When he again regained his senses, he was in the CP of the 2nd Panzer Division where he was interrogated by the intelligence captain who threatened to murder him.

Six days afterward, Fuller was deep in Germany, marching up and down snow-covered hills at the head of a long column of Americans who had been captured in the Ardennes. Weak from hunger and exhaustion, the GIs shouted for the German guards to slow down, but they kept moving at a steady pace.

Word was passed up to Fuller that several men, too weary to continue, had fallen by the wayside and were shot by the guards. Other GIs who stopped to relieve themselves were bayoneted in the posteriors.

Infuriated, the colonel took charge. Turning around, he held up both hands and shouted for the POWs to halt and fall out for a ten-minute break.

As the Americans collapsed on the ground, the confused German guards didn't know how to react. This had never happened before. This upstart colonel had issued orders as though he were in command.

While Fuller was seated in the snow, the German major in charge of the march rushed up and shouted something at the colonel. A GI told Fuller, "He says he's going to shoot you if you don't get the POWs on the march again."

Looking up at the frustrated major, Fuller said, "Tell him that we're exhausted and we're going to take a short break."

Infuriated, the German reached for his pistol, but had second thoughts.

Sensing that he was getting the better of the march commander, Fuller told the GI, "Tell him if he'll let me be in charge of the march, we'll make better time."

As this pronouncement was being translated, the German's face reflected astonishment. Then the major snapped a few words and walked away.

"What'd he say?" Fuller asked the GI.

"Colonel, he said that you are now in charge!" Fuller got to his feet and called out, "All right, men, let's get going."

Nearly a month later, in late January 1945, the last-gasp effort by Adolf Hitler to earn at least a negotiated peace in the West had been smashed, and the German Army was limping back into the Reich. At the same time, Colonel Fuller and other POWs were marching along a road in Poland, a few hundred miles east of the Ghost Front. Off in the distance, he could hear the faint rumble of Soviet guns, and knew the Red Army was approaching from the East.

Among the guards was a friendly German, Paul Hegel, who had been secretly aiding Fuller during the march of the column of POWs. On January 29, Hegel helped the colonel take charge of the entire marching prison camp when it reached a small Polish village. As though he were directing his own regiment, Fuller sent his unarmed GIs to barricade all entries to the town, which was turned over to the Red Army the next day after the German guards had fled—except for the amiable Paul Hegel.

Fuller, knowing that Hegel might be shot by the Russians or sent to a Siberian labor camp for years, put him in an American uniform, and the German was escorted through southern Russia and on to safety in Italy.[6]

# An Allied Spy's Dilemma

THROUGHOUT THE WAR, the Western Allies high command had been notified in advance about most of Adolf Hitler's tactical plans by an ingenious monitoring and decoding process called Ultra. Suddenly, on December 12, 1944, four days before Adolf Hitler launched his last-ditch offensive in the Ardennes region of Belgium, radios on the German side went "dead."

Radio silence was a customary clue that an attack was imminent. However, few if any, at Allied headquarters outside Paris read anything sinister into the fact that Ultra was failing to pick up German wireless messages in recent days. Nazi Germany, the Allies knew, was *kaputt*.

When the Germans struck with enormous impact in what was to become known as the Battle of the Bulge, the Allies, from the private on outpost duty to the supreme commander, were taken by total surprise.

In desperation, American commanders called on Captain Ray Brittenham, a young lawyer from Chicago who was in charge of an Office of Strategic Services (OSS) detachment whose task was to recruit Belgians for espionage missions behind German lines. Brittenham was urged to slip agents through the lines and report back on German gun batteries, infantry positions, and panzer movements.

One of Brittenham's favorite Belgian spies was a man named Louis, who completed four short infiltrations and returned with a wealth of valuable intelligence during the Battle of the Bulge. On his returns, Louis went to his home in a Belgian village that was in Allied hands.

Soon Louis pleaded with Brittenham for a fifth hazardous mission, but the OSS officer rejected the idea. Louis, he knew, was already a fugitive from the law of averages, a prime candidate to be apprehended while behind German lines.

Louis continued to plead his case. When behind German lines, he explained, he often holed up in a barn or unoccupied house and knew total serenity. But when he came back to Belgium and his wife, he also encountered his live-in mother-in-law, who, he stressed, "makes life hell for me."

Louis said he would much rather risk being caught and shot as a spy by the Germans than to engage in hassles with his mother-in-law.

Fortunately for Captain Brittenham, he was spared having to make a crucial decision. American forces had flattened the Bulge and it would no longer be necessary to infiltrate spies behind German lines in Belgium.[7]

# Marooned amid the Foe

WITHIN HOURS after Supreme Commander Dwight Eisenhower concluded that Adolf Hitler's attack in the Ardennes was a full-blooded offensive, U.S. airborne units that had been in reserve far to the rear in the Rheims region of France were rapidly loaded onto flatbed trailers and into trucks and headed hell-bent for Belgium.

Private First Class Milo C. Huempfner was driving an ammunition truck at the tail of the 551st Parachute Infantry Battalion convoy on December 20,

*Private First Class Milo C.
Huempfner shared a town
with a German unit.
(Courtesy Dan Morgan)*

1944—four days after the Germans had struck. When highballing through Leignon, Belgium, at night, his truck skidded on ice, careened into a ditch, and was badly damaged.

With the aid of other soldiers in the convoy, the ammunition was rapidly shifted to another truck, and Huempfner was told to stay put until a wrecker could be sent. Huempfner spent the night alone in the small, dark town. He was armed only with a rifle and a .45 Colt.

As dawn was breaking, the stranded GI heard a sound in the distance, and presumed that it was the wrecker. However, the noise turned into an enormous roar, and he saw a frightening sight: a column of fourteen German panzers with perhaps fifty soldiers riding on them, were clanking down the street toward Huempfner. He quickly doused his truck with gasoline and set it afire.

"I really took off like a jackrabbit," Huempfner recalled much later. "I don't know why the Krauts didn't see me, because it was nearly light."

Huempfner dashed into the railroad station and Victor DeVeille, the stationmaster, quickly hid the "fugitive" in a tiny waiting room. "There were Germans all over the place," Huempfner remembered. "I could see them through a small window. I thought my goose was cooked."

Two German officers strode into the station and asked DeVeille if there were any Americans in town. Huempfner was only a few feet away and could hear the conversation. DeVeille assured them that there were none, and the Germans left the station.

Huempfner felt like a trapped animal. His plight was intensified when he recalled hearing reports that German SS troops were shooting prisoners. Concerned that eventually he would be discovered if he remained in the station, the American stole out the back door.

Despite his precarious situation, Huempfner felt it was his duty to create as much damage to the German force as possible. Spotting two parked half-tracks, he disabled them with hand grenades placed in the engines. Then he set fire to a barn, scurried away for fifty yards, and hid behind thick, snow-covered brush. Minutes later, he was delighted to see the results of his handiwork: some fifty SS soldiers, thinking that they were under attack, bolted out of the burning barn and began firing their weapons wildly at unseen "enemies."

When darkness fell over the Ardennes, the mercury dropped to almost zero. If he were going to survive, Huempfner knew he would have to get inside a warm house. Taking a chance that the Belgian civilians in one home would not betray him, he tapped gently on the front door and was ushered inside. His trust had not been misplaced.

The Belgian couple told the American that there was a Boche (German) tank, guarded by a lone sentry, parked by the town church. So Huempfner left the house, sneaked up on the iron monster—and was seen by the sentry. Thinking that the shadowy intruder was a comrade, the SS soldier called out a friendly, *"Hallo!"*

Huempfner responded by putting a bullet through the German's head, then the American hightailed it back to the Belgian couple's house. He felt convinced that a lone pistol shot in the night would not cause concern among the Germans. War is often a succession of weapons firing, even in an area where no battle is raging.

For four days and nights, Huempfner holed up in various houses amidst the Germans. On the fifth day, Christmas, a Belgian burst into his hideout and cried out excitedly: "The Boches are gone!" Minutes later, the American could hear the grating sound of tracked vehicles approaching. Were the Germans returning?

Soon Huempfner emerged from his house to greet the tanks of the U.S. 2nd Armored Division, which were inflicting an enormous disaster on German spearheads that had run out of fuel.

Huempfner's elation over being rescued was soon tempered. Because he didn't know the current password which usually changed daily, he was taken into custody by a military police lieutenant, who suspected that the paratrooper was actually a German in an American uniform. Otherwise, why would the suspect have spent five days and nights inside a town swarming with German troops?[8]

# Trapped in an Attic
# for Eight Days

"I'M GETTING TO HELL out of here—tonight!" Captain Carlos C. Alden Jr. whispered to a companion.

"You're crazy!" the other replied. "You'll either freeze to death, die of starvation, or be shot—maybe a little of each!"

"Well, I'll take my chances," said the thirty-three-year-old Alden, surgeon of the crack U.S. 509th Parachute Infantry Battalion. He had been captured a few days earlier while far in front of friendly lines tending to a pair of mortally wounded comrades during the Battle of the Bulge.

Doc Alden and several other American POWs had been marching all day and now were being held for the night in an abandoned building in eastern Belgium. It was January 28, 1945.

Escaping from German captivity was nothing new to Alden. While alone behind enemy lines in Italy the previous year, he had been apprehended on three occasions. Each time he had escaped and spent many harrowing days and nights playing hide-and-seek with German troops before returning to his unit.

Alden was not the typical army combat surgeon. After seeing two of his unarmed medics—wearing red crosses on their helmets—get shot down deliberately during the fighting in North Africa, he went into battle armed with a Tommy gun, two pistols, a trench knife, and a few grenades. He was an expert with these weapons, and had often used them while he was with the point of his battalion's attacks. Among his chestful of decorations was the Distinguished Service Cross, America's second highest award for valor.

Now, hoping that the German guards had settled in for the night, Alden stole down a long corridor to a door leading outside. Surely there would be a guard there, Alden reflected. But to his astonishment, the door was unlocked and there were no Germans in sight. No doubt the guards had sought shelter to escape the fifty degrees below zero windchill.

Stepping into a freezing blast of wind, Alden began walking rapidly. About a hundred yards from the building, he bumped into two Germans who had their machine pistols aimed at him. Without a word, he turned around and went back to the building with the two Germans right on his heels. Soon the surgeon fell into an exhausted sleep.

Prior to daylight, Alden and the other POWs were awakened by the shrill and demanding voices of German guards, "*Rous mitten! Rous mitten!*" (Out with you! Out with you!) Without breakfast, he and several others were hustled into a truck that headed eastward. Two miles along the way, the vehicle skidded off the icy road and became stuck in a high snowdrift.

"*Rous mitten!*" When the POWs leaped down, they were ordered to push and dislodge the truck. Alden saw that the two guards were standing in front of the vehicle, so he sauntered into the nearby field and waded through deep snow for two hundred yards.

There were strident shouts: "*Halten! Halten!*" A bullet angrily hissed past Alden's head. He shrugged and returned to the truck, which was now dislodged.

The POWs were driven to Prum, a small German town twelve miles east of the Belgian border. Alden and five others were put in a fourth-floor, twelve-foot-by-ten-foot room in a former hospital. The surgeon immediately disclosed that he was going to escape that night. The others tried to discourage him. "There're lots of Krauts at the doors downstairs," one said. "How do you think you're even going to get out of the building?"

"You'll see," Alden replied. He went to the opening of a dumbwaiter, peered down the chute, and saw that the basket was settled in the basement five levels below. Hauling up the rope, he cut it with a razor blade he had stolen from a German guard.

As silently as possible, the surgeon opened the window and glanced down to make certain there were no guards on the ground. Then he fastened the rope to a sturdy metal pipe and dangled the strand out the window. "Don't wait up for me!" Alden quipped to the others. He put a leg over the windowsill and began lowering himself. After he reached the ground, his companions hauled the rope back up.

Bracing himself against blasts of Arctic winds, the lightly-clad doctor set out cross-country in a direction he hoped would eventually take him to friendly forces. After struggling through the night for five hours, his clothes were saturated with icy water and his boots were filled with melting snow. A hundred yards ahead, he spotted the dim silhouette of concrete bunkers and knew that he was heading in the right direction. These fortifications were part of the Siegfried Line along the German border.

Near collapse, almost frozen to the bone, and weak from hunger, Alden knew he had to get inside a bunker where he could be shielded from the wind. But were there Germans in the fortifications? He slipped up to one bunker, paused to listen, heard nothing, and pushed open the steel door. Stumbling inside, he sprawled onto the concrete floor and fell fast asleep.

Soon after dawn, Alden awakened in misery, gripped by severe cramps and hunger pangs. Emerging from the bunker, he continued his arduous journey. Walking over a knoll, he came to an abrupt halt. A platoon of SS troops was sitting on the ground eating frozen field rations.

An SS officer carrying a Schmeisser machine pistol came up to Alden and inquired in flawless English: "And where do you think you're going?" There was no animosity in the question. Rather he sounded like a father who had caught his urchin with his hand in a cookie jar.

"Well, I guess I'm going with you," the American said.

*Highly decorated Captain Carlos C. Alden Jr., America's greatest escape artist. (Author's collection)*

"You certainly are!" the German responded.

Alden was taken by truck back to Prum, but it was found that the POWs had been moved to Gerolstein, fifteen miles deeper into Germany. So he and a few other GIs were driven there in a vehicle and locked in a large bombed-out factory building.

Since his capture two weeks earlier, Alden had lost much weight. His uniform hung in folds on his frame, and his belt had been taken up four notches. Yet twenty-four hours after arriving in Gerolstein, he hatched another escape plan. This time two POWs, Lieutenant Virgil McCall and Private Henry Aldrich, would go along.

That night, the three Americans stole out of the building, evaded guards, and walked westward along a snow-packed road heavy with German military traffic. The escapers did not scamper off the road and take cover when vehicles approached. It was dark and their rumpled uniforms looked like those worn by countless displaced civilians who were wandering throughout a disintegrating Third Reich.

Dawn was breaking when the nearly frozen Americans reached Prum. Although they might be detected by civilians who would notify German soldiers, the escapers decided to take the risk and enter the town. If they were to survive, they would have to get out of the icy wind blasts for a short rest.

Selecting a house that seemed to be unoccupied, the Americans cautiously sneaked inside and stopped to listen for an indication that someone was there. They heard nothing. "Let's go down in the basement," McCall suggested. "Americans are pounding the town with artillery and it will be safer down there."

"Safer, yes, and a hell of a lot colder," Alden responded. "Besides, we won't be able to see what's going on outside. Why don't we go upstairs?"

Aldrich and McCall agreed. Unknown to any of the three, it was one of the wisest decisions of their lives.

The Americans climbed the rickety stairs to the upper level, which was a small attic. There was laundry equipment at one end and two mattresses were on the floor.

Fatigued and sleepy, they flipped a coin to see who would stand guard first to warn of approaching danger. Aldrich "lost." An hour later, Alden and McCall were awakened by a tugging of their shoulders. "Krauts!" Aldrich whispered.

An army truck carrying Germans and towing a large howitzer halted beside the house. Moments later, the front door could be heard opening, and hobnailed boots striding on the wood floor echoed throughout the house. Trapped, the Americans could only remain silent.

Peeking through a crack in the attic floor, Alden counted eight Germans. The minutes ticked past, then the hours. The escapers felt that it was only a matter of time until one or more of the Feldgrau came upstairs to poke around.

Darkness arrived. Through the crack in the floor, the GIs could see that the Germans had wrapped themselves in blankets and fallen asleep. The fugitives held a whispered powwow. They planned to dash down the steps and strangle the slumbering Germans or bash them with pieces of furniture. The scheme was promptly rejected. The Americans were far too weak to conduct such a violent venture.

Five days after their arrival in the attic, the plight of the fugitives got even worse. Long-range American artillery began firing a newly-developed "secret weapon"—a shell with a proximity fuse—which triggered an air burst as the projectile neared a solid object, cascading jagged shrapnel downward. A few skybursts sent white-hot metal fragments through the roof of the escapers' hiding place. For forty-eight hours, shell explosions shook the house periodically. Miraculously, perhaps, the Americans were unscathed.

After seven days and nights trapped in the cold attic without food or water, the Americans were suffering constant hunger cramps and their throats were parched, lips cracked and bleeding, and bodies aching. Henry Aldrich said he was going to make a run for it that night.

"You won't get a hundred yards," Alden advised. McCall nodded in agreement.

"I might get caught, but at least I'll get something to eat," Aldrich replied.

Waiting until the Germans below were asleep, Aldrich opened a small window, squeezed through, and dropped softly to the ground. Minutes later, the two escapers in the attic heard German shouts from down the street. Aldrich had been caught.

With the arrival of dawn, heavy German traffic began moving past the house, retreating farther into the Third Reich. Glancing out a window, McCall and Alden saw long columns of bedraggled infantrymen also trudging eastward. The procession continued through the day and into the night. But the eight German artillerymen remained on the first floor of the house.

Night was starting to draw its veil over the region when Alden and McCall heard the stairs creaking. Obviously, a German was coming to the attic. Discovery and possible execution were imminent. GI hearts beat faster. Moments later, a voice from below called out: *"Kom hier, Fritz, wir gehen sofort!"* (Come back, Fritz, we're pulling out!)

There was the sound of boots going down the stairway. The Americans let out silent sighs of relief.

At dawn, German soldiers were no longer in Prum. "Let's get the hell out of here!" Alden said. Stealing down the stairs, he and McCall went out the front door and walked westward.

A few miles after leaving Prum, the two men saw a column of soldiers in snow capes coming toward them. Some units on both sides wore white camouflage, so the escapers could not discern if they were Germans or Americans.

"We've got to get undercover," Alden said. Moving as rapidly as their weakened legs could carry them, they scrambled into an unoccupied farmhouse.

Peeking outside, Alden and McCall saw a squad of riflemen less than a hundred yards away, heading for the house. Clearly, the fugitives had been spotted. Minutes later, the soldiers were at the front door.

"Come out, you Kraut bastards!" bellowed a voice with a southern drawl. "We know you're in there!"

Alden and McCall smiled broadly. "That's the most beautiful GI cursing I've ever heard!" the surgeon exclaimed.[9]

# Love and War at a German Post Office

ADOLF HITLER'S THIRD REICH was crumbling. Allied armies were driving toward Berlin on three sides of the beleaguered nation. Yet, with Teutonic efficiency, the civilian postal service continued to operate. At the post office in Landshut, northeast of bomb-battered Munich (the birthplace of Nazism), a beautiful young German woman, Paula Vorholzer, had six American POWs working under her direction in early 1945.

One of the GIs was Bill Cottrill, who had been captured when his 29th Infantry Division outfit had been overrun in a heavy German attack near Aachen, Germany, the previous October. Soon after he was assigned to Land-shut, loading and unloading boxcars of mail, the twenty-one-year-old Cottrill and his supervisor, Paula, became attracted to one another.

They began stealing kisses in dark rooms and behind large mail crates. She sneaked extra food to him. Food in Germany was scarce, but she divided her portion with the American. Against regulations, the postal worker also secretly permitted the emaciated Cottrill and the other POWs a chance to rest numerous times during the fourteen-hour workdays.

The intimate relationship was fraught with peril. Had it been discovered by German authorities, both Bill and Paula might have been hurled into bru-tal concentration camps, or even executed. U.S. forces were closing in on the Landshut region. Rumors were rife that the Germans were going to murder all POWs as a final act of vengeance.

April 29, 1945, would be the couple's last night together. After darkness, with the aid of another German post office employee, Paula helped Cottrill and forty-seven other American prisoners to escape. She led them to a remote swamp where the POWs could hide until friendly troops arrived.

Paula, in tears, gave Bill a photograph of herself and a gold chain from around her neck. With one long final kiss, she vanished into the night.

Back home after the war, Cottrill planned to return to Germany to find Paula. But the Reich was in chaos, millions of homeless people were wander-ing around, and his chances of locating her seemed almost impossible. More-over, the cost would be expensive, and, like other GI veterans, he had little money.

The years rolled past, and periodically Bill tried to reach the woman who had saved his life, using the mail and other means. There was a good reason for his failure. In 1955, he learned, gorgeous Paula had taken her own life.[10]

# MacArthur "Visits"
# a Japanese CP

As a dark sky gave way to the first faint tinges of dawn, imposing Mount Santo Tomás, at 7,407 feet, seemed to frown on the American intruders squat-ting in Lingayen Gulf on the main island of Luzon in the Philippines. In the haze were nearly one thousand U.S. ships carrying 280,000 of General Dou-glas MacArthur's soldiers—the most powerful armada yet assembled in the Pacific. It was S-Day (Invasion Day), January 9, 1945.

*General Douglas MacArthur, leading two aides in a combat area, was on a similar trek when he came upon a Japanese command post. (U.S. Army)*

At 7:00 A.M. an enormous roar swept across the gulf and reverberated off the towering green mountains inland. Navy warships were pounding the invasion beaches. A half hour later, assault troops, burdened with weapons and heavy combat gear, climbed over the railings of their transports, made the hazardous descent down slippery rope ladders, and dropped into bobbing landing craft. Fifteen minutes later, the invaders charged ashore.

Except for a handful of Japanese stragglers who fired rifle shots before fleeing into the thick jungle, there was no opposition at the beaches. Just as MacArthur had hoped, the Japanese had been taken by total surprise.

With no obstacles except the terrain—a combination of sand and marsh—the invaders struck southward for the key objectives of the war in the Pacific: Manila and its rock fortress of Corregidor, 125 miles away.

Typically, MacArthur had waded ashore almost on the heels of the assault troops. He rapidly located German-born Lieutenant General Walter Krueger, the Sixth Army commander, and urged him to "get to Manila as fast as you can."

On the road to Manila, the Japanese were fighting a delaying action campaign. They would resist bitterly, then fall back, then fight again tenaciously. All the while, MacArthur, who in a few days would be observing his sixty-fifth birthday, was dashing about the battlefields like a man possessed. His aides had become deeply concerned about "the boss being constantly in or near the frontlines, or ahead of them."

One morning, MacArthur and his physician, Dr. Roger O. Egeberg, were in the general's jeep bearing a five-star pennant and looking for the scene of the fighting about fifty miles north of Manila. They got lost. Continuing forward on foot, the pair came upon a GI crouched behind a tree. "Better get down!" the soldier called out. "They're Japs up ahead!"

"Thank you, Corporal," MacArthur replied, continuing to stroll forward with a nervous Egeberg following reluctantly. The general found a strand of communications wire in a thicket and said, "Let's follow this. It'll take us to our nearest CP [command post]."

The two men trudged forward beside the wire. Suddenly, Egeberg was stricken by panic: This was a thinner wire than the American kind—this was *Japanese* wire and they were behind enemy lines and heading for a Japanese CP.

Struggling to keep his voice calm, without much success, Egeberg pointed out his discovery. However, MacArthur shrugged and continued to walk forward. Minutes later, the pair emerged from a thicket. Off to the left, they saw what apparently was a Japanese CP. It was guarded by three manned machine guns.

One of the Japanese gunners spotted the two Americans and shouted something at them. "I guess we had better go back," MacArthur said evenly. Egeberg did not protest. The two men melted into the jungle and returned a half hour later to the general's parked jeep.

As they drove away, Egeberg could still feel his heart pounding from the jaunt behind Japanese lines. MacArthur never brought up the adventure again. Presumably the general had felt that this was just another day at the office.[11]

# A Patrol's "Pigeon Air Force"

AMERICAN, BRITISH, CANADIAN, AND FRENCH armies were aligned on a 450-mile front along the German border, stretching from Holland in the north to Switzerland. Allied foot soldiers were battling two ferocious enemies: the cold, nasty weather and the German Feldgrau. It was early February 1945.

Preparations were underway for the Allies to launch an all-out offensive that would reach the Rhine River, the final barricade to invasion of the Reich heartland. No hostile force had crossed the Rhine in more than 130 years.

General Courtney H. Hodges's U.S. First Army was confronted by the normally serene Roer River, which flows parallel to the Rhine thirty-five miles to the east. Hodges had the crucial task of capturing the monstrous Schwammenauel Dam, a structure as high as a twenty-five-story building and eight hundred feet long.

Allied leaders regarded the Schwammenauel as a serious impediment to reaching the Rhine. If the Germans blasted the dam, a steady stream of water would charge into the Roer, turning that mild little river into a swollen, raging torrent.

As feared, German engineers did blow a huge hole in the dam's tough hide. Until the 22 billion gallons of pent-up water would finish emptying in two weeks, the First Army could not force an assault crossing. The planned drive to the Rhine had to be put on hold.

During the flood-caused stalemate, the First Army sent patrols to the other side of the now broad Roer almost nightly to seek intelligence. Late on the bitterly cold night of February 13, Sergeant William M. McIlwain and six comrades of the U.S. 104th "Timberwolves" Infantry Division negotiated the treacherous Roer, climbed onto the far bank, and began creeping and slithering through the mud.

McIlwain had volunteered for this "sleeper patrol," meaning it would infiltrate German positions, prowl around deep behind German lines, hole up at dawn, then slip back across the Roer on the following night. The mission was to locate German gun emplacements, barbed-wire entanglements, minefields, and headquarters.

An unusual feature of the patrol was that the Timberwolves brought with them a "pigeon air force." Although great strides had been made in technology during the war years, these two birds would wing back across the Roer with the intelligence the patrol collected.

As the GIs trudged onward in the blackness, always alert for signs of danger, they were thoroughly miserable—soaked to the skin, shivering from the cold, nearly exhausted from the physical and mental strain, and always candidates for sudden death. "I must be crazy to have volunteered for this job!" McIlwain reflected.

Suddenly, Platoon Sergeant Walter Flores, the patrol leader, thrust his hand into the air. The column halted. McIlwain felt his heart pounding furiously. Then Flores motioned his men to join him and pointed downward. By the muted rays of the moon, McIlwain and the others looked at a German soldier sleeping soundly in a muddy foxhole.

Not a word was spoken. The Americans knew their business. One man whipped out his razor-sharp trench knife, knelt beside the German and held the blade to his throat. This German would either live or die depending upon whether he awakened and tried to spread an alarm. The other GIs stole silently away, and soon the man holding the knife followed. The slumbering Feldgrau snored away, unharmed.

McIlwain and the others stole deeper into German territory. Again the column was brought to an abrupt halt. Sergeant Flores had spotted antipersonnel mines. The patrol gave the field a wide berth, and from that point on, the Americans lived in dread of the thought that each step might activate a mine and blow off a foot or leg. It was a terrifying reflection: if anything went

*U.S. soldiers cross the Roer River after waters receded. The Timberwolves patrol and its "pigeon air force" earlier had operated behind German lines on the far shore. (U.S. Army)*

wrong, there was nothing comrades could do to help, and the victim would suffer excruciating agony until he bled to death.

Cautiously moving in single file, McIlwain and the others neared a house that had been picked out in aerial photos as the patrol's observation post. The column froze. A shaft of light was seeping out of one window, and from inside came loud German voices raised in a favorite ballad of the Wehrmacht, "Lili Marlene." It was obvious that a raucous drinking bout was going full blast.

"I can't attend the party," a GI whispered. "I left my tuxedo back across the Roer!"

The Americans climbed into large bomb craters near the house to watch and to listen. The excavations were partially filled with water, and the men lay freezing in the icy wetness, damning themselves for going on the patrol.

Suddenly, a door opened a crack and out staggered a German soldier without a helmet or overcoat. He stumbled almost to where two Americans were huddled in a dark hole, halted, and proceeded to urinate. The GIs held their breaths. If discovered by the drunken German, he would shout a warning to his comrades. However, the Feldgrau finished his ritual and wobbled back inside.

Eventually, dawn arrived, but instead of a warming sun, the shivering Americans were greeted by a murky sky, heavy winds, and rain. One of the men reached into his gas-mask cover and pulled out one of the two pigeons he had been carrying. A terse message was attached to its leg and the bird was released. It headed deeper into German territory, then got its bearings, banked, and flew off toward its roost on the American side of the Roer. McIlwain and the others watched breathlessly until the pigeon was out of sight.

The Americans peered over the rims of the bomb craters and saw German soldiers starting to move about on all sides. Suddenly, a new peril surfaced: "friendly" shells from across the Roer began exploding around the patrol's holes, exposing them to the fire that was to have protected them in the designated house.

Throughout the day, the GIs observed German activities and spotted several artillery and machine-gun positions. Despite the tenseness of the situation, McIlwain realized that he was enjoying spying on the unsuspecting Feldgrau from right in the midst of their positions. But he and the others greeted the arrival of dusk with relief.

It had also been a productive mission. The patrol had counted Germans, spotted a 120-millimeter gun, sketched trench networks, and marked the large strip of Roer shoreline saturated with mines into which they had nearly stumbled. This information was sent back over the Roer by the second member of the "pigeon air force"—a communications technique reminiscent of wars of yore. But there was good reason for the feathered messengers: if the patrol did not make it back, at least its intelligence findings would get there.

That night, the Timberwolves patrol had nearly reached the Roer on the return trip. Just as the men were entering the water, a German machine gun opened fire, and bullets hissed past them. However, they reached the west bank unscathed. All agreed that it had been the longest twenty-four hours of their lives.

When the Schwammenauel had nearly finished emptying its water, General Hodges set the assault crossing of the Roer for February 23. Two days before the attack, Captain William Stelling, a Timberwolf intelligence officer, was studying reports in the damp, frigid basement of a shell-torn house in the village of Merken, less than a mile from the Roer.

Stelling had grown highly alarmed, a not unfamiliar state of mind among those engaged in trying to divine an enemy's capabilities and intentions. Fragments of information seemed to indicate that the Germans had sneaked several more units into positions along the far riverbank. There was no time to mount a patrol to cross the Roer. But that night, a lone German soldier provided a ray of hope for Stelling. The Feldgrau negotiated the river and surrendered to a Timberwolf machine-gun post. He was rushed to Captain Stelling.

Shivering from the freezing water that had saturated his uniform and poured inside his hobnail boots, the Feldgrau, a man about thirty years of age, tried to be cooperative. He declared he had deserted because he was fed up with Adolf Hitler, fed up with the Nazis, and fed up with the war. Aware that a man-made tornado of steel and explosives was about to strike the Germans along the Roer, he exclaimed that he had no desire to gain the honor of being killed for the führer in a lost cause. "Hitler *kaputt!*" he cried out.

When Stelling asked for specific information about the identity of German units now facing the 104th Division, the prisoner pleaded that he had rushed toward the river so rapidly that he had not had time to talk with any Germans there. Desperate for up-to-the-minute information and sensing that the Feldgrau was telling the truth, Stelling was struck by an innovative scheme. He would send the German back over the Roer that night and have him ask each German he encountered the designation of his unit. Without hesitation, the POW agreed.

Yet Stelling was nagged by doubt. Was this German sincere, or had he been sent to gather intelligence on American plans for assaulting the Roer? Maybe the entire scenario had been hatched by clever German intelligence officers as an elaborate *ruse de guerre* (war trick).

"If you're lying and double-cross us, you're a goddamned dead Kraut!" the German was told, illogically, because he would be back with his comrades on the far side of the Roer.

Just past midnight, Lieutenant Burleigh Sheppard and six of his engineers escorted the German to the water's edge and ferried him to the other side at a place the POW said was unmanned. After the Feldgrau obtained the intelligence, he was to make his own way back over the Roer to the American side.

Captain Stelling waited anxiously for word that his converted spy had returned. He kept glancing at his watch . . . 3:00 A.M. . . . 3:30 . . . 4:00 . . . 4:30 . . . still no sign of the German. Stelling's field telephone suddenly jangled impatiently, and as he picked up the instrument and listened to the voice on the other end a broad smile spread across his face. It was an outpost along the Roer bank. The spy had just climbed out of the river after swimming back.

Stelling soon learned that the information the German had obtained was far in excess of what he had hoped for. The enemy soldier had checked in with several German outposts along the Roer and confirmed that a new division had recently moved into position. The information would prove to be precisely accurate.[12]

# A German Boy-Soldier
## Saves Two GIs

COLONEL RUPERT D. GRAVES, leader of the U.S. 517th Parachute Regimental Combat Team, was seated at a desk in an old house in Bergstein, Germany. Known to his men as the Gray Eagle, he was poring over orders for a nightmare mission his outfit had just received. It was February 5, 1945.

*Adolph Hitler pats the cheek of one of his new soldiers, a thirteen-year-old boy. Another youngster that same age saved the lives of two Americans in bloody Huertgen Forest. (National Archives)*

Graves's paratroopers were to jump off from Bergstein at midnight, fight their way through the treacherous and heavily defended Huertgen Forest, cross the swift-flowing Kall River in a deep ravine, scramble up the far side, and seize the high ground a mile and a half from the line of departure (LOD).

Bloody Huertgen, the forest was called. Since September of the previous year, four different U.S. divisions had suffered a total of 21,900 casualties while trying to penetrate Huertgen. Sprawled among the trees now were the corpses of hundreds of American soldiers, grotesque and rigid, just emerging from the deep snow that had preserved them all winter.

Located southwest of Cologne, bloody Huertgen was a seemingly impenetrable mass, honeycombed with minefields, barbed-wire barricades, thick-walled pillboxes, and scores of machine guns with interlocking fields of fire.

Promptly at the stroke of midnight, two battalions of Colonel Graves's men trudged out of Bergstein eastward in the freezing blackness. Fluorescent stripes were stuck to the back of each man's helmet; a trooper in the rear was to follow the white blob three feet to his front.

For the first six hundred yards, it was deathly still. Only the crunching of boots in the icy snow. Suddenly, a cacophony of noise erupted as the Germans raked the Americans with machine-gun fire and pounded them with artillery and mortars. The troopers, their faces ghostly in the glare of brilliant German flares, were cut down in large numbers.

Throughout the night, the Americans tried to inch forward. Screams split the blackness as men were blown to pieces by "Bouncing Bettys," especially fiendish mines that hopped upward before exploding at face level.

Caught in the hailstorm of fire, a company commander, Captain George Giuchici, and his men, crawling and slithering, tried to circle around behind the German force. One of them, Myrle Traver, a Browning automatic rifleman, recalled later: "Machine guns and flares were keeping me scared to death. But somehow we got through the minefield and began moving up and down hilly trails. After awhile, I looked back—no one was with me."

At dawn, Traver, disoriented in the confusion of the night, started cautiously walking. Soon artillery shells exploded around him—"friendly" fire. Now he knew that he was far behind German lines.

Eventually, Traver came across Captain Giuchici, who was also alone and lost. "Follow me!" the officer said. The two men began jogging back toward American lines—or so they thought. Actually, they were going even deeper into German territory.

Soon they bumped into a pint-sized German soldier, whom they judged to be about thirteen years of age. The GIs were aware that Adolf Hitler had been scraping the bottom of his manpower barrel in recent months, drafting boys and elderly men into the army. Giuchici and Traver disarmed the German and he started to cry. His body was shaking and he begged his captors not to kill him.

"Let's take the boy with us," Giuchici said.

At dusk, the captain made a fateful decision. Instead of trying to sneak back through German lines, they would get into a large bomb crater and wait for their regiment to catch up with them. The two men had no way of knowing that American casualties had been horrendous, causing the attack to be cancelled.

That bitterly cold night, Giuchici, Traver, and the German boy huddled miserably in the crater. Suddenly they could hear the crunch of footsteps in the snow. Two Germans walked up to the edge of the crater and stood talking for several minutes. Giuchici understood the German language sufficiently to grasp the topic: their officers were idiots.

The fact that the newcomers were openly smoking cigarettes in the darkness confirmed what the Americans already suspected: there were no friendly troops for great distances, or else the Germans would not be risking their lives from the glow of the lighted cigarettes.

Perhaps three minutes after the two Germans paused for a smoke, Giuchici reached up and touched one of their boots—"just for the hell of it." With no sign that their comrades in the 517th Parachute Infantry were approaching, the Americans and their captive remained in the crater all day and into the second night. At about 2:00 A.M., Giuchici emerged from fitful slumber and shook Traver awake. "The boy's gone!" the captain whispered.

Just after dawn, five German soldiers stole up to the crater, leveled their rifles at the Americans, and said they were going to kill the *Schweinhund* (bastards). Before they could pump bullets into the pair, the German boy who had been with the Americans, suddenly appeared.

"They didn't kill me when they could have," the kid soldier pleaded. "So you shouldn't kill them!"

For long moments, there was tense silence. Then the weapons were lowered and the five Germans and the boy walked off, disappearing into the forest.[13]

# A Scheme to Trigger an Uprising

JANE FOSTER, A CAREFREE SPIRIT, an unreconstructed rebel, was one of the handful of women assigned to the U.S. Office of Strategic Services (OSS) posted at Ceylon, a large island in the Indian Ocean, south and east of India. At Kandy, an inland town in southern Ceylon, British Admiral Louis Mountbatten, supreme commander of the South East Asia Command (SEAC), had his headquarters.

It was April 1944, when Foster and a few other OSS females arrived at Kandy to begin work in a group of palm-thatched huts surrounded by barbed wire.

Although technically under Mountbatten's command, the OSS detachment managed to maintain its status as a U.S. agency. Orchestrated by the OSS at Kandy, behind-the-lines operations were conducted throughout a wide swathe of the region—Sumatra, Dutch East Indies, Siam, Burma, Malaysia, and French Indochina (later Vietnam).

Foster belonged to the Morale Operations (MO) of the Kandy-based OSS contingent. MO consisted mainly of skilled professionals in the mass communications field—journalists, Hollywood scriptwriters, advertising and public relations experts, and authors. They cranked out "black"—or covert—propaganda and hatched devious schemes to undermine enemy morale and encourage natives behind Japanese lines to resist and torment their country's military occupiers.

Jane Foster had been born into a wealthy San Francisco family. After graduating from an exclusive college, she traveled extensively in Europe, where she was appalled by the iron clamps Adolf Hitler had on Germany and Benito Mussolini had on Italy.

After returning to the United States, Jane met and married a Dutch bureaucrat who took her to Java for two years. Then she returned to San Francisco and obtained a divorce. In mid-1939, she joined the Communist Party.

A short time before a woefully unprepared United States was bombed into global war at Pearl Harbor on December 7, 1941, Jane married a Russian,

George Zlatovski, whom she had met in New York City, where they were both active in promoting Communist causes.

When her husband entered the U.S. Army and was sent overseas, Foster, a talented writer and artist, was recruited by the OSS, which was aware of her Communist background. That political affiliation was subtly ignored by Major General William J. "Wild Bill" Donovan, holder of the Congressional Medal of Honor from World War I and, much later, founder and head of the cloak-and-dagger agency.

Although in his sixties, Wild Bill hopped around the globe regularly to visit his outposts. In early 1945, he popped up in the Ceylon hut occupied by MO people. He noticed that Foster and two native women were busily engaged in some activity at a large table. Edging closer, Donovan, a rich Wall Street lawyer who thought he had seen everything there was to see, was astonished to note that the women were stuffing messages into rubber condoms.

Watching the operation, the general saw the women blow air into the condoms, tie knots, and throw each one into a large pile.

When Foster saw the Big Boss looking on with a bemused yet puzzled look on his face, she said, "These are messages being smuggled to Indonesians urging them to launch an uprising against the Japanese. Our agents release hundreds of them from airplanes along the coastline."

Donovan asked no more questions and conducted a rapid strategic withdrawal.

Earlier, after Jane had hatched the "airborne scheme," she had great difficulty in obtaining the condoms. When she called at the OSS physician's office, he came out for what he believed to be a patient visit. A quizzical look spread across his face when Foster said she needed some condoms. Because the operation was secret, she did not disclose the reason. He thought they were for her personal use.

When the doctor asked how many she wanted, he again received a jolt. "About five hundred," she replied. He dropped his stethoscope and stared at her in disbelief.[14]


# Uninvited "Guests" on Corregidor

A BRIGHT SUN was ascending into the heavens over the Philippines on the morning of March 4, 1945, as five-star General of the Army Douglas MacArthur climbed into an eighty-foot PT boat in Manila. It cast off and headed for Corregidor, a rock fortress three and a half miles long and one and a half miles across that was perched in Manila Bay.

Three years earlier, MacArthur and a woefully weak United States had suffered a bloody and humiliating defeat at the hands of the Japanese Army, which captured Corregidor and subjected its defenders to a sixty-mile march to a POW camp that resulted in agonizing deaths to hundreds of American soldiers, marines, and navy men.

Before Corregidor had fallen, President Franklin D. Roosevelt ordered MacArthur—three times—to escape to Australia, sixteen hundred miles to the south, to build an army to retake the Philippines.

On his arrival Down Under, MacArthur had solemnly pledged, "I shall return!" Corregidor, he said, was a Holy Grail. "It symbolizes within itself that priceless, deathless thing, the honor of a nation," the general declared. "Until we lift our flag from its dust, we stand unredeemed before mankind."

Eventually, MacArthur did "return," and in mid-February 1945, the 503rd Parachute Infantry Regiment bailed out onto Corregidor's 500-foot high Topside, and a battalion of the U.S. 24th Infantry Division fought its way ashore at Bottomside, the low area. Intelligence had stated that 600 Japanese were on the Rock.

Typically, the defenders fought to the death. When organized resistance ended, 4,506 Japanese corpses were counted, but many hundreds more had been sealed in the maze of caves when they refused to emerge.

Now, General MacArthur and a galaxy of American brass stepped ashore from their PT boat on Bottomside. It was the single most momentous episode of MacArthur's brilliant career—a triumphant return to the Holy Grail.

Masking the deep emotions that no doubt engulfed him, MacArthur got into a waiting jeep and, with the other brass trailing, his cavalcade began a tour of The Rock. First, he went to Malinta Tunnel, his headquarters during the agony of three years ago. Colonel George M. Jones, the thirty-three-year-old leader of the U.S. forces that had recaptured Corregidor, accompanied MacArthur on the tour.

Much later, Colonel Jones recalled: "This was an anxious period for me. I could visualize some die-hard Japanese marine popping up in his spider hole [foxhole] and shooting General MacArthur."

When the MacArthur parade of jeeps reached Topside, Colonel Jones took his place in front of his battle-weary but proud honor guard in their soiled and torn uniforms. A few had blood-stained bandages.

MacArthur strode briskly to a point facing Jones, who saluted smartly and said, "Sir, I present you Fortress Corregidor!"

Speaking under a brilliant blue sky, MacArthur declared that Rock Force had carried out "one of the boldest feats in military history." The supreme commander said: "I see the old flag pole still stands. Have your troops hoist the colors to the peak, and let no enemy ever haul them down."

As hundreds of American eyes—many welled with tears—watched Old Glory waving in the breeze, proud were hearts filled with grief over the heavy price to repurchase Corregidor: 223 men killed, 1,107 wounded or injured— nearly one-third of the entire Rock Force.

On New Year's Day 1946, ten months after MacArthur had returned to Corregidor, eighteen bedraggled Japanese soldiers, leaving their weapons and ammunition behind, emerged from a cave and surrendered to an amazed GI of a U.S. Graves Registration Company posted on The Rock. Through an interpreter, one Japanese explained that he had left his group's hiding place in search of water the previous night and found a Tokyo newspaper that said Emperor Hirohito had surrendered four months earlier.

These Japanese "guests" had, in essence, been lurking behind American lines and could have killed The Rock's handful of caretakers had they chosen to do so.[15]

# Eavesdropping behind Japanese Positions

ON A DARK NIGHT, Lieutenant Edward McLogan, a platoon leader in the elite American outfit of volunteers known as Merrill's Marauders, was concerned about shouts from a Japanese force to his front in mountainous northern Burma. It seemed clear that the enemy unit was about to launch an assault against his dug-in platoon.

McLogan called for Sergeant Roy A. Matsumoto, a Nisei (second generation Japanese-American), who was serving as a frontline interpreter. "What're they jabbering about out there?" the lieutenant asked. Matsumoto replied that he would get closer and eavesdrop. It was early March 1945.

A few weeks earlier in another locale, Matsumoto had been with a battalion of Merrill's Marauders when he found and tapped into a Japanese telephone line connecting the front and rear echelon. The Japanese talked freely, no doubt secure in the knowledge that Americans could not understand their language.

Matsumoto intercepted one conversation between a frustrated and upset Japanese sergeant who gave his position away. He told the rear echelon that he had only three men with rifles to protect a large ammunition dump and that he feared the Americans were about to attack. He pleaded for "help and advice."

The Japanese sergeant's plight—and location—were relayed to the Marauder's leader, Brigadier General Frank D. Merrill. An accommodating fellow, he agreed to provide "help and advice" to the ammunition dump. It was delivered by a flight of fighter-bombers that blew up the hidden cache of explosives.

Now, with Lieutenant McLogan's platoon, Matsumoto slithered and crawled forward in the blackness until he was behind Japanese positions. There he lay stone-still for nearly an hour and listened to conversations.

Matsumoto returned from the high-risk mission and reported that the Japanese planned an attack after dawn on a forward slope of a hill held by McLogan's platoon. The platoon leader pulled his men back to the top of the elevation where they could bring down fire on the attackers.

At daybreak, shouts of *Banzai!* split the air as a contingent of Japanese broke out of a woods and charged up the slope, hurling hand grenades at the foxholes McLogan's men had abandoned two hours earlier. Then they stormed the position with bayonets fixed, firing wildly into the empty foxholes.

The fact that the Americans were not where they were supposed to be did not delay the assault for long. Led by a sword-waving officer, the Japanese rushed on up the hill.

McLogan and his men held their fire until the Japanese were within twenty yards of the top. Then the Marauders loosed withering bursts from rifles and machine guns that cut down the attackers like a huge scythe hacking off cornstalks.

Perhaps fifty bodies were sprawled in front of the Americans. But minutes later, a second wave of attackers bolted up the hill. Perhaps seeing the corpses of so many comrades, the Japanese flopped to the ground. Then Roy Matsumoto shouted in Japanese from the crest of the hill, *"Charge! Charge!"* Not knowing from where the command had come and ever obedient to orders, men of the second wave scrambled to their feet and dashed forward—right into the muzzles of spitting machine guns and rifles.

Now an eerie quiet descended upon the bloody elevation. Thanks to the quick-thinking Nisei, the Japanese force had been wiped out without the loss of a single Marauder.[16]

# Eisenhower's Spy in Berlin

IN HIS APARTMENT in suburban Berlin, forty-nine-year-old Carl Johann Wiberg, a Swede who had been a businessman in the Reich capital for nearly thirty years, was clandestinely listening to a newscast over BBC radio in London. Powerful U.S., British, and French armies under General Dwight D. Eisenhower were over the Rhine River, four hundred miles west of Berlin, and had launched an end-the-war offensive. It was late March 1945.

Although Wiberg was a foreigner, he was well liked by his neighbors, who regarded him as a "good Berliner" first and a Swede second. Although Allied bombers had been pounding Berlin for more than four years, Wiberg remained, unlike other foreigners, in the city.

Friends especially admired Wiberg because he never complained though he had lost nearly everything. His wife had died in 1939, his two small factories had been destroyed by bombs, and he was almost broke.

There was good reason for the Swede to stay in Berlin and risk death almost every night: he was a spy, an agent of the U.S. Office of Strategic Services (OSS). His mission was monumental: locating Adolf Hitler so that the Allies could arrest him when they reached Berlin, probably in mid-April, about three weeks away.

On the same day that Wiberg had learned that the Western Allies were heading toward Berlin, he paid a call at his favorite bar, Harry Rosse's on Nestorstrasse. It was one of the few still doing business in the Swede's region. As any competent spy knows, much valuable information can be obtained by eavesdropping on the conversations of others. And Rosse's was no exception. Its clientele included German military officers, Nazi big shots, a few business executives, and secretive men Wiberg concluded were Gestapo agents.

The atmosphere was convivial and schnapps and wine loosened tongues. Wiberg seemed to be a curious type, and he engaged in friendly conversation with patrons to inquire about damage done by the previous night's bombing raid, how the *Herrenvolk* (people) were holding up against the almost constant air attacks—and especially he sought clues concerning the whereabouts of Adolf Hitler.

"Who knows?" a *Heer* (army) major replied after downing a large shot of booze. "That's the most closely kept secret of the war!" Wiberg had already reached the same conclusion.

That night, the Swede covertly contacted high-ranking friends in the *Heer* and the Luftwaffe, but they knew nothing either. Only a handful of the führer's confidants knew that he, his mistress, his German shepherd Blondi, and an entourage of aides were holed up in the bombproof bunker below the Reichskanzlei (German chancellery).

Wiberg's apartment had miraculously escaped the heavy bombings, at least up until now. But he shuddered to think of the consequences if it were hit. He would immediately be exposed as a master spy. Over the years, his lodgings had turned into an espionage warehouse. Hidden in rooms were a large amount of German currency (sent by the OSS), and a wide variety of drugs and poisons. In his cellar and adjoining garage was a small arsenal of hand weapons and ammunition.

Wiberg was especially nervous about a suitcase packed with highly volatile explosives. If a bomb were to hit nearby, the apartment—and Wiberg—would be blown sky-high. He settled that gnawing concern by stashing the suitcase in an innovative hiding place: a large safety deposit box in the vault of the Nazi-controlled Deutsche Bank.

The Swede's thoughts were mixed about the possibility that a bomb might hit the bank's vault. No doubt the ensuing explosion would be spectacular, but he would regret the deaths of many ordinary German workers.

Less than three weeks after the Western Allies jumped off from the Rhine, a courier arrived from Sweden and brought shocking news to Wiberg: don't expect the Americans and British.

For months, Wiberg had been sustained in daily risking his life by the thought that the Western Allies would eventually capture Berlin. He had already made extensive plans for distributing his large cache of weapons and ammunition to his agents in the capital to be put to use when the British and Americans were nearing the city.

Wiberg had no way of knowing the reasoning of General Dwight D. Eisenhower and his top commanders in suddenly changing the plan to seize Berlin—and, hopefully, collaring Adolf Hitler and the key figures in his Nazi regime. At the time Berlin had been targeted as the ultimate objective over a year earlier, no Allied general could have foreseen that the Soviet army in the East would have advanced within forty miles of Hitler's bunker in downtown Berlin and that the Western Allies would still be more than two hundred miles to the west.

In light of this unexpected development, Eisenhower now had doubts about taking Berlin and sought the views of his closest confidant, U.S. General Omar N. Bradley. "I think it will cost us one hundred thousand casualties to capture Berlin," Bradley declared. "A pretty stiff price for a prestige objective." He pointed out that President Franklin D. Roosevelt and Prime Minister Winston S. Churchill had already conceded the eastern region of Germany to the Soviets.

Eisenhower's viewpoint also was greatly influenced by a haunting report from a mystery source in Berlin: Hitler and other Nazi bigwigs would abandon Berlin in the next two weeks and flee to a National Redoubt in the towering Bavarian Alps of southern Germany, where a quarter of a million die-hard SS troops would barricade themselves and prolong the war for months—or years.

Only much later would the Allies learn that the National Redoubt had been a colossal hoax, and that it succeeded in diverting the Western Allies from Berlin. The "mystery source" that had spread this widely believed report was Josef Goebbels, the Nazi propaganda genius.

In the days ahead, Carl Wiberg tuned to BBC on his secret radio and his spirits plunged when it became apparent that some Allied spearheads had been sent to capture the nonexistent National Redoubt and other U.S. and British forces had halted at the Elbe River, some ninety miles from Berlin, to await the arrival of the Soviet army after it had captured the German capital, now largely a colossal pile of rubble.

"We have been abandoned," Wiberg sadly told one of his undercover agents. "We have risked everything—for nothing!"[17]

# Father Sam and
# His Hidden Radio

EARLY IN MARCH 1945, an American colonel, James Alger, was a new arrival at Stalag II-A, northeast of Berlin. He was an exceptionally clever man, and within a few days, he had sized up the "goons" (as the POWs called all German guards) and contacted the candidate to be bribed.

Colonel Alger's psychoanalysis proved to be accurate. Through the guard, a radio was smuggled in piece by piece. Now the great problem was finding a suitable place to conceal the radio, because the Gestapo made frequent and thorough inspections of the barracks.

Alger, who had been captured only recently, knew that BBC in London was broadcasting instructions to Allied prisoners and, with the war in Europe drawing to a close, it was essential to comply with these orders.

Soon a hiding place for the illegal radio dawned on Alger. Because Captain Francis L. Sampson, a Catholic chaplain, would be deeply involved, he checked with him. Sampson readily agreed, and even took an impish delight in being a participant in the scheme.

Alger got in touch with a POW who had skills as a carpenter and had him build a small pulpit for the chapel where Sampson had been conducting Mass. The POW did a masterful job in fixing a little trapdoor near the top of the pulpit, and covered it entirely with a piece of blanket material. Then he inserted into a hole a long spike that kept the trapdoor shut. By pulling out the nail, the door would fly open, and the radio could be put to good use by the POWs.

Captain Sampson, who had been awarded the Distinguished Service Cross for valor in Normandy, had been captured at Bastogne, Belgium, where his 101st Airborne Division had been surrounded during the Battle of the Bulge when he had gone far in front of friendly lines searching for wounded troopers. He and other American POWs had then trudged for 190 miles through the bitterest European winter in a quarter-century to reach Stalag II-A.

Now, soon after the secret radio had been installed, Sampson happened to be in the makeshift chapel when a squad of Gestapo agents burst in and began tearing things apart in customary fashion while searching for escape gear, weapons, and any other *verboten* items—especially radios. Sampson tried to look casual as the secret police closely inspected the altar and looked over the pulpit.

The chaplain knew that the Germans had a "plant" among the prisoners, a German who had lived in the United States, spoke flawless English, and was presumably above suspicion. In GI terms, he was a squealer. Colonel Alger and Sampson felt they knew his identity, but they were not certain.

*Captain (Chaplain) Francis L. Sampson. (Author's collection)*

Now it appeared that the plant had tipped off the Gestapo about the hidden radio, although its presence was kept from most of the POWs. Sampson breathed a sigh of relief when the German agents left without finding incriminating items.

On a Sunday morning a few days later, Father Sam, as the Catholic priest was known, was conducting Mass and he was about to launch into his sermon. On the previous night, he had been listening to the BBC instructions and had neglected to replace the spike securely in the trapdoor on top of the pulpit.

Sampson rested his arm on the pulpit and began talking: "Seek ye first the kingdom of God and His justice, and all these things shall be added unto you." Suddenly, the trapdoor flew open and the radio dropped out in front of the entire congregation, which included several German guards.

POWs found few things about which to laugh. But now, after a few moments of total silence, they broke out in gales of laughter. Trying to act nonchalant, the priest picked up the radio and stuffed it back into the pulpit. He tried to continue with his sermon, but the snickering was so intense that he soon gave it up and resumed the Mass.

Despite the GI merriment, it was a most ticklish situation. Would the German guards report the verboten radio to the camp commandant, resulting in serious punishment for Sampson and others?

When the Germans went to Communion, the chaplain felt confident that they would keep their silence. They did.

Soon after this episode, the suspected plant made a major mistake: he talked in his sleep—in German. A couple of days later, the squealer suffered a mysterious accident and had to be hospitalized.[18]

# Intelligence Coup on a Train

ON A BLEAK MORNING in early March 1945, Feldwebel (Sergeant) Hans Steinhauser and Schütze (Private) Heinrich Nowatny were on a train that pulled out of the railroad station in Vienna and headed westward. Steinhauser whispered to his companion, "If we're about to be collared by the military police while we're moving, we'll have to jump off the train and take our chances."

There was good reason for the apprehension: The two German soldiers were spies for the U.S. Office of Strategic Services (OSS) and had been sent to Vienna on an espionage mission.

"Steinhauser" actually was Fritz Molden, twenty-one years of age, who had been born in Vienna. He had fought with the German Army against the Soviets and later was opposing the Americans after the Allied landings at Anzio, in Italy, early in 1944.

Molden had always been anti-Nazi, so when he had the chance, he fled from the Anzio battleground into the nearby Appenine Mountains. There he contacted Italian partisans, who helped him slip into his native Austria where he joined the underground.

When Molden seemed to be in danger of arrest by the Gestapo, he was smuggled across the border into neutral Switzerland. Under cover of night, he stole up to a building at Herrengasse 23 in the picturesque, medieval section of Bern. Squinting in the dim glow of a streetlight, Molden discerned the lettering on a small sign next to the front door:

Allen W. Dulles
Special Assistant to the
U.S. Minister

The sign was merely part of the games that those involved in international intrigue play. Dulles, as nearly all of the scores of German and Allied spies roaming about Switzerland knew, was actually the OSS station chief in Switzerland, a hotbed of espionage.

Dulles was fond of tweed jackets and bow ties, wore rimless spectacles, and was seldom caught without his briar pipe—a stereotype of Hollywood's version of a kindly college professor. Despite his deceptively mild appearance, the fifty-two-year-old one-time missionary in India was tough-minded and shrewd.

Dulles was no novice to the cloak-and-dagger business. During World War I, he had been posted in Bern, ostensibly as an employee of the U.S. State

Department. Then he had the same task as he had a war later—collecting intelligence from inside neighboring Germany and Austria.

Fritz Molden held a conversation with Allen Dulles and offered his services as a spy. After investigating Molden's background, Dulles promptly gave him a perilous mission: establishing a chain of agents in and around Vienna in anticipation of the arrival of U.S. forces from the west or Soviet armies from the east.

Going with Molden to Vienna would be "Private Nowatny," whose real name was Ernest Lemberger, a Jew, which made his task even more hazardous. At thirty-eight, Lemberger was eighteen years older than his companion, Molden.

Lemberger had to flee his native Austria after Adolf Hitler took over that small country in March 1938, settled in France, and joined the French Army.

After the Nazi war machine had conquered France in only six weeks, Lemberger adopted the *nom de guerre* (war name) "Commander Jean Lambert" and fought the Nazis with the French underground. When the Allies liberated France in 1944, he was recruited by the OSS.

Wearing their German army uniforms and carrying forged credentials crafted by OSS technicians, Molden and Lemberger took a train to Vienna, where they linked up with an anti-Nazi group that called itself O-5. For three weeks, the two OSS agents traveled from town to town in the region, setting up an underground cell of four or five Czechs at each place.

Lemberger and Molden had completed their mission to Vienna, and were returning to Switzerland by train to report to Dulles when they saw a military policeman checking identity papers and moving toward them. They were trapped. Minutes later, the German MP was inspecting the papers of "Sergeant Steinhauser" and "Private Novatny." The two spies tried to act casual, but they were alarmed when the other German jotted something on a small pad.

Molden and Lemberger got up from their seats and headed for the coach door to leap from the racing train. But the German MP who had checked their credentials returned and told the pair to follow him to the train commander, an army captain, in another coach.

Clearly the two men's masquerade had been detected. Before the procession reached the coach door, the train went through a tunnel, blocking any chance to leap out. Molden unsnapped his pistol holder and whispered for Lemberger to do the same. They would take a few Germans down with them before they, themselves, were killed.

Before they could pull their weapons, the train emerged from the tunnel and they soon found themselves in the presence of the train commander, who was elderly for his modest rank. The captain apologized for inconveniencing them, but he knew from their papers that they were members of Abwehr, the intelligence service. He had only the one military policeman, so would the two soldiers mind checking papers on the front half of the long train?

The gods of espionage had smiled on Molden and Lemberger. Instead of being shot, they had stumbled onto an intelligence bonanza. Moving down the aisle, the two spies inspected orders of military men and could piece together a portrait of German army deployments in Austria.

On March 4, Lemberger and Molden were back in Switzerland where they gave the OSS chief Allen Dulles and his aides an hour-long briefing on the positions or movements of German tank, artillery, and infantry units in the Austria region.[19]

# Nazi Frogmen on the Rhine

TO THE GERMAN PEOPLE, the broad, majestic Rhine River, stretching from Switzerland northward for seven hundred miles, had always been the symbol of their national heritage and strength. In Richard Wagner's operas, the Nibelungen ring, made from the gold guarded by Rhine maidens deep in the river's waters, gave its possessor power over all the world.

Not since the time of Napoléon Bonaparte in 1806 had an invading army managed to cross the Rhine, because it could be turned into a vast defensive moat simply by blowing up its bridges. Now, in early March 1945, with Allied armies driving steadily toward the heart of the Fatherland, preparations were made to transform the Rhine into an impregnable barrier.

As the last German troops and panzers retreated behind the Rhine, Adolf Hitler issued strict orders for all of the bridges to be blown on the approach of enemy forces. Then, if the Allies tried to force an amphibious crossing, the führer was convinced that they would be repulsed in a bloody disaster.

On March 8, Hitler received shocking news in his bunker below the Reich Chancellery in bomb-battered Berlin. General Alfred Jodl, his trusted confidant, informed him that the Americans had seized intact the Ludendorff Bridge at Remagen, and troops and tanks were pouring across the Rhine.

Hitler flew into one of his most violent tirades of the war. Red-faced and trembling with fury, he shouted that he had been the victim of "cowards and traitors." The supreme leader demanded scapegoats, so he sent for SS Major General Rudolf Hübner, a staunch Nazi.

Hübner arrived at the Berlin bunker and was told to form a Flying Special Tribunal West, which would be empowered to conduct on-the-spot courts-martial and immediate execution of sentences.

Two days later, General Hübner launched trials in a large farmhouse thirty miles east of the Rhine. Seated on a rickety divan, the three SS colonels on the panel listened impassively as Wehrmacht legal officers presented the "evidence" against the "cowards and traitors" who had "permitted" the Americans to get across the Rhine.

*German frogmen almost reached the Ludendorff Bridge at the Remagen before being discovered and wiped out. (U.S. Army)*

Hübner, presumably a spectator, played his role to the hilt, shouting at each defendant that he was a miserable coward and deserved to be shot. The trial of each of six officers lasted less than ten minutes.

Major Hans Schiller explained that the one thousand combat troops he had been promised to protect the Ludendorff had never arrived. So he had only thirty-six elderly and infirm security guards to thwart the strong American force. Schiller was dragged outside and shot.

Twenty-two-year-old Lieutenant Karl Peters, who had been in charge of four antitank guns, was found guilty of high treason for leaving one of his weapons on the west side of the Rhine when American tanks were nipping at his heels. He was shot.

Major Hans Ströbel and Major August Kraft told the court that they had not blown the Ludendorff because the one thousand tons of explosives promised by a higher headquarters failed to appear. That "excuse" was unacceptable, Hübner yelled. A firing squad riddled the two highly decorated majors.

While loyal German officers were being shot at Remagen because of bungling at high levels, Hitler demanded that the bridge be destroyed before more Americans and tanks could cross the Rhine. Obsolete Stuka dive bombers and revolutionary new jets attacked the bridge and were greeted by a torrent of antiaircraft fire. They failed to score direct hits.

At the same time, the Karl howitzer, an enormous 540-millimeter weapon, lobbed shells weighing more than two tons each from a distance of twenty miles.

After firing several rounds and missing, the howitzer needed repairs and was put out of action.

The führer's *Vergeltungswaffen* (vengeance weapons), huge supersonic rockets that had been pounding London and the Belgian port of Antwerp for eight months, were turned against the Ludendorff. Eleven of the rockets were fired from bases in the Netherlands. All missed the target by considerable distances.

In desperation, Hitler ordered frogmen to blow up the span. By now, the Americans had built a bridgehead on the east bank of the Rhine nine miles deep and fifteen miles long. So to even reach the Ludendorff, the frogmen would have to swim for perhaps eight miles behind American lines. Moreover, the Rhine temperature would be near freezing, causing the frogmen to get cramps and perhaps drown. It would take a near miracle for the mission to succeed.

An hour after darkness descended on March 17, nine days after the first squad of American infantrymen had dashed across the Ludendorff, eleven furtive figures, burdened with heavy loads of explosives, stole along the banks of the Rhine and into the rapid current ten miles north of the bridge. Lieutenant Hans Schreiber, leader of the frogmen, had been a champion swimmer while in a Berlin university; he and each of his men wore skin-tight rubber suits, rubber foot fins, and carried an apparatus to breathe underwater.

After superhuman effort in battling the strong current and the frigid river temperature for three hours, the frogmen had negotiated nearly five miles behind enemy lines. Suddenly, when two miles from the bridge, the nearly exhausted swimmers were virtually blinded by powerful searchlights that played over the water from both banks of the Rhine.

A torrent of machine-gun and rifle fire peppered the helpless Germans. Several of them were hit by bullets and disappeared below the surface. Those who survived struggled to reach the bank and were captured—including the crestfallen Lieutenant Schreiber, who had been fully aware that Adolf Hitler had sent him and his men on a suicide mission.[20]

# VIP Hostages Saved by Fate

AS THE END NEARED for the Third Reich in April 1945, some top Nazi leaders began agonizing about war crimes trials the Allies had promised to conduct. It was decided to transfer a group of high-profile prisoners out of reach of the approaching Allied armies. These prominent figures could be used as hostages for barter.

A plan was hurriedly concocted. The captive bigwigs would be rounded up from concentration camps and taken southward through the Brenner Pass which connects Germany and Italy. In charge of the secret operation was SS

General Gottlob Berger, who had earned high praise in Berlin for his ruthless actions in "pacifying" the population of Prague, Czechoslovakia, in 1944.

In a final discussion of the barter plan, Adolf Hitler declared that if the hostage overtures to the Allies were to be unreceptive, Berger was to "shoot them all."

At dawn on April 27, a convoy of trucks and buses carrying the VIPs with an escort of SS troops rolled into a small village in northern Italy, a region still held by German troops under Generalleutnant Heinrich von Vietinghoff, the supreme commander in Italy. What Hitler did not know was that Vietinghoff had been engaged in clandestine negotiations with the U.S. Office of Strategic Services (OSS) operatives for surrendering his forces in Italy.

Among some 120 prisoners were Léon Blum, who had been the first Jew to be premier of Catholic France; Kurt von Schuschnigg, chancellor of Austria prior to its Nazi takeover; German Pastor Martin Niemoeller, internationally hailed for his opposition to Nazism; Hjalmar Schacht, former economic minister in Hitler's regime; and Fritz Thyssen, a German armaments baron who was arrested when he tried to flee the Third Reich in 1940.

Now, after the group of VIP prisoners reached the Italian village, the vehicles were parked while General Berger, confused by his instructions, left to seek clarification from Berlin. While he was away, one of the prisoners, Colonel Fritz von Bogislave Bonin, bluffed his guards and reached a nearby town that was the headquarters of General von Vietinghoff.

Bonin and the German commander in Italy had been longtime army friends, and the colonel quickly whispered that help was urgently needed back in the village. An hour later, a sizeable detachment of *Heer* (army) soldiers arrived there, surprised and disarmed the SS guards, and took charge of the VIPs. The hostages were protected until they were freed by U.S. troops on May 4, 1945.

Only much later would the VIPs learn that an urgent order from the SS head and Gestapo chief, Reichsführer Heinrich Himmler, had been sent to General Berger in Italy. The hostages were to have been shot immediately.[21]

# A Stroll through 145,000 Germans

AFTER THE RHINE RIVER, Germany's ancient barrier to invasion from the west, had been breached at several points along its 450-mile length, Allied forces were charging ahead at often spectacular speeds. By April 3, 1945, elements of three U.S. armies had forged a ring of steel around the Ruhr, the heart of Adolf Hitler's industrial might.

Trapped in a space about half the size of New Jersey, some 325,000 haggard German soldiers, along with 29 generals, were captured when the Ruhr Sack, as it became known, was flattened on April 18.

Meanwhile, on April 11, the U.S. Ninth Army north of the Ruhr reached the Elbe River, one hundred miles from Berlin, where it was ordered to halt and await the arrival of the Soviet Army, which was closing in on the nearly demolished German capital.

On the night of April 30, Red Army soldiers were but two blocks from Hitler's bunker in Berlin. Minutes after being married to his longtime companion, Eva Braun, the führer put a Luger pistol's muzzle to his head and pulled the trigger. Two days later, the Russians captured all of the city.

On May 1, the same day that Radio Berlin announced the "heroic death" of Hitler, elements of the U.S. 82nd Airborne Division launched an assault, crossing the Elbe River by boat, north of the Ruhr. After a bridgehead was carved out on the far bank, engineers built a pontoon bridge under murderous artillery fire, and on the second day, the U.S. 740th Tank Battalion rolled across the Elbe.

Tankers and paratroopers hooked up as a team. The seven Shermans, with airborne men atop each one, clanked forward. A tank commander near the front radioed back to his squadron leader: "Believe it or not, Captain, four paratroopers on bicycles just passed my tank and are now spearheading the attack!" A few minutes later, he radioed again: "Good God, here comes a horse and buggy loaded with seven paratroopers—and they're passing me, too!"

Then a third call: "Captain, this is the damnedest thing I ever saw. Over there on the left, there's about twenty 82nd Airborne troopers galloping along on horses and rounding up Krauts!"

There was much more than just the customary spirit of paratroopers in play. The 82nd Airborne wanted to end its war in Europe in a blaze of glory by being the first outfit to link up with the oncoming Soviets.

Consequently, on the morning of May 3, thirty-three-year-old Colonel Reuben H. Tucker, leader of the 504th Parachute Infantry Regiment, got into a command car and headed eastward. Also known as "Rube" or "Tommy," Tucker had been a four-sport star at high school in Ansonia, Connecticut, and a cadet corps leader at West Point. With him on the safari into the unknown was Lieutenant Chester A. Garrison, one of his staff officers, who had been seriously wounded when a platoon leader during the fighting in Sicily in mid-1943.

Tucker was a fiery, gung-ho leader known for his courage on the battle-field. Garrison kept his own counsel, but he wondered if his boss was not being grossly reckless. A day earlier, Lieutenant General Kurt von Tippelskirch had surrendered his 21st Army of 145,000 men. But had all of his troops got the word?

Tucker's command car drove along a road cluttered with hordes of Germans moving west on foot or in decrepit vehicles. Many of the Feldgrau were

*Colonel Reuben H. Tucker and an aide marched through hordes of Germans, many of them armed, in an effort to meet the Soviets. (U.S. Army)*

fully armed, and they scowled at the passing Americans. When the vehicle could no longer penetrate the flow of humanity, Tucker and Garrison got out and continued on foot.

The parachute officers were a curiosity to the Germans, the first Americans they had seen close up. Groups of sullen SS troops stared at the two men smolderingly. Some of the SS officers, in a symbol of defiance, fired their pistols into the air.

Wary that some embittered German could easily shoot Tucker and himself without detection, Garrison pulled and cocked his revolver, knowing how futile that action was, and strode onward with his eager-beaver leader.

Years later, Chester Garrison recalled: "We were the American point with thousands of unpredictable Germans, many fully armed, between us and our 82nd Airborne comrades. We marched for about three miles until it was clear we were far behind the 21st Army. When darkness was falling and the Russians failed to appear, even Colonel Tucker's ardor finally faltered."

Garrison tried to conceal his enormous relief when the colonel said, "We'd better go back." But would the return trip be that simple? The two officers would have to negotiate their way on foot through at least three miles of presumably "captured" Germans, many of whom probably were not aware that they were, technically, prisoners of war.

Soon it was dark, making the passage through throngs of Germans all the more precarious. Garrison drummed up visions of his and Tucker's corpses never being recovered by the Americans. However, compassionate gods of war shielded the two men, and they arrived back with friendly troops after the bizarre adventure behind enemy lines.

Three days later, Colonel General Alfred Jodl, who had been Adolf Hitler's most trusted military confidant since the war began in September 1939, walked briskly into the redbrick schoolhouse that served as General Dwight Eisenhower's headquarters in Reims, France. A few hours later, the Allied supreme commander sent a dispatch to the Combined Chiefs of Staff in Washington: "The mission of this Allied force was fulfilled at 0241 [2:41 A.M.] local time, May 7, 1945."[22]

# Mobilizing Twenty-Eight Million Civilian Killers

"WE WILL TURN THE TIDE of the war by meeting the [Americans] on the homeland," General Suichi Miyazaki, the Japanese Army's chief of military operations, told his commanders at Ichigaya, headquarters of the Imperial Army in Tokyo. "By pouring twenty divisions into the battle when the enemy lands, we will annihilate him entirely."

It was mid-June 1945. Miyazaki was setting forth the theme of Ketsu-Go (Operation Decision), a plan for the last-ditch defense of every foot of the home islands that most Japanese held sacred, believing them to have fallen as drops from the sword of an ancient god.

There would be three million Japanese warriors to defend the homeland. Each man was keenly disciplined and highly motivated. There was no greater honor for him than to die in battle for the emperor. His allegiance to the emperor was reinforced almost daily when he faced in the direction of Tokyo and recited parts of the "Imperial Rescript to Soldiers and Sailors."

The Rescript contained the Code of Bushido which demanded "honor, obedience, and valor." It told what was expected of the samurai warrior: "The soldier and sailor should consider their loyalty their essential duty . . . a duty is weightier than a mountain while death is lighter than a feather. . . . Never by failing fall into disgrace and bring dishonor to your name."

Hundreds of miles away in Manila, U.S. General Douglas MacArthur, who would command ground forces for Operation Downfall, the invasion of Japan set for November, told the Pentagon in Washington that it might take ten years and cost over one million casualties to American forces alone to conquer the home islands. Perhaps as many as five-to-ten million Japanese military men and civilians would perish.

*In July 1945, construction was finished on these buildings and six miles of chambers bored into a mountain 100 miles northeast of Tokyo. The secret complex would house the Imperial General Headquarters and 10,000 employees to direct the last-ditch defense of Japan. (U.S. Army)*

Even while tenacious Japanese soldiers were fighting to hold their final piece of territory on the island of Okinawa, 350 miles below Tokyo, far behind their lines the warlords in Japan were mobilizing twenty-eight million able-bodied civilians—men, women, and youngsters between the ages of twelve and sixty—to join with three million combat troops in defending the homeland. The civilians were armed with ancient rifles, grenades, explosives, and even bows and arrows and point-sharpened bamboo spears.

Women were determined to sell their lives dearly in hand-to-hand combat. Sachiko Ishikawa, a nurse, explained why she and others like her had been ready to die: "It was the kind of education we received earlier. When we left [nursing] school, we were told that, if necessary, we should be prepared to die for our country."

A young Japanese housewife, who had lost her home to bombs from B-29 Superfortresses, said grimly: "I have never thought of quitting. I will sacrifice even my children and fight to the death."

A woman who was unable to find a weapon was urged to use pepper from her kitchen to blind an unsuspecting American soldier. Then she was to take a butcher knife or meat cleaver hidden under her kimono and hack the invader to death.

Preteen boys and girls were taught how to strap explosives on their backs, then sneak under American tanks and detonate the charges. A teenage girl, Yukiko Kasai, was given a carpenter's awl by her teacher and told, "When the Americans come, you must draw on your Japanese spirit and kill them. You must rip out the enemy's abdomen."

Elsewhere, a large group of Tokyo girls, who had been evacuated to rural areas to escape heavy bombings, were trained with and became skilled in the use of long, hook-bladed *naginata* spears, a weapon dating back to the Middle Ages. The scythelike instrument was intended to cut off an American soldier's leg.

The civilians were trained for their last heroics by army drillmasters. Each day before dawn, the citizens would assemble for that day's schedule. There were strenuous physical exercises, and then groups lined up in front of life-sized targets made of straw bundles held by sturdy uprights. Men and women, old and young, lunged, parried, and thrust long bamboo spears for seemingly endless hours, shouting obscene curses at the imaginary "American soldiers."

Japanese propagandists spread scare stories in case the civilian warriors might waver when the Americans landed. Tokyo newspapers carried grisly accounts of how American soldiers had pillaged and raped and committed other atrocities as they overran enemy countries in Europe.

At the same time, Radio Tokyo broadcasts sought to steel the wills of the military and civilian sectors by assuring that secret weapons were ready to inflict mayhem and carnage on the "white devils." Unlike the false canards about the atrocities committed by American soldiers in Europe, the secret weapons disclosure was quite accurate.

Ten thousand kamikaze planes with 500-pound bombs were ready to dive into ships of an invasion armada. Scores of one-man suicide torpedoes were scattered along the coasts. Hundreds of Shinyou suicide powerboats, each carrying a 4,406-pound warhead fused to detonate on impact, were hidden in coves and ready to crash at full speed into an approaching fleet.

Civilians would join in the suicide attacks. Hundreds of obsolete training planes were trucked into the mountains overlooking likely invasion beaches. The old aircraft would be loaded with bombs and manned by teenagers or university students with little or no flying experience. When ready to go into action, these planes would slide down long, skilike ramps, hurtle into the air, and plunge into American ships and landing craft.

The kamikaze spirit was regarded as an example for every civilian warrior to follow in the looming battle to kill thousands of Americans and drive the remainder from their holy soil.

For those Japanese who still had hope, "Victory in the last five minutes" became their slogan. Others without hope pledged to die for the emperor.

On August 6, 1945, a B-29 Superfortress piloted by thirty-year-old Colonel Paul W. Tibbets approached Hiroshima, a city of 350,000 that was a center for the manufacturing and distribution of military weapons. Suddenly, a brilliant flash split the blue sky. Much of the ancient town vanished; perhaps 50,000 Japanese died.

On August 18, forty-four-year-old myopic Emperor Hirohito, a figure so sacred to the Japanese that they had never even heard his voice, broadcast a recorded message over Radio Tokyo: "The enemy has begun to employ a new and most cruel bomb, the power of which to do damage is incalculable."

Hirohito ordered an end to hostilities at 4:00 P.M. that day. His action avoided the greatest slaughter of the human race since the Mongol warlord Ghengis Khan and his armies swept across northern Asia and eastern Europe in the early 1200s.[23]

# Notes and Sources

## Part One—Darkness Falls over Europe

### 1. Post Office Shoot-Out Launches a War
Herbert Kriegheim, *Die Geheimnisvollen Brandenburger* (Berlin: Bernard & Graefe, 1958), pp. 47–48.
Donald McLachlan, *Room 39* (New York: Athenaeum, 1968), p. 245.
Author's archives.

### 2. Wiping Out Hitler's Spy Network
Author's archives.

### 3. The Gestapo Cracks an Espionage Ring
Anthony Reed and David Fisher, *Colonel Z* (New York: Viking, 1985), pp. 230, 235.
Author's archives.

### 4. Masquerading Germans Pace the Invasion
Time-Life Books Editors, *The Shadow War* (Alexandria, Va: Time-Life Books, 1991), p. 157.
*Illustrated Story of World War II* (Pleasantville, N.Y.: Reader's Digest, 1969), p. 77.
Author's archives.

### 5. A Streetcar Spearheads an Attack
Jacques Benoist-Mechin, *Sixty Days that Shook the West* (New York: G. P. Putnam's Sons, 1963), p. 72.
Author's archives.
C. L. Sulzberger, *The American Heritage Picture History of World War II* (New York: American Heritage Publishing, 1966), p. 74.

### 6. Hitler Order: Kidnap Queen Wilhelmina
Eddie Bauer, ed., *Illustrated Encyclopedia of World War II*, vol. 2 (London: Cavendish, 1966), p. 215.
*Lightning War* (Alexandria, Va: Time-Life Books, 1991), p. 31.
Anthony Cave Brown, *Bodyguard of Lies* (New York: Harper & Row, 1975), p. 243.
Author's archives.

### 7. A Legal Diamond Thief
Obituary of Montague R. Chidson, *The Times*, London, October 4, 1957.
Author's archives.

8. **Rommel Personally Captures a Unit**
   Peter Young, *Rommel* (London: Collins, 1950), p. 32.
   Walter Goerlitz, *History of the German General Staff* (New York: Praeger, 1954),
      p. 392.
   Author's archives.
   Liddell Hart, *Rommel Papers* (New York: Obolensky, 1951), p. 101.

9. **A General's "Impossible" Escape**
   R. Harris Smith, *OSS* (Berkeley: University of California, 1972), p. 47.
   Edward L. Spears, *Assignment to Catastrophe*, vol. 1 (New York: Wynn, 1954), p.
      157.
   Author's archives.
   Robert Murphy, *Diplomat Among Warriors* (New York: Doubleday, 1964), p. 123.

10. **"The Cat" Was a Triple Agent**
    Mathilda Carré, *I Was the "Cat"* (London: Four Square Books, 1961), pp. 37, 102,
       187.
    Hugo Bleicher, *Colonel Henri's Story* (London: Kimber, 1954), pp. 82, 143, 162.
    Author's archives.

11. **Prowling behind German-Held Coast**
    Report on Combined Operations (London: His Majesty's Stationery Office, 1943).
    Author's archives.

12. **Cat-and-Mouse Game**
    Ladislas Farago, The Game of the Foxes (New York: McKay, 1971), pp. 235–236.
    Author's archives.

13. **A Personal Telegram for the Führer**
    Author's archives.

14. **Who Was the Mysterious Max?**
    Author's archives.

15. **Underwater War at Gibraltar**
    *London Sunday Express*, December 25, 1949.
    *Reader's Digest*, November 1950.
    Author's archives.

16. **Polish Spies Invade Germany**
    David Irving, *The Mare's Nest* (London: Kimber, 1964), pp. 19, 34, 36.
    Reginald V. Jones, *The Wizard War* (New York: Coward, McCann & Geoghegan,
       1978), p. 127.
    Josef Garlinski, *Hitler's Last Weapons* (New York: Times Books, 1978), pp. 53, 150.

17. **A Leg Is Parachuted to a British Ace**
    Paul Brickhill, *Reach for the Sky* (New York: Norton, 1954), pp. 234, 244.
    Edward H. Sims, *The Greatest Aces* (New York: Harper & Row, 1967), pp. 78–79.

18. **Sudden Death for the "Blond Beast"**
    Henri Michel, *Shadow War* (New York: Harper, 1972), p. 223.
    Anthony Cave Brown, *C* (New York: Macmillan, 1989), p. 411.
    Walter Schellenberg, *The Labyrinth* (New York: Harper, 1956), pp. 336, 338.
    Author's archives.

19. **Parachuting in a Boat**
    Author's archives.


## Part Two—Freedom's Time of Crisis

1. **A Ruse to Spy on Cherbourg**
   Author's archives.
   Richard Collier, *Ten Thousand Eyes* (New York: Dutton, 1958), p. 113.

2. **"Hunting" Germans in Canoes**
   Bernard Fergusson, *The Watery Maze* (London: Collins, 1961), pp. 31, 52.
   Graeme Cook, *Commandos in Action* (London: Taplinger, 1974), pp. 98, 106.
   Author's archives.

3. **Jewish Raiders in Disguise**
   Virginia Cowles, *The Phantom Major* (London: Collins, 1958), p. 114.
   Philip Warner, *The Special Air Service* (London: Kimber, 1972), pp. 136–137.
   Author's archives.

4. **A Conspiracy to Capture Cairo**
   Time-Life Books Editors, *The Shadow War* (Alexandria, Va: Time-Life Books, 1990),
       p. 82.
   Anthony Cave Brown, *Bodyguard of Lies* (New York: Harper & Row, 1975), p. 119.
   Author's archives.

5. **Intruders at a Secret Airport**
   Cecil Carnes, *Behind Rommel's Lines* (New York: Bobbs-Merrill, 1943), pp. 127,
       130, 135.
   Samuel W. Mitcham, Jr., *Triumphant Fox* (New York: Stein and Day, 1984), pp.
       83–84.
   Author's archives.

6. **A Special Medal for Burma Tribesmen**
   U.S. Secretary of War Henry L. Stimson Diaries, January 13, 1942. New Haven,
       Conn.: Yale University Library.
   Barbara Tuchman, *Stilwell and the American Experience* (New York: Bantam,
       1972), p. 385.
   *Reader's Digest*, June 1945.
   Author's archives.

7. **American Medics Save Ho Chi Minh**
   Author's archives.

8. **A Hoax at Soviet Oil Fields**
   Herbert Kriegheim, *Die Geheimnisvollen Brandenburger* (Berlin: Bernard & Graefe, 1958), pp. 164–165. Author's archives.

9. **A Woman Heads an Escape Apparatus**
   Author's archives.
   Airey Neave, *Saturday at M.I.9* (London: Hodder and Stoughton, 1969), pp. 129, 134.

10. **The Ranger Wore Bedroom Slippers**
    Author's archives.

11. **The Countess and the Commandos**
    Lucas Phillips, *Cockleshell Heroes* (London: Hutchinson, 1949), pp. 17, 43, 184.
    Airey Neave, *The Escape Room* (New York: Doubleday, 1969), pp. 210, 212, 214.
    Author's archives.

12. **"Blow Up Rommel's Railroad!"**
    Author interview with Dan DeLeo, 1992.
    Author correspondence with Roland Rondeau, 1990.
    Author interview with Charles Doyle, 1992.

13. **Reconnoitering Hostile Beaches**
    Author's archives.
    Russell Miller, *The Commandos* (Alexandria, Va: Time-Life Books, 1981), pp. 124–125.
    Peter Young, *Storm from the Sea* (London: Kimber, 1959), p. 147.

14. **A Master of Disguises**
    Author correspondence with Alyce M. Guthrie, PT Boats, Inc., Memphis, Tenn., 1993.
    Author's archives.

15. **Deceiving an Italian General**
    *Time*, July 21, 1943.
    Author's archives.

16. **The Canal Saboteurs**
    Author's archives.

17. **Strange Places for Secret Radios**
    Author's archives.

18. **Saved from a Firing Squad**
    Hugh Pond, *Sicily* (London: Kimber, 1962), p. 147.

Francis de Guingand, *Operation Victory* (New York: Scribner's, 1947), pp. 298–299.
Author's archives.

## Part Three—Hitler's Empire under Siege

### 1. Old Popski Invades a German Headquarters
Author's archives.

### 2. The GI with the Too-Short Pants
Author interview with Lieutenant General William P. Yarborough (Ret.), 1996.
Author interview with George Fontanesi, 1990.
Author interview with General Mark W. Clark (Ret.), 1984.
Author's archives.

### 3. The New York Subway Connection
*Yank*, October 1944.
Author's archives.

### 4. Nose-Thumbing at the Germans
Author's archives.

### 5. The Chef Had Bombs on His Menu
Author's archives.

### 6. Spying from a Church Steeple
Author's archives.

### 7. The Black-Hearted Devils
Author interview with wartime member of the First Special Service Force William S. Story, 1991; wartime paratrooper and OSS operative Herbert Schumacher, 1992; and Lieutenant General William P. Yarborough (Ret.), paratrooper leader on Anzio, 1996.

### 8. A Scheme to Go under German Lines
Author's archives.

### 9. A New Baby Stymies Normandy Planning
Allen Andrews, *The Air Marshals* (New York: Morrow, 1970), p. 135.
Author's archives.
Anthony Cave Brown, *Bodyguard of Lies* (New York: Harper & Row, 1975), p. 582.
SHAEF, *Military Objectives for Aerial Bombardment*, 1944, Washington, D.C.: National Archives.

### 10. Sabotage Campaign by Railway Men
Author's archives.
*New York Times*, May 24, 1944.

11. **A Close Encounter with Two Jungle Beasts**
    Theodore H. White, *The Stilwell Papers* (New York: Sloane, 1948), pp. 178, 184.
    War Diary of the 5307th Composite Unit (Provisional), China-Burma-India Thea-
        ter, pp. 328, 347. Washington, D.C.: National Archives.
    Charlton Ogburn, Jr., *The Marauders* (New York: Harper, 1956), pp. 98–99.

12. **"Baby Sergeant York"**
    Author's archives.

13. **A Millionairess Resistance Leader**
    Author's archives.
    E. H. Cookridge, *They Came from the Sky* (London: Crowell, 1967), pp. 136, 138.

14. **A Woman OSS Agent and "Cuthbert"**
    Author's archives.

15. **Panzer Watchers and Phony Laundries**
    Author's archives.
    Anthony Cave Brown, *Bodyguard of Lies* (New York: Harper & Row, 1975), p.
        692.
    Dwight D. Eisenhower Diary, Eisenhower Library, Abilene, Kans.

16. **The Supersecret X Troop**
    Author's archives.

17. **Miracle at a Normandy Convent**
    Author interview with Major General Francis L. Sampson (Ret.), 1997. As a
        Catholic chaplain in the U.S. 101st Airborne Division in Normandy, he had
        visited the destroyed convent soon after the bombing and talked with the
        mother superior about the "miracle."

18. **A Luftwaffe Pilot Declines to Take Bait**
    Author's Archives.

19. **Jealousy Thwarts a German Scheme**
    Author's archives.

20. **A British POW Saves His Captor's Life**
    Ronald H. Bailey, *Partisans and Guerrillas* (Alexandria, Va: Time-Life Books, 1978),
        p. 128.
    Author's archives.

## Part Four—Beginning of the End

1. **"Hell, We're Halfway to Berlin!"**
   Author interview with Leonard A. Funk, 1994.

2. **Alone in a German-Held Town**
Author interview with General Maxwell D. Taylor (Ret.), 1987.
Author's archives.

3. **Two Admirals Go Souvenir Hunting**
Author interview with General J. Lawton Collins (Ret.) 1984.
Author interviews with Vice Admiral John D. Bulkeley (Ret.) 1989, 1994.
Author's archives.

4. **An American General's Strange Odyssey**
Lloyd R. Shoemaker, *The Escape Factory* (New York: St. Martin's Press, 1989), pp. 189, 192, 197.
Delmar T. Spivey, *POW Odyssey* (Attleboro, Mass: Colonial Lithograph, 1984), pp. 135, 187.
Author's archives.

5. **Mission: Kidnap Field Marshal Rommel**
Author's archives.
Anthony Cave Brown, *Bodyguard of Lies* (New York: Harper & Row, 1975), pp. 800–801.

6. **A Soviet Spying Mission Fizzles**
Author's archives.

7. **A "Dead" GI Returns**
Author interviews and correspondence with various members of the wartime U.S. 509th Parachute Infantry Battalion, 1988 through 1993.

8. **Operation Sauerkraut**
Author's archives.
Materials pertaining to Operation Sauerkraut. Washington, D.C.: National Archives.
*Washington Post*, October 10, 1944.

9. **A POW Haul in a Saloon**
Hugh M. Cole, VIII Corps Operations, *Operation Cobra* (Washington: Chief of Military History, 1962), p. 212.
Author's archives.

10. **"The Madman of St. Malo"**
Author's archives.
Colonel Chester B. Hansen Diaries, 1943–1945. U.S. Army Military History Institute, Carlisle, Pa.

11. **The "Terrorist" Was a Lady**
Author's archives.

12. **Jeds behind the French Riviera**
Author interview with Colonel Aaron Bank (Ret.), 1989.

Author interview with Lieutenant General William P. Yarborough, (Ret.), 1998.
Author's archives.

### 13. The Mysterious Lady in Red
Author's archives.

### 14. An Escape by Eight "Policemen"
Author correspondence with Colonel Vincent M. Lockhart (Ret.), historian of the
U.S. 36th Infantry Division, 1990.
Author's archives.

### 15. An Endangered Pilot Is Saved
Author interview with former PT-boat skipper L. Rumsey Ewing, 1999.
Author correspondence with Rear Admiral John Harllee (Ret.), 1991.
Author's archives.

### 16. Shooting Up an "Iron Kraut"
Author interview with Lieutenant General James M. Gavin (Ret.), 1988.
Author's archives.

### 17. Hiding a "Pregnant" Glider Pilot
John C. Warren, *Airborne Operations in World War II, European Theater* (Maxwell
Air Force Base, Ala, 1956), pp. 118, 129, 131.
Gerard M. Devlin, *Silent Wings* (New York: St. Martin's Press, 1985), pp. 265, 267.
Author's archives.

### 18. The "Lone Raider" on the Prowl
Author interview with Ted Bachenheimer's wartime associates: Colonel Warren
Williams (Ret.), 1988; Virgil F. Carmichael, 1996; Lieutenant General James
M. Gavin (Ret.), 1988.
Author's archives.

### 19. A Secret Mission in the Alps
Author interview with Duffield W. Matson (1991); Lieutenant General William P.
Yarborough (Ret.), 1993; and Jim Phillips, 1994.


## Part Five—Peace at Last

### 1. "League of Lonely War Women"
*Washington Post*, November 10, 1944.
Elizabeth E. McIntosh, *Sisterhood of Spies* (Annapolis, Md: Naval Institute Press,
1998), p. 65.

### 2. Curious Doings in a POW Camp
Author interview with James W. Collins, 1990.
Author's archives.

3. **POWs Parachute into the Reich**
   U.S. Seventh Army Daily Log, August 2 to December 12, 1944.
   *The Invasion of Southern France* (Washington, D.C.: Chief of Military History, 1952), pp. 174, 182.
   Joseph E. Persico, *Piercing the Reich* (New York: Viking, 1979), pp. 108, 112, 114.
   Author's archives.

4. **The Good Samaritan of Leyte Gulf**
   Author's archives.

5. **"Scarface Otto" Creates Mass Hysteria**
   Charles Foley, *Commando Extraordinary* (Costa Mesa, Calif: Noontide Press, 1988), pp. 126, 132.
   Author interview with General J. Lawton Collins (Ret.), 1984.
   Otto Skorzeny, *Skorzeny's Special Missions* (London: Robert Hale, 1957), p. 132.
   Harry C. Butcher, *My Three Years With Eisenhower* (New York: Simon & Schuster, 1946), pp. 314, 327.
   Author's archives.

6. **A POW Colonel Takes Command**
   John Toland, *Battle* (New York: Random House, 1959), pp. 132–133, 247.
   James M. Gavin, *On to Berlin* (New York: Viking, 1978), p. 209.
   Dwight D. Eisenhower, *Crusade in Europe* (Garden City, N.Y.: Doubleday, 1948), p. 345.
   Author's archives.

7. **An Allied Spy's Dilemma**
   Author's archives.
   Joseph E. Persico, *Piercing the Reich* (New York: Viking, 1979), p. 188.

8. **Marooned amid the Foe**
   Author interview with Milo C. Huempfner, 1991.
   Author's archives.

9. **Trapped in an Attic for Eight Days**
   Author interview with Colonel Carlos C. Alden (Ret.), 1993.
   Author interview with Virgil McCall (1993).

10. **Love and War at a German Post Office**
    *The Twenty-Niner*, newsletter of the 29th Infantry Division Association, March 2000.
    Author's archives.

11. **MacArthur "Visits" a Japanese CP**
    Author's archives.
    William Manchester, *American Caesar* (Boston: Little, Brown, 1978), p. 413.
    General Charles A. Willoughby, *MacArthur* (New York: McGraw-Hill, 1954), p. 178.

12. **A Patrol's "Pigeon Air Force"**
*U.S. VII Corps History of Operations in Europe* (privately printed), 1945, pp. 179, 181, 183.
Author's archives.
Leo A. Hough and Howard J. Doyle, *Timberwolf Tracks* (Washington, D.C.: Infantry Journal Press, 1946), pp. 168, 172–173.
General J. Lawton Collins, *Lightning Joe* (Baton Rouge, La.: Louisiana State University Press, 1979), p. 299.

13. **A German Boy-Soldier Saves Two GIs**
Author correspondence with Lieutenant General Richard J. Seitz (Ret.), 1991.
*Stars and Stripes*, March 26, 1945.
Author's archives.
Author correspondence with Allen R. Goodman, who had been a corporal in the 517th Parachute Regimental Team, 1991.

14. **A Scheme to Trigger an Uprising**
Jane Foster, *An Unamerican Lady* (London: Sidgwick and Jackson, 1979), p. 120, 160–162.
Author's archives.

15. **Uninvited "Guests" on Corregidor**
Author interview with Brigadier General George M. Jones (Ret.). 1993.
Author's archives.

16. **Eavesdropping behind Japanese Positions**
Theodore H. White, ed., *The Stilwell Papers* (New York: Sloane, 1948), p. 226.
Charlton Ogburn, Jr., *The Marauders* (New York: Harper, 1956), pp. 117, 205.
Author's archives.

17. **Eisenhower's Spy in Berlin**
Kenneth Botting, *From the Ruins of the Reich* (New York: Crown, 1985), p. 87.
Cornelius Ryan, *The Last Battle* (New York: Simon and Schuster, 1966), pp. 23, 366.
Author's archives.

18. **Father Sam and His Hidden Radio**
Author interview with Monsignor (Major General, Ret.) Francis L. Sampson, 1996.

19. **Intelligence Coup on a Train**
Joseph E. Persico, *Piercing the Reich* (New York: Viking, 1979), pp. 228, 231.
Allen W. Dulles, *Secret Surrender* (New York: Harper & Row, 1966), pp. 162, 179.

20. **Nazi Frogmen on the Rhine**
General Omar N. Bradley, *A Soldier's Story* (New York: Holt, 1951), p. 306.
Field Marshal Albrecht Kesselring, *A Soldier's Record* (New York: Doubleday, 1954), p. 284.

Joseph B. Mittelman, *Eight Stars to Victory* (Washington, D.C.: Infantry Press, 1948), p. 268.

Author's archives.

21. **VIP Hostages Saved by Fate**

Ulrich von Hassell, *The von Hassell Diaries* (New York: Doubleday, 1947), p. 205, 207.

William L. Shirer, *The Rise and Fall of the Third Reich* (New York: Simon and Schuster, 1960), p. 1074.

Author's archives.

22. **A Stroll through 145,000 Germans**

Author interview with Virgil F. Carmichael, a wartime lieutenant in Colonel Tucker's regiment, 1993.

Author correspondence with participant Chester A. Garrison, 1993.

23. **Mobilizing Twenty-Eight Million Civilian Killers**

Author's archives.

# Index